Eleven Years
in Soviet Prison Camps

ELINOR LIPPER

Eleven Years
in Soviet Prison Camps

HENRY REGNERY COMPANY

CHICAGO, 1951

This authorized translation from the original German, *Elf Jahre in sowjetischen Gefängnissen und Lagern* (Zürich, Verlag Oprecht, 1950), was made by Richard and Clara Winston.

Copyright 1951
HENRY REGNERY COMPANY
Chicago 4, Illinois

Manufactured in the United States of America
by American Book–Knickerbocker Press, Inc., New York

Foreword

IN THIS BOOK I have described my personal experiences only
to the extent that they were the characteristic experiences
of a prisoner in the Soviet Union. For my concern is not
primarily with the foreigners in Soviet camps; it is rather
with the fate of all the peoples who have been subjugated by
the Soviet regime, who were born in a Soviet Republic and
cannot escape from it.

The Russian people, and the other peoples of the Soviet
Union, cannot be equated with the Soviet government.
Though they may have brought it into being, they are now the
helpless victims of a ruling caste whose arbitrariness they must
endure in silence. They have not the slightest chance to
control their rulers. It is easy to condemn "the Russians"—
but to do so is to do the Russian people a great injustice.
For only would-be suicides and heroes can raise their voice
against the decisions of their government in Russia. There
are few such people in Russia, as there are few everywhere
in the world. And it is not only that speaking out is courting
death; objectors will be liquidated in absolute secrecy and

can be certain that scarcely anyone will ever hear about their resistance.

Let us therefore avoid passing judgment on the Russian people. They are already condemned to the most horrible kind of existence: living in perpetual fear.

Who are the so-called counterrevolutionaries who make up the majority of the prisoners in Soviet camps? Are they guilty, are they innocent? There can be only one answer. From the standpoint of objective, non-Soviet justice, and from the standpoint of the strictest kind of class justice as well, these people are innocent. Of all the millions of persons in Soviet prisons and camps, very few have consciously taken action against the government in speech or in writing, by demonstrating or by attempting to escape from the Soviet Union. Their number is so small that they are insignificant in the great mass of prisoners. Only after spending many years in camp is one likely, with luck, to meet up with a "genuine" counterrevolutionary.

It is courting error to suggest hard and fast rules about the reasons for imprisonment. The machinery of injustice, once it has begun moving, behaves illogically and wantonly. It is not for nothing that we speak of "blind" terror. Nevertheless, the so-called counterrevolutionaries fall into two main categories.

1) Those who by reason of their origin, their education, their nationality, their past political behavior or their general cultural level are or could be potential opponents of the regime. This need not mean that they have ever committed the slightest offense. On the contrary, though as members of Soviet society they could not help feeling discomfort, most of them were not even conscious of any such feeling until

the moment they were arrested. They did not want to be conscious of it. That is especially true of the members of the Communist Party and the Young Communist League, whose eyes were opened to the results of their own work only after they were imprisoned.

2) The second, and by far the largest group, consists of "counterrevolutionaries" who were politically and socially neutral and who have obviously been arrested solely to increase the supply of slave labor.

One consequence of all these arrests has been complete intimidation of the people. No one knows what group will be struck tomorrow, whether it will be "undisciplined" workers, or peasants whose harvest proved too small, or national minorities, or "insubordinate" Russians, or government officials, or army officers, or members of the intelligentsia who today are proud of being "proletarian intellectuals" and who tomorrow may be denounced as corrupt cosmopolitans. There is no security for anyone in the Soviet Union, just as the word "security" does not exist in the Russian language—the only word covering that concept means "lack of danger."

And so a generation of children is growing up there whose first word is "Talin" (Stalin), and who speedily learn that there are questions which must never be asked, answers which can never be given. Throughout life all the members of a great nation are forced to mask their faces. Millions of human beings struggle to prove their guiltlessness anew every day, without ever being able to prove it completely. For when the day of arrest comes, nothing counts, neither work nor merit, neither heroism nor submissiveness, neither wisdom nor silence. There are so many who die in the camps, and the gaps must be filled.

I have not based this book on any notes I took during my imprisonment. Taking notes is suicidal in the Soviet Union. But during eleven years of imprisonment everything that happens in the world beyond the barbed wire becomes as intangible and unreal as a dream. The only reality is the land of wooden watch towers—our land, the land of prisoners. Reality is the one white highway along the ridge of the white ravine where the frozen river flows, a highway of loneliness and howling snowstorms which leads straight into the silence of the white forests. If you have shoveled the endless snow upon that road, you never forget it. If you have jolted mile after mile over that road in a jammed truck, incapable of moving your numbed limbs from under your neighbor's numbed limbs, you will not forget that road.

Everything we once knew—lines from our favorite poems, foreign languages, history—more and more vanished from our minds. At last we even forgot how to despair over this sinking down into a dull, brutish indifference. The number of ounces in the bread ration became more important than all the dates in world history. We can no more forget how many ounces were distributed where and when than we can forget those places which often had no names, just a number in kilometers, but which meant life or death to us.

The events I describe are the daily experiences of thousands of people in the Soviet Union. They are the findings of an involuntary expedition into an unknown land: the land of Soviet prisoners, of the guiltless damned. From that region I have brought back with me the silence of the Siberian graveyards, the deathly silence of those who have frozen, starved, or been beaten to death. This book is an attempt to make that silence speak.

Contents

Contents

Contents

xi

Contents

1. The Beginning

Moscow—1937

E VERY NIGHT a few more persons vanished from the hotel which housed the professional revolutionaries from every country of the globe. In the morning there would be large red seals pasted on the doors of a few more rooms.

The others waited tensely to see who would be next. Social intercourse stagnated. Each Party member, after returning from meetings where he had inveighed against traitors, spies, and saboteurs, and passed lengthy resolutions calling for the liquidation of the enemies of the people, settled down in his room to brood about the arrest of Comrade Z. Each wondered: Can it possibly incriminate me?

But how could anyone imagine that Z, such an old Bolshevik. . . . Of course Z had once been accused of right deviations from the Party line back in 1923. But after all that was a long time ago, and an accusation wasn't a crime. There must be some other reason for his arrest. The NKVD knew what it was about. But what had he done, what had he done? Could people conceal their true selves so thoroughly? After all, Z was an old friend. That was just it; that could get you into trouble. The best thing to do was not to associate with anybody.

The guests of the hotel kept away from one another. They began weighing every word carefully before they spoke. They observed one another, slyly, suspiciously. Why did the Party secretary give me that queer look today? And the boss left the office without saying good-by! Are there any charges against me? But I haven't done anything; I'm completely innocent.

They were all innocent, and they were all afraid. They were innocent, and they started up whenever they heard an unfamiliar sound on the stairs. They were innocent, and they tossed sleeplessly in their beds at night.

Until it happened—and the torment of waiting was replaced by the torture of the prison cell.

They came at night, when the last worrier in the big hotel had finally fallen asleep.

Arrest

I started up. Was it a dream, or had someone knocked? There it was again, once, twice, three times—a loud, harsh, insistent knocking. It sounded like the roll of thunder, loud enough to wake everyone in the hotel. A man's voice called out, "Open the door!"

I had to get something on—quickly. I could not find the sleeves of my robe. Why was I trembling so? I had done nothing. I had committed no crime against the state.

Again the impatient, threatening voice: "Open the door!"

Three officers entered. The stripes on their uniforms showed that they were members of the NKVD, the state political police. They were stiff but courteous.

"Your name?"

"Elinor Lipper."

The Beginning

He found the name on the list and nodded. One of the others leafed through a sheaf of papers. He extracted one and handed it to me. All I knew of Russian was the alphabet. But I could make out a few international words. "O-r-d-e-r . . . A-r-r-e-s-t. . . ." And my name.

While I dressed the three tall men considerately looked away. I sat for a moment on the edge of my couch, uncomprehending. I was stunned, without a thought in my head. And I felt nothing, neither hope nor fear nor indignation. Then they began searching my room. They did not finish until nine o'clock in the morning.

Instead of taking the elevator they walked me down the six flights of stairs to the street, in plain view of the whole hotel. Familiar and unfamiliar faces stared at me, paled and turned away. No one greeted me; no one indicated that he knew me.

I took my last automobile ride through the streets of Moscow. One NKVD officer sat beside me, another beside the driver. I was taken to Lubyanka, the central NKVD prison in the heart of Moscow. Iron double doors opened. The soldiers on guard saluted. The inside courtyard was surrounded by a high brick wall. The sun glared on the asphalt pavement.

I was inside of the first of my ten Soviet prisons. The first day of eleven years of imprisonment had begun.

Reception in Prison

The first search of my person. An indifferent woman guard "shook me down" with practiced hands. My papers, watch, ring, money, and pocketbook were taken away. Then the iron door of a small cell was shut behind me, and six women began talking to me all at once. I wanted to tell them that I did not understand Russian; then I realized that my voice was choked with tears. Without a word I sat down in a corner.

That same night I was taken to another prison. Not in an ordinary automobile this time. I sat inside the dark cavern of a prison van that carried me swiftly into the unknown. My stomach contracted with fear. Now they were going to kill me. Nonsense, why should they?

The van raced through the streets.

If I had been arrested for nothing, I could be shot for nothing. Take it easy, take it easy, I said to myself; you're a coward. How hard it was to breathe inside this gloomy box.

The van raced through the streets.

Now they are going to kill me. My forehead was wet with cold perspiration. I clambered out of the van. More iron doors, courtyards, walls and iron doors. I entered the huge vaults of Butyrka Prison. And everywhere there were soldiers, soldiers, and more soldiers.

Each prisoner who is brought to Butyrka Prison is first taken to a room where she must strip naked. A woman guard runs her fingers through the prisoner's hair, examines her ears and nostrils, pokes around in her mouth, looks under her armpits and into her anus, then makes the naked prisoner do knee bends, and finishes with a gynecological examination. All buttons, hooks, eyes, and elastics are removed from her clothes and all pockets and seams are searched. Then the prisoner is allowed to get dressed again.

I walked down endless corridors and stairways, then more corridors filled with an ominous silence. Infrequently, a low murmuring from one of the cells was audible. Still more corridors. Wire nets were stretched between flights of stairs to prevent the possibility of suicide as a way of escaping interrogation. An iron door was opened and closed behind me.

6

The Cell

A collective cell for women. It seemed like a mass tomb. The cell did have windows, but like all windows in Soviet prisons these were not only barred but also masked with boards, so that you could never see anything but a small segment of the sky. Heavy stone pillars rose up to the vaulted ceiling, in the center of which hung a naked electric bulb that burned day and night. The gray stone walls, stained by huge spots of moisture and mold, were alive with thousands of bedbugs. One corner of the floor was covered by inches of water. Some seventy women sat on a platform of rough boards laid about half a yard above the stone floor and covering the entire cell from wall to wall, except for a small space near the entrance. There were neither blankets, mattresses, nor straw sacks. A few lucky women owned prized blankets which they had been allowed to take with them when they were arrested. An oppressive stench took your breath away when you came in; it was the mingled odors of seventy cramped, perspiring women's bodies, and of the moldy stone walls.

I did not know where to step, for every inch of space was taken up by the bodies of half-dressed women. This cell had been intended originally for twenty-four prisoners. It now held seventy; later the number was to increase to eighty and ultimately to ninety-five.

One of the prisoners, called the cell orderly as I later learned, pushed her way through the mob of women and measured out a space for me about sixteen inches wide. Then she gave me a wooden spoon and a tin cup.

Butyrka Prison in Moscow holds an average of thirty thousand prisoners, but it is only one of the five large Moscow prisons for suspects still under examination—that is, persons

7

not yet convicted of any crime. The others are Lubyanka, Lifortovo Military Prison, Navinka Prison and Targanka Prison. The two last-named are also used for criminals; the other three are reserved for political prisoners.

In all the cells in Butyrka the custom is to allot space for each prisoner according to the length of time he has been in prison. The best places near the window are given to those who have been in custody longest. The newcomers are assigned to the corner near the slop bucket, which in all Russian prisons is poetically called *parasha*—actually a diminutive of *Praskovia,* a common woman's name. When a prisoner is taken out of the cell, the rest move up strictly according to the order of their arrest. No exceptions are made for sickness or age.

In general it is amazing to a foreigner to see how little consideration a modern Soviet citizen shows for the aged or the sick. In the tough life of the Soviet Union a person can get along only by jabbing hard with both elbows, and apparently no one has the time or the wish to perform even the slightest service for the old and infirm. In addition, nothing in Soviet education inspires young people to respect age as such, without regard for special merits.

From the moment he is arrested the prisoner is kept in constant suspense. No matter what is done to him or where he is taken, he is given no explanation. This permanent uncertainty and complete helplessness in the grip of a silent, uncanny power, produces in every prisoner exactly what it is expected to produce: fear. He begins to fear every change in his condition. Perhaps it may be a change for the better—but he is afraid anyhow. And the NKVD plays with virtuoso skill upon this fear. Even when the prisoner is not called for interrogation, he is never allowed to settle down. The big col-

lective cells are continually being reorganized and the inmates distributed among other cells. At least once a month
the entire cell is called out for a physical search, which the
prisoners call "the dry bath." Again you are made to strip
naked; the last button is cut off your dress; ribbons that you
painfully wove out of threads are confiscated, as well as the
sewing needles which all the women make out of the teeth
of combs. Then again you will be called out for finger-
printing, and again to be photographed for the rogues' gal-
lery. From both these procedures most women returned sobbing.

The prisoners are eternally suspicious of one another, for
there is at least one person in each cell who informs the
authorities of everything her fellow prisoners say. These informers are also supposed to urge the other prisoners to confess to whatever they are charged with, since there is no use
resisting.

Prisoners who are subjected to specially strict interrogations (in other words, physical abuse) are generally kept in
Lubyanka or Lifortovo prisons, or in the special section
(*osoby korpus*) of Butyrka, where they occupy single or double cells. But occasionally, as an object lesson to the others,
a few of these black-and-blue and swollen victims of long
interrogations are put into the collective cells to demonstrate
to the newcomers that the threats of the examining judges are
not empty talk. But the months of waiting for the first interrogation is in itself enough to wear down the prisoners. Most
prisoners enter the cell with the quiet assumption that they
are innocent. Soon enough they become anxious, sleepless
hysterics who all night long start at every sound and leap to
their feet whenever anyone cries out.

For seven and a half months I sat in various collective cells without being called for interrogation a single time, without even having my personal data taken down. At first I expected hourly that my arrest would prove to be a mistake. I pictured the whole scene in detail—how they would apologize to me: "Regrettable error, particularly regrettable since you are a foreigner. . . ."

I sent a petition to Vyshinsky, then chief state prosecutor of the Soviet Union, pointing out that it was unconstitutional to hold a prisoner for more than six months without informing him of the charge against him. My petition was of course not answered.

And so I had plenty of leisure time to look back upon the path that had led me to this prison.

How I Came to the Soviet Union

I heard about Russia for the first time when I was nine years old. A lady who was not particularly well informed told me about a country where there were no longer any rich people or poor people, where everybody had to work equally, and where all received just as much money as they needed for food and clothing.

"Do you like the idea?" she asked me.

"No, I don't," I said after thinking it over for a while.

"Why not?"

"Because then nobody would have money to give presents."

When I was eleven years old my father told me and my brother about the Belgian workers' children who had emptied their savings banks to help starving Russian children. Both my brother and I listened to the tale with obstinate indifference, and neither of us rushed off to fetch his savings bank. What did we know about Russia and her famine? Hurt by our heartless reaction, my father silently walked out of the room. I have never forgotten his look of disappointment, although I did not understand his emotion until much later. He was thinking that something was wrong with our normal, secure, middle-class upbringing if it made children so unfeeling about the sufferings of others. (We were carefully shielded from suffering, of course.)

When I was fourteen my schoolmates and I laughed heartily at a teacher of ours who took part in the workers' demonstration on May 1. To think of a teacher making herself ridiculous by tramping through the streets with such a parade! None of us thought about what might lie behind this parade. But I felt real sympathy for the sorrows of the Dutch fisherwomen whom I saw waiting at the port on stormy days in November, and often waiting in vain for their menfolks to return.

When a girl-friend asked me whether I had read a certain article in the newspaper, I answered with sixteen-year-old haughtiness that I never looked at the newspapers. "They're all full of filth," I said. My political views at that time were confined to two simple principles: war and capital punishment should be abolished. Why should I waste my time on newspapers when there were Wassermann, Dostoyevsky, Rilke, and Stefan George to read?

When I graduated from high school my principal asked me what I expected to study for. When I told him I was still hesitating between medicine and the liberal arts, he said smilingly, "Why not—editor of a pacifist magazine?" My classmates roared with laughter.

In 1931, when I began studying medicine in Berlin, student life was full of political tensions. The Chinese wall behind which I had lived so peacefully in my native Holland was beginning to crumble. For the first time I met students who were working their way through the university. They spoke enthusiastically about a country where gifted young people could go to school without paying for their tuition. That country was the Soviet Union. (In 1942 fees for higher education were reintroduced there.) We had endless discussions about free love and women's right to have abortions. There was one country in the world which gave this right to women—Soviet Russia. (In 1935 abortion was forbidden by law in the Soviet Union and was declared a crime punishable by eight years in a labor camp [Paragraph 148]. If the abortion took place after four and one half months of pregnancy the charge was murder and the sentence provided was ten years. Aiding and abetting an abortion was punishable by eight years imprisonment. Later, when I was in camp, I met a woman who had had an abortion which was not discovered until she was again pregnant. Because of changed circumstances she wanted this second child. She was arrested and the baby was born in prison. She was convicted, given an eight-year sentence, and the baby was taken from her and given to her family at the time she was moved from prison to camp. The baby had been breast-fed, and the sudden separation from its mother was too much for it. It died soon afterward. The woman prisoner brooded and brooded over this: "I am being locked up for eight years on account of an unborn child, but my living child is torn away from me so that it will die. . . .")

While I was at Berlin University I worked during vacations in the municipal hospital. For the first time I saw human misery close up. With other students I helped distribute milk among the children of the unemployed. To this day I can see an unemployed epileptic's six children staring at us with dumb suspicion, the oldest about ten years old, all with colorless faces, overlarge heads and rachitic legs. Once your eyes were opened to social injustice it was impossible for you to shut them again, especially during the years 1931 and 1932 in Berlin. Men out of work loitered on every street, and political discussions went on at every street corner.

What first led me to socialism was a purely emotional reaction to this misery. It was only later that I fortified my belief by reading theoretical writings on socialism. The menace of the Nazi monster with its hateful ideology was coming dangerously near, while the Social Democratic government of Germany retreated step by step before it. It seemed impossible for a thinking person not to take a stand. I entered the "Red Student Group."

I thought I was casting my lot for a social order which would use modern technology for the benefit of the masses, rather than for a privileged upper crust, by nationalizing the land and the means of production:

A social order which by intelligent application of technology would make possible a six-hour working day and a five-day working week (achievements of the Russian Revolution which have long since been abolished), with the leisure time thus saved being used for the development of the individual personality.

A social order which would not resort to war to further its ends, because its people felt linked with the masses all over the world. Which recognized force as an evil and would use it only in the period of transition and only against those who used force against it.

A social order which freed its artists, architects and scientists from concern for their daily bread, so that they could devote their full energies to their artistic and scientific tasks.

A social order where there was no incentive or cause for

13

crime because all men were guaranteed a minimum livelihood that would enable them to live like dignified human beings. A few criminals would still exist, the heritage of former social conditions, but they would be re-educated rather than punished. We assumed that born criminals were relatively rare and that there would be very few such pathological cases.

That was and is my conception of socialism. For the sake of this ideal I left Germany in 1933. The same ideal impelled me to go to the Soviet Union in 1937. There I worked for two months in a publishing house that specialized in foreign literature. (Until 1934 I had tried to continue my medical studies in Italy, but I was unable to get the necessary academic documents out of Germany.)

After my first two months I was arrested.

The political path that had led me to the Soviet Union was perfectly clear, perfectly straightforward. Nothing I had done, said or planned could have justified my arrest. My only fault was my boundless naïveté in imagining that the Soviet Union was the realization of my ideals.

Even today, after my return from the Soviet Union, the idea of socialism seems to me the most reasonable solution to the social problem and its achievement the only guarantee that wars can be averted in the future. But today I know that the Soviet Union has no interest in the realization of this idea. The Soviet Union has betrayed socialism to the world; it has drowned the idea in blood. A believer in socialism cannot believe in the Soviet Union, for it is impossible to defend the slaughter of millions of innocent human beings and to claim at the same time that one is striving to benefit suffering humanity.

But at that time I did not yet know this. At that time I sat in my cell completely dazed, and waited. And I endured what thousands of women in this same prison endured. I was shifted from one collective cell to the other. I picked up Russian and heard my fellow prisoners' stories. Each new story that I heard made me see more and more, until at last I realized what I vainly tried not to realize: that all these people were as innocent as I was. Then my own suffering began to merge into the vast suffering of them all.

It is impossible to enumerate all the grotesque charges that bring people to Soviet prisons. Every one of the stories I have set down here is the story, with slight variations, of thousands and tens of thousands of unhappy Soviet people.

The Inmates of My Cell

In 1937 and 1938 about half of the inmates were Communist Party members or Young Communists. Three fourths of these were members of the Russian Communist Party; the rest belonged to the Polish, Latvian or German parties. There were also some Hungarians and Rumanians. The rest of the inmates were housewives from every segment of the population. Some of them had been arrested on informers' charges; others because they were the wives of more or less prominent men.

Mrs. Rakovski, the wife of Soviet Ambassador Rakovski, was a Rumanian, a white-haired, sickly woman who suffered severe heart attacks every few weeks. Her neighbor in the cell was a dark-eyed, dark-haired, and stately woman, the wife of Prince Obolenski, who for years held a high position in the Soviet state and was a frequent visitor of Stalin's. Then there was a frail, slender, nervous person, a former student of philosophy, who was the wife of Alexander Serebrovsky, head of a huge copper trust. There was a full-bosomed woman with dyed blonde hair who tripped around the cell on high heels.

She was the wife of Commander Silko. Lacking face powder, she powdered her nose with tooth powder when she was called to interrogations. This did not help her; like the others she was sentenced to eight years in camp for belonging to the family of a traitor. Rebuchkova, the wife of a high state functionary, was a woman in her fifties who had obviously been very beautiful in her youth. She suffered from gallstone attacks and would writhe on the floor, screaming piteously. Lisa Geller, who had worked for the Soviet Trade Mission in Berlin, wept bitterly about her two small children whom she had left behind. The first wife of a member of the government, Meshlauk, was a woman of about forty with a tight-lipped, unyielding face. She was a fanatical communist and a person of great self-assurance. On suspicion of espionage she was sentenced to eight years in camp; she died of dysentery in 1938 while in the transit camp at Vladivostok. Mrs. Kossior, who had accompanied her husband on a foreign mission to Berlin, attempted suicide the night after she was convicted and sentenced to ten years for counterrevolutionary activity. She served her sentence in a Siberian camp near Mariinsk. Voronova, who was assistant to the People's Commissar for Light Industry, had formerly been a textile worker. By means of devotion to her work and absolute submissiveness she had risen to her high position. She was sentenced to ten years in prison for counterrevolutionary activity. In memory of her husband she had never remarried. He had died during the Civil War when the Whites surrounded and set fire to a stable in which he and his soldiers had barricaded themselves.

The secretary of Madame Stassova, chief of the International Red Aid (MOPR), was named Shvalova. When she was placed in our cell she did not speak to anyone and refused to answer our questions about events in Spain. She thought that we were all dangerous counterrevolutionaries and that she alone was innocent. A military court sentenced her to fifteen years imprisonment. She was sent to Kolyma in northeastern Siberia and stayed there until she died at the beginning of the war.

Irina Kun, wife of the famous revolutionary Bela Kun, was given eight years on suspicion of espionage. She too was sent to Kolyma. She was frail to begin with, became incapable of work in Kolyma and was finally transferred to an invalid camp at Mariinsk.

These names represent only a portion of all the revolutionaries or the wives of revolutionaries whom I met in prison and camp. All of them, after more or less brutal interrogations, were given long prison sentences, whether or not they renounced their husbands, whether or not they had lived with them during the years before their arrest, whether or not they had children or were pregnant. They were convicted and sentenced even when their husbands had committed suicide a year before their arrest—as was the case with the ballet dancer, Madame Lercher, of the Bolshoi Theater in Moscow. This charming, cultured dancer was an altogether unpolitical person. For a short time she had been married to a people's commissar of light industry who committed suicide after the first big Moscow trial in 1936. After his death he was accused of Trotskyism. A year later Madame Lercher was arrested on the same charge and sentenced to eight years in camp on account of her marriage to a man who had held a high post up to the moment of his death and who had been branded as a traitor only after his suicide. It was terribly moving to watch this woman persisting with dance exercises and gymnastics. Losing her suppleness meant for her losing her livelihood, and so she kept up her routines in the furthermost corner of the cell, because all such exercise was strictly forbidden. Her eyes filled with the sadness and the resignation of the prisoner, she moved her feet with magical lightness and performed lovely figures and pirouettes on the rough boards of the cell.

One prisoner who was a great consolation to us was Berta Alexandrovna B. A kindlier person than this near-sighted, enormously well-padded woman could not be imagined. Again and again she got into difficulties with the cell orderly because she could not lower her loud, hearty voice; she was always shouting encouragement to someone, with her head thrust close to the other's face so that she could see her. Her glasses had been taken away, of course, for anyone who had glass might use it to cut open her veins.

After the evening count, when each of us lay with her head between the often none-too-fragrant feet of her neighbor (we lay alternately, one with head and one with feet toward the wall, to take up less space), we could hear for a long time Berta Alexandrovna whispering loudly to her neighbor. It was a gross breach of regulations, but like many of us she suffered from insomnia. Now and then someone made her way awkwardly over the sleeping bodies to the bucket. We waited in suspense for Berta's turn to come. At last, slowly and majestically, the huge figure in the lavender dressing gown would rise. For a long time she would stand hesitantly looking for a free space for her first step. The massive raised leg would hover threateningly over the innocent sleeper; the near-sighted eyes appeared to detect an inch of clear space; and then she stepped down. There followed immediately the terrified shriek of the first victim. Berta, who was always considerate of everyone, would murmur an alarmed apology. The same ritual would be repeated, and she would take her second step, and then her third, each time convinced that she had really found a passage, and each time stepping on a head or stomach with the sureness of a somnambulist. Ten steps—ten cries of agony, curses, angry shouts, but rarely a helping hand. Ten times Berta, growing more and more disconcerted, would murmur polite apologies. It was very funny, and very sad.

Every morning she also took advantage of the confusion in the cell, as we prepared for being let out into the washroom, to try a few forbidden gymnastic exercises. She could not resign herself to this ban, for even during Tsarist times when she had served her first prison sentence, she had been allowed daily calisthenics. At that time she had been an active social revolutionary like her husband, who had also been arrested, although both had abandoned political action after the creation of the Soviet state. In order not to make trouble for their two sons, she and her husband had made no attempt to influence the children politically. The sons had followed the regular course of Soviet youth, belonging first to the Pioneers, then to the Comsomols, the youth organization. Both became engineers and both were arrested in 1937—because their parents had been arrested.

In spite of her family tragedy Berta had never lost a deep interest in other people, other countries, and in art, literature, and above all poetry. Her particular type of cultivated revolutionary has by now practically died out in Russia. The last representatives of the class vanished behind prison walls during 1937 and 1938. Foreigners who always think of Russians as an amalgam of Dostoyevsky and Gorky would be bitterly disappointed today. The search for truth, the urge to understand the meaning of life, is wholly alien to the younger generation which has passed through the school of the Communist Youth Organization. For them, all problems have been solved; there is a standard answer to every question. The language of these intellectually impoverished young people is larded with ready-made phrases. They quote Stalin instead of thinking for themselves; they derive their opinions from *Pravda* editorials. They are arrogant and complacent, and everything that pertains to them is the greatest thing there is: their country, their power, their leader. Theirs is also the greatest misery and oppression, but they are unaware of this, for they have never known anything but Soviet life. The members of this younger generation have neither sympathy nor understanding for their elders; there is no bond between them. If anyone puts forth a thought which does not fit into the pattern laid down by Stalin, they do not argue against it, but they react with such suspicion of the other's true intentions and hidden thoughts that he quickly learns to keep his ideas to himself. They are primitives who hate the unfamiliar.

There were a number of arrested Young Communists in our cell, and their attitude toward Berta Alexandrovna was a combination of suspicion and contempt. She spoke several foreign languages fluently and could become as enthusiastic about Michelangelo's sonnets as they about the dubious successes of the Five-Year Plan. Everything about Berta's emotional and intellectual world was foreign to the Young Communists, and therefore Berta—who had spent years of her life in Tsarist prisons for the sake of her ideals—was an enemy to them.

People like Berta Alexandrovna were doubly isolated. They were alone as every prisoner is, and they were cut off from the mass of the prisoners. Later I saw her again at Kolyma, when we had both been ten years in prison. Her grayish hair had turned snow-white; she had lost a great deal of weight, and folds of empty skin hung loose all over her body. Dead tired, she dragged her still-ponderous legs back to camp from work every evening. She was not likely to think of calisthenics now; every movement was a wearisome effort to her. She no longer talked about poetry; her eyes no longer flashed with emotion—they too had been dulled by suffering. Her husband had died in camp; her older son was also dead; she did not know what had become of the younger son. Soon she would be free. Free to crawl into a corner somewhere and die.

2. In the Machinery of Justice

Evening in the Cell

OPPOSITE OUR CELL and separated from it by a rather narrow yard lay the wing which contained the offices of the examining judges. During the day there was nothing remarkable about this wing. But as soon as darkness fell, the ordinarily silent prison was filled with sounds.

In our cell the last whispers died away. We all listened. Listened to the steadily mounting shrieks and screams from that wing, listened to the interrogators shouting curses at their victims. The voices of the prisoners could be distinguished only when they cried out in fear, pain, or despair.

A hoarse voice: "You bastard, I'll make you talk."

Then more silence—the blows were inaudible to us—and suddenly a clear, pleading cry: "Comrades, comrades." The cry grew louder, more hopeless: "Comrades, comrades."

Then again something happened that we could not hear, and the same voice called out, "Mama, my head, mama, my head! Mama, mama, mama, my head."

We in our cell listened, choked with fear and pity.

There was an old woman in the cell who never wept, even

when she returned from a hearing with her chest beaten black and blue. Now tears rolled quietly down her wrinkled face.

"Mama, my head. . . ."

A few peasant women crossed themselves.

The newcomers sat pale and wide-eyed, thinking of their own first hearing and what would happen to them.

"Mama, mama. . . ." Others listened knowingly, thinking that this was already behind them and wondering whether Heaven would preserve them from further hearings.

"Mama, mama," the man screamed.

There were a few who still believed that nothing of the sort could happen to them, because after all they were innocent—whereas you could never be sure that anybody else was innocent.

"Mama, my head. . . ."

I thought about the fact that the man had gone on calling his torturers "comrade" when they were already beating him; he could think of no other word for them and called them "comrade" when they fell upon him like beasts—until he understood and in his agony cried out to the only loyal name that was left to him: "Mama."

And I thought how fortunate it was that those unknown mothers somewhere in Moscow, weeping for their imprisoned sons, were not there to hear him screaming and screaming: "Mama, my head, mama, mama, mama, my head," until they carried him off and there was left only a confused medley of voices, screams and curses.

Hunger Strike

A hunger strike by a prisoner, like any strike in the Soviet Union, is considered a counterrevolutionary action.

If a prisoner embarks on a hunger strike, the fact is recognized only if he informs the prison authorities in writing. But since we could send in "slips" only once every two weeks, no notice was taken of a hunger strike that occurred meanwhile. There was no way for the authorities even to know that a prisoner in a collective cell was hunger-striking.

I recall the case of one woman who started a hunger strike from the moment she was placed in the cell. Every morning and evening at count time the cell orderly informed the guards that one of the eighty-two inmates was on hunger strike. Before long the woman was so weak that she could no longer stand. Still the prison administration did not react, since the woman had not yet had the opportunity to announce her hunger strike in writing. She had not been strong when she was brought in, so that before long she lay half-conscious on the boards, failing rapidly.

At last she was taken to the prison hospital where such cases are force-fed. Two attendants held her while the nurse introduced the feeding tube into her nose. This painful procedure is continued until the prisoner realizes that his resistance is pointless, since because of the forced feeding he is not credited with being actually on a hunger strike.

Mass hunger strikes in the camps no longer take place, since experience has shown that the NKVD replies to such actions by mass shootings. I know of only one case of a successful hunger strike. This took place in a camp for Polish prisoners of war. For eleven days the inmates refused to take any nourishment but water, as a protest against their starvation rations. Threats and solitary confinements had no effect. Had they been Soviet citizens the NKVD would have taken care of them soon enough. But a thousand Poles, that is, foreigners, could not be liquidated outright.

At last a commission put in an appearance and announced

that the camp rations would be improved. The improvement actually lasted for a while. Then the customary speculation and embezzlement by the camp authorities were resumed, and the food became unbearably vile again. Once more the camp started a hunger strike which lasted for six days this time. The inmates were promised that their demands would be met, and they ended the strike. But by this time the NKVD had had enough of Polish solidarity. The camp was dissolved and the inmates distributed among various other prisoner-of-war camps.

The Mother

One of the many mothers in our cell was Smirnova, wife of a high government official. After her husband's arrest she had been evicted from her apartment in Moscow. Let the wife of an enemy of the people see where she could live with her three children. She found a wretched shelter in a suburb of Moscow, where she rented a *dacha* or country cottage—actually it was a primitive peasant's hut. After much searching, for no one wanted to employ the wife of an enemy of the people, she succeeded in getting work in the post office. In rest periods she had to rush home to nurse her two-month-old baby. The next child was a girl of six who watched the baby while the mother was at work. The oldest, a fourteen-year-old boy, was going to school.

The little girl frequently asked after her father, and the mother invented innumerable stories about a long trip from which the father would soon be returning. The boy asked no questions. He had been present when the father was arrested and he could not forget his father's look of complete amazement and incredulity when he was handed the warrant for arrest. The boy had stood at the window and watched the automobile speeding away with his arrested father. That moment had marked the end of his childhood. A world which had hitherto seemed so harmonious collapsed abruptly. His father was an enemy of the people. His father had gone to prison for no crime. That fact outweighed all the humiliations he had to swallow from then on. None of his former friends spoke to him, for he was the son of an enemy of the people. His favorite teacher, with whom he had had a close and friendly relationship for years, now became formal, cold and unapproachable. No one wanted to sit next to him in class. Every recess became a torment for him, for he was left strictly alone. Almost every day, in classes or at school assemblies, anathemas were called down upon the enemies of the Soviet state and the pupils were urged to be on guard against them. Then the eyes of dozens of merciless children pierced him from all sides.

At fourteen this boy was a despised outcast. The whole world stared at him out of hostile, hate-filled faces. The only person who still loved him was his mother. With the tenderness and sensitivity of the sufferer he drew close to his mother, who daily endured humiliations a hundred times worse than his own.

During the early period after the father's arrest the family expected his return daily, hourly. But months went by and he did not come back—none of all the millions of innocent persons come back once the prison gates of the Soviet Union shut behind them.

But the police did come back. One night they were there to take the mother away. Quivering, pale, the boy stood in front of her to protect her. It did not help. Nor did it help when the little girl, awakened out of her sleep, clung sobbing to her mother. It did not help when the mother, almost mad with despair, snatched up her baby. The police pushed the boy and girl aside, laid the screaming baby back in its cradle, and dragged the resisting mother into the waiting car. The boy stood at the window until the car vanished into the darkness of the night.

Iron gates swung open and closed. She was locked within the three-foot-thick walls of Butyrka Prison.

She was searched. When it was over she tried with shaking hands to braid her hair—even her hairpins had been taken away. She turned to the guard:

"Citizeness, how long will this go on? Where am I being taken? I must get back home! I've left my baby home, a nursing infant. She will die of starvation without me; she's had only my milk. I must go to her."

The guard's face showed no flicker of expression. Her eyes remained dull, indifferent, bored. She did not answer. No one but the examining judges are allowed to talk with prisoners beyond giving them essential orders.

She was locked up in one of the temporary cells which the prisoners call doghouses. It was about four feet long and two feet wide. On one wall was a stone bench; high above the iron door was a tiny hole which let in a little light from the corridor. Here she sat for hours, obsessed by the thought: My children, my baby. . . . Her breasts hurt her; they became swollen with milk for which her hungry baby at home must be crying.

Toward evening she was taken to the hearing. With an ironic smile the examining judge looked at the woman's distracted face, framed in loose braids, at her wrinkled stockings and her hands, which were convulsively clutching her buttonless dress to keep it together.

"Tell us about your husband's counterrevolutionary activity."

"My husband was not a counterrevolutionary."

"What's that? You've been married to him for fifteen years and you claim you know nothing about his seditious activities, which he himself has confessed to?"

"That can't be. I've lived with him for fifteen years and I know everything he thinks. He can't be a traitor."

"Then you won't talk? You want to shield this scoundrel? All right. Maybe the cell will change your mind."

"The cell? I must go home. I've left my three children all alone. My baby will starve if I'm not allowed to nurse it."

"Sign this statement that you were informed of your husband's seditious activities and you will see your baby."

"I can't sign it. He's innocent."

The examining judge pressed a button. His orderly appeared. "Take her away. Cell forty-nine."

She stood in the cell like a sleepwalker. She was unable to understand the questions of the other prisoners. She did not notice anyone in the throng. The scene of wretchedness all around her was banished by the terrible vision of her abandoned children.

When she was given her spoon and cup, like all newcomers, she took them quickly and sat down on the boards close to the bars of the open window, with her back to the others, in search of a little privacy. Then she pressed the milk out of her bursting breasts into the tin cup. One of the women emptied the cup into the stinking bucket near the door. A low murmur passed through the cell: "They've put a nursing mother into prison."

The mother did not hear them. She could hear only the crying of her hungry baby.

28

Next day the examining judge interviewed her again.

"Well, have you thought it over?"

"Tell me what has been done with my baby," she implored him.

"Sign this statement that you talked over his seditious activity with your husband and I will tell you about your baby."

"You want me to be my innocent husband's murderer. I cannot sign this lying statement."

"Is that all you have to say to me?"

"Let me go to my baby. She will die without her mother. At least tell me where she is. Have mercy on the helpless child."

She pleaded, wept, moaned. She did not know that an examining judge of the NKVD cannot be moved to pity. Instead of answering her, he laid the statement down for her to sign.

"My baby will never thank me if I ruin her father for her sake." She pushed the document away.

The examining judge shrugged and had her taken out. That night she was called out once more. A nurse bandaged her breasts to stop the flow of milk.

After a few months, without any charge being made against her personally, she was sentenced to eight years loss of freedom "as a member of the family of a traitor." She never found out what had happened to her children.

The Procedure

A Soviet citizen who is charged with counterrevolutionary activity is arrested on the basis of a warrant signed by the state prosecuting attorney. A similar warrant authorizes the search of a home. In the large cities arrested persons are brought to special prisons and do time before trial apart from

criminals. In smaller towns where there is limited space, pretrial prisoners are put into mixed cells with criminals. Even
the smallest town in the Soviet Union has a prison, and everywhere the prison is being enlarged.

For counterrevolutionaries the period of detention while
awaiting trial is often longer than a year and sometimes
stretches on to two or three years. But on the average, especially for female prisoners, it lasts six months. A law exists
which provides that a prisoner must be informed of the
charge against him within two weeks after his arrest, but in
practice this law is seldom observed. I did not learn of the
charge against me until my fourteenth month in prison. The
written indictment is handed to the prisoner by the examining judge and the defendant is supposed to sign it. If he refuses to sign, a guard signs a statement that the indictment
was read to the prisoner in his presence.

All defendants are classified under Paragraph 58 of the
criminal code: Counterrevolution. This paragraph is divided
into various articles, and the indictments rest on one or more
of these articles. There are numerical gaps in the following
list because my knowledge of the articles is derived from
meeting prisoners who were indicted under them. I never
met any prisoners indicted under Articles 2, 3, 5 or 13.

Article 1: Treason
     a. by civilians
     b. by military personnel
Article 4: Support of a foreign state against the Soviet
     Union
Article 6: Espionage
Article 7: Sedition
Article 8: Terrorism

Article 9: Diversion
Article 10: Agitation and propaganda
Article 11: Organization and formation of groups
Article 12: Failure to denounce
Article 14: Sabotage

The defendant may be charged directly under one of these articles of Paragraph 58, or he may be charged, under Paragraph 17, with complicity in the crimes specified under Paragraph 58. Members of the family of persons who are convicted under Paragraph 58, Article 1 are held to be guilty under the same clauses.

It is the business of the examining judges to draw up a deposition demonstrating the defendant's guilt, and to persuade the defendant to sign this deposition. If he steadfastly refuses to sign, incriminating statements against him are extorted from his fellow defendants, so that his determination does him no good. But if his signature is indispensable, methods of examination are applied which ultimately always succeed—because there are limits to the resistance of the human organism.

It is very rare for the defendant to be confronted with witnesses or codefendants, and then only when their testimony is against him.

Indicted counterrevolutionaries do not have defending lawyers.

A prisoner awaiting trial is not permitted to communicate with his family or with any other person. Twice a month, however, he has the right to address petitions to one of the following authorities:

The prison warden
The examining judge

31

The State Attorney
The People's Commissar (now Minister) of the Interior
The Central Committee of the Communist Party
The Supreme Soviet
Stalin

Almost all defendants write several letters to one or another of these authorities. They offer proofs of their innocence, name witnesses who can testify in their favor, point to their unsullied life or Party history, and protest against the methods of the examiners. I know of not a single case in which the afore-mentioned authorities (assuming the communications actually were transmitted to them) intervened in behalf of a defendant or even answered his letter.

The defendant is informed when the examination is completed.

There are two different ways in which counterrevolutionaries are convicted. Either a court-martial (or a military commission) tries the case, or the verdict is passed administratively by an invisible commission of judges. The court-martial passes death sentences or sentences of imprisonment from ten to twenty-five years. The verdict of a court-martial always involves confiscation of personal property and loss of civil rights for from three to five years after completion of the sentence. These verdicts are based upon one or more articles of Paragraph 58. The "special commission of judges of the NKVD" (Russian abbreviation: OSO) metes out sentences up to ten years in camp, in the absence of the defendant. This commission is never empowered to order confiscation of property or loss of civil rights. Its verdicts are not governed by the articles of Paragraph 58; in the formula used by this court the defendant is convicted of general counterrevolutionary intentions, but of no specific crimes.

Except for the show-trials which reach the world press, all trials of counterrevolutionaries are held in secret. After the trial the convicted person is placed in a cell reserved for convicts. But here too he is not permitted to see any members of his family or to inform them of the verdict.

Those who are sentenced to prison terms are moved to the so-called *polit-izolators*—political-isolation prisons. After about three years in such a prison the terms of most sentences are commuted, although the prisoner himself usually has not asked for any revision of sentence. The new modified sentence provides for the prisoner's being sent to a camp. (That is how I was able to learn details concerning the inmates and the regime of the political-isolation prisons.) The revision of sentence does not take place automatically, however; the prisoners to be shipped to camp are always selected individually.

In 1937 and 1938 most cases were settled by the invisible commission of judges. The panel of judges and the defendant never saw one another. The defendant had no opportunity to make any statements about the information extorted from him by the examining judge, nor to say a word in his own defense. Hundreds of thousands of human beings were sentenced by a stroke of the pen. The phrases most frequently used in imposing sentences of up to ten years imprisonment were the following:

1. For counterrevolutionary activity (Russian abbreviation: KRD). Sentence of five, eight, or ten years.
2. For counterrevolutionary Trotskyist activity (Russian abbreviation KRTD). Sentence of five or eight years.
3. As a socially dangerous element (Russian abbreviation: SOE). Sentence of five years.

4. For *suspicion* of espionage (Russian abbreviation: PSh). Sentence of eight years.
5. For counterrevolutionary agitation (Russian abbreviation: KRA). Sentence of five to ten years.
6. For counterrevolutionary Trotskyist agitation (Russian abbreviation: KRTA). Sentence of five or eight years.
7. As a member of the family of a traitor (Russian abbreviation: TSh/S). Sentence of five or eight years.

How easy it was for the commission of judges, since they could convict a person on mere suspicion of espionage. And this was the case, not in time of war, but in peacetime, in 1937 and 1938.

But what is the meaning of "suspicion of espionage" in the Soviet Union?

Every Soviet citizen is suspected of espionage if he has ever been abroad or ever associated with a foreigner. Naturally every foreigner is suspect.

Association means any correspondence with relatives, friends, acquaintances or professional colleagues abroad. People who were earlier sent abroad by the state itself for study or training are suspected of espionage because of these very journeys. So are the employees of diplomatic and trade missions abroad. Similarly, any encounter with a foreigner inside the Soviet Union can be dangerous. Thus the employees of Intourist, the state organization which handles the traveling of foreigners in the Soviet Union, must perpetually look forward to the prospect of being accused of espionage because of their work.

In 1937 the Comintern, which for so many years had been considered an instrument of the world revolution, was denounced in thousands of Party meetings throughout the

Soviet Union as a vehicle for smuggling foreign spies into the Soviet Union. Political exiles from Fascist countries were also castigated as spies.

Until the sale of the East Chinese Railroad (KWShD), whose administrative center was in the Manchurian city of Harbin, thousands of Soviet citizens worked alongside of Chinese and Japanese on the railroad. In 1934 the Soviet Union sold its share of the KWShD to Japan, and all the Soviet workmen who had been employed on the road returned with their families to the Soviet Union. During 1937 and 1938 almost every one of them was arrested, and their families with them, so that often three generations of the same family were in the same prison at the same time. One and all, they were charged with suspicion of espionage for Japan, no matter what they had been: switchmen and executives, the aging mother of an engineer or an enthusiastic Young Communist girl who had already done time in a Chinese jail for her beliefs.

All of them were sentenced by administrative decree, that is, by the invisible commission of judges, and given eight years in camp. When the usual question was put to them: "What are you in for?" they would answer laconically, "Harbin." That was enough; there was no need to ask further.

For thirty years the frontiers of this vast country have been hermetically sealed. For thirty years the few citizens who are sent abroad have been sifted over and over, weighed, measured, tested, and probed to determine whether they are firm enough to meet the peril of contact with foreign countries. For thirty years there have been no amnesties at all for political prisoners.

How little the rulers must believe in the myth of a happy and free life in the Soviet Union when they fear to let their citizens be contaminated by the slightest knowledge of life abroad. Or is the Soviet citizen so ready to sell himself as a spy? Certainly not. The Soviet people love their country and are as ready to make sacrifices for it as any other people on earth.

At bottom it is not espionage that the rulers fear. It is the possibility of comparison between life in Russia and life abroad. They must inevitably fear this. For thirty years the Soviet people have been given a totally twisted, unreal, carefully censored and distorted picture of the non-Soviet world.

It is true that foreign films are shown in the Soviet Union, but the best are never shown, only the second-rate films. In spite of their superficiality and the crudity of their plots these foreign films are always an event for the Soviet citizens. People in Russia talked for years about pictures like *A Hundred Men and a Girl* or *The Great Waltz*. This pleasure in mediocre films is an expression of the Soviet citizen's tremendous fatigue. He is sick to death of heroism, of being urged to inhumanly superhuman accomplishments, of the religion of hate in the name of a questionable love for the unborn generations of future centuries. In the foreign films he finds a little of the element he is starving for: human, unheroic, untroubled, relaxing entertainment. What joy it is for him when for an entire evening no one is glorified.

In order to appease this obvious hunger of the people for unpolitical moving pictures a number of very pretty fairytale films have been made in the Soviet Union. But it is significant that the themes for the pictures had to be taken from fairy-tales, because there is nothing high-spirited and innocently charming in the real Soviet world.

Some foreign literature is obtainable in the Soviet Union. But how minute, how ridiculously small is the number of

36

foreign authors who are translated into Russian. Few Soviet citizens are in a position to read foreign works in the original because they can never order a book from abroad or find it in a bookstore. Soviet citizens are able to read only what the state censors deem healthful. What would become of the "bulwark of socialism" if its citizens began constructing their own independent picture of foreign countries and contrasting it with Soviet misery? There must be no grounds for comparison whatsoever, for only then can the Soviet rulers convince the Soviet masses that strictest censorship of every word of printed matter in the Soviet Union is true freedom of the press; that it is a sign of true freedom of opinion when a man is shot for printing an illegal leaflet; that shooting striking workers is proof of a true democratic spirit; that confirming the choice of the sole candidate on the slate is true electoral freedom; that it is revolutionary progress when no worker can change jobs without permission from the authorities and when tardiness of twenty minutes can mean a six month jail sentence; that the constant incarceration of almost ten per cent of the male population in prisons and forced labor camps is the normal condition of society and marks the country as "the only genuine democracy in the world."

The Judges Too

When Yagoda, chief of the NKVD, was convicted of counterrevolution in 1937, the staff of examining judges was thoroughly overhauled. The old staff vanished. A large percentage of them had been Latvians who fought in the Revolution and Civil War on the Soviet side, but now simply disappeared. Those who had spent part of their lives abroad suffered the same fate. Many prisoners found considerable satisfaction in meeting their own examining judges, who had bawled the accusation of counterrevolutionary and spy at them, in prison on the same charges.

Since the tremendous influx of prisoners could no longer be handled by the normal staff of the NKVD, new assistants were installed, ridiculously young boys who were given a slip of paper with the standard questions, at which they glanced now and then during the hearings to refresh their memories. None of them knew anything about conditions abroad, but two general principles were impressed upon them: everyone who had had the slightest contact with adherents of a non-Communist party was a counterrevolutionary; and everyone who had been arrested abroad and then released was an agent of the foreign police, that is, a spy. Where the case concerned Soviet citizens who had never been abroad, the criteria were the following: a person whose work had always been above reproach was undoubtedly covering up counterrevolutionary activities. But should there have been any instance of trouble or any accident in the defendant's place of work, that was proof of his sabotaging activities. If the defendant admitted having observed anything suspicious in the private or professional life of a superior who was also under indictment, he was guilty for not having denounced his superior. If the defendant had observed nothing suspicious, he was guilty of a lack of revolutionary alertness. If a woman repudiated her husband once he was arrested, she thereby admitted that she thought him a counterrevolutionary and was therefore guilty for having lived with him. If she did not renounce him, she was guilty of questioning the infallibility of the NKVD.

It did not matter how the defendant behaved—he was always guilty. A Party member was told: For the higher interests of the Party you must admit that you knew about X's counterrevolutionary activity. If the defendant fell for that—and the idea of Party discipline was so deeply ingrained in most of them that they did—he was convicted, for he had admitted his guilt by association. If he refused to perform a service for the Party, he was guilty of insubordination. There was no escape, quite aside from all the other methods which could be used to force a Communist to declare that he was a counterrevolutionary.

For the remarkable aspect of all these trials is the fact that 99 per cent of all the defendants are favorably disposed to the government when they are arrested and can be forced to confess their guilt only by subtle methods and torture. It is only after they are sentenced that these people's eyes are opened to the true nature of the Party which they loyally supported up to the moment of their arrest.

What is most terrible is the cynicism of the trials. It is always possible to find examining judges who will perform their ugly task. For the examining judges know just as well as the defendants what is going on. They know the prisoners are innocent. After an examiner has finished with thousands of people who suffer the most unbearable moral and physical torments before they will confess to a crime which is repugnant to them and inconsistent with their whole lives—and the examining judge learns every detail of their lives—he cannot help realizing that he has condemned innocent persons. When the examining judge says to the defendant after the very first hearing: "Sign it. Why drag the matter out? You'll sign in the end. They all sign"—he knows that these signatures do not confirm the defendant's guilt. Rather, they are proof of the infallibility of the methods of interrogation.

The accusers as well as the defendants know the score, but

the accusers dare not withdraw from the game—for if they do they are lost.

The "Conveyor"

We remained in our cell and could not believe that innocent people were being convicted. Prisoners are kept completely isolated before trial. We never saw anyone but the inmates of our particular cell.

But one time there was a slip-up and a convicted woman was returned to the cell for pretrial prisoners. She was Cara Jessinskaya, the wife of the Polish writer Jessinski, who died in 1938, one of the many thousands of victims of the spotted-typhus epidemic in the transit camp of Vladivostok. She had been divorced from him for many years; nevertheless, she had to pay for having once been close to him. When she came back to our cell we stared at the plump, good-natured, always somewhat disheveled person. We were unable to believe that she had just been sentenced to ten years in prison. Like Jessinski she had thought to find a home in the Soviet Union. Like him she was now convicted of being a Polish spy.

As the twentieth anniversary of the Revolution approached (November 7, 1937) we abandoned ourselves to optimistic fantasies that there would be a grand amnesty in honor of the day. In actuality the penal system was everywhere tightened up. The pretrial cells became so crowded that many women fainted and suffered heart attacks due to the lack of air. Moral and physical torture began to be applied more frequently. The most common type of torture was one the prisoners called "the conveyor," after the conveyor belts that are used in assembly lines. The prisoner is not allowed to sleep. Every four hours the examining judges relieve one another. Their sole duty is to keep the prisoner from sleeping. This goes on for days. Again and again the dazed victim is asked to sign the document the examiner has prepared, confessing to his alleged crime. He refuses. His feet and legs swell; he can no longer stand erect.

"Stay awake, stay awake. Stand up against the wall."

The prisoner reels, collapses, falls unconscious to the floor. The examining judge presses a button. A doctor comes in and gives the defendant an injection. He comes to.

"Sign it."

He shakes his head and his eyes shut. He is shaken awake, and again he stands against the wall until he collapses once more. Then he is taken to his cell.

He scarcely touches the cold supper that his fellow inmates have saved for him. They lay him on the floor and by the time they have folded a coat and placed it under his aching, swollen legs, he is asleep. After ten minutes the slot in the door opens and the defendant is called to another hearing. His comrades shake him awake, hold him up, encourage him, but he neither sees nor understands. With eyes red, swollen and wild with fatigue, he staggers into the corridor where a guard with expressionless face is waiting for him. He staggers up steps and down halls, staggers into the small examining room where endless torment and a fresh, well-rested interrogator are waiting for him.

"Sign the paper—then you can sleep. Why are you tormenting yourself? You'll sign sooner or later. They all sign. Stay awake. Stand up. What kind of posture is that? Don't lean against the wall."

He continues to hold out. Three days, four days, eight days. Sleep, sleep. If only he could sleep a full hour. Why is he torturing himself so? His fellow defendants have already signed—the examiners show him the confessions. Those others have given up already. Sign and you can sleep. No, never. Ten days, eleven days. . . . Sleep, sleep. He can think of nothing else. Let them shoot him. If only he can sleep again. On the sixteenth day he signs.

Then comes the trial. It takes place in Lifortovo Military Prison. Since this is a capital case, the prisoner is present at his trial. Judges and prosecutor sit at a long table draped with a red cloth. The statement prepared by the examining judge and signed by the defendant is read. The prosecutor makes a brief closing address. There are no witnesses, no lawyer for the defense. The defendant is given a brief final word. He swears to his innocence, swears that his signature was extorted under duress. The court retires and returns in a few minutes with the verdict, which has been settled beforehand. Dazed, the defendant hears as though from far away: "Guilty. Sentenced to death by firing squad."

The Boots

Lifortovo Military Prison is notorious for its methods of torture. In 1937 men sat in the death cells of Lifortovo and waited.

First came the torture, then the sentence, then the waiting. Alone, or by twos, threes, and fours.

In the death cells they sat and waited.

In the death cells they sat and moaned.

In the death cells they sat and screamed.

When they screamed the guard would rap on the iron door with his keys. And they would quiet down, would sit waiting silently.

When a step sounded in the corridor, they looked away from one another. Not because of their own fear. That was past increasing. They looked away in deference to the fear of the others, which was there in the others' eyes, so naked and so terrible. They averted their gaze in order not to shame their cellmates.

Footsteps in the corridor. They're coming. Whom are they coming for? There are still three left in this cell. Not me, not me!

Footsteps pass by and die out along the corridor.

In the death cell they sit and wait.

One man went out of his mind and whimpered, like a dog at his master's deathbed. Day and night he whimpered incessantly. A second rocked back and forth from the waist up, praying. His lips moved incessantly, for time was short and perhaps he did not know the right prayers. All his life he had known only one prayer, the Communist Manifesto, and only one faith, the Party. If he had been asked now, "Do you believe in God," he would probably have answered still, "I don't know." Or he would not have answered at all, for now nothing in the world existed for him but footsteps in the corridor and his own prayer.

The two others in the cell were army officers, a young lieutenant and a gray-haired colonel. They were still wearing their uniforms and had not lost their military self-control. But here and there the lieutenant's uniform looked threadbare, and when the madman on the stone floor in the corner whimpered, the lieutenant trembled.

The colonel's uniform was of stout cloth, and he betrayed no nervousness. Every morning he dusted off his high, close-fitting black top-boots and paced up and down the cell. The cell was four paces wide—four paces forward, four paces back. The gleaming black boots creaked softly at each step. Now and then he talked with the young lieutenant about trips he had taken, people he had loved, artists or books that had moved him. And in between they listened, listened to the footsteps in the corridor. Listened and waited, day and night, for weeks and months.

The man who prayed sat rocking on his cot; the madman writhed on the floor and whimpered; the young lieutenant cried out at night, but only in his sleep when such weakness could not shame him; and the colonel paced back and forth, back and forth.

The first to be fetched was the colonel. His name was called, he was ordered to be prepared, and the slot in the door was closed again. It was like being called out for a walk or a hearing or to use the washroom. But it was none of these things. This time it was death.

The madman had crawled on his knees to a rear corner of the cell. The other had stopped his prayers. Two tears ran down the lieutenant's white face.

The colonel put on his tunic and his long army coat. He glanced at the mad creature in the corner who had once been a sensible and friendly human being. Then he silently shook hands with the others and turned toward the door.

The guard opened it.

"One moment, please," the colonel said, turning back to the others. "I almost forgot." And with quick, practiced movements he drew off his high boots. "One of you may be able to use these," he said, and he put on the madman's rent, crumpled shoes. "I won't need boots any more."

Then he stepped out of death's waiting room into the main office. Flanked by two silent guards he walked down the silent corridors with their arched stone ceilings. In a barred room an officer was waiting for him with a document in his hands. So now they were going to read him his death sentence again. He knew all about that. It had been read out to him

44

three months ago. Every word was engraved on his memory. He scarcely listened as the dry official voice indifferently ran through his name, rank and so on. If only it were all over. Then he looked up in amazement. This was not the familiar text.

". . . The Supreme Military Tribunal has decided to alter the death sentence to ten years of incarceration in a correc- tive labor camp."

Commutation. Life!

Years later he told the story at a campfire in Kolyma. He came to the end.

"How I could have used those boots," he said with a sigh. "How much bread I could have traded them for."

Trotskyists

A new prisoner entered our cell. At first we were struck by the red shawl printed with large yellow flowers which covered her head and shoulders. When she removed it with a graceful gesture, we saw the wrinkled face of an aging woman whose eyes were vivacious and intelligent. She sat in her place on the boards with the relaxed and natural posture of a lady in her drawing room, the colorful shawl spread across her knees. And while her manicured fingers toyed with the red and yellow fringes, she rained caustic remarks—in the obligatory whisper—down upon the heads of her amazed, overjoyed, or distinctly hostile neighbors. She was the only one of us who openly made fun of the innocent lambs who still tried to de- fend the Party and the NKVD which had put them here, and who still offered the usual hypocritical explanations for the inexplicable: you can't make an omelette without breaking eggs; better to liquidate ten innocent persons than to let one guilty one get away; spies are everywhere; revolutionary alertness is essential. And then, of course, there were those who asserted piously: "Even if I have to clean toilets in Siberia, I'll do it gladly, because even there I shall be serving the Soviet Union."

Into this typically Soviet atmosphere of suspicion, insincerity, secrecy, and cliquishness in which all participated—old and young Party members, non-Party members, wives of great men, and intimidated peasant women—there suddenly entered a woman who candidly spoke her mind for all to hear, including those who did not want to hear.

For this woman who cast a spell over all the inmates of the cell had nothing more to lose. She was Ida L, the widow of one of the best-known adherents of Trotsky in the Soviet Union. L himself had luckily died a natural death in the Far East, while she herself until the day of her arrest had headed the world-famous Yiddish Theater in Moscow. She had no illusions about what awaited her. For aside from the fact that her husband had been an oppositionist, she herself had a huge circle of friends, most of whom had also been arrested and forced to give incriminating evidence against her. For many months she was subjected to the severest interrogations and was finally convicted and sentenced by a military court to ten years imprisonment. I never found out what happened to her afterwards, but I have not forgotten those evenings in the cell with her, when she talked animatedly about people and events in her life—a life that had been as colorful as the shawl she held in her nervous, delicate hands.

Irina was another of our cell mates. We called her "the Marquise" on account of her fragile aristocratic beauty.

Tennis would seem to be a harmless occupation, but it proved to be young Irina's nemesis. She had not been a member of any party. And although her personal life became con-

46

siderably more difficult for her after the Revolution, since she came from the landed aristocracy, she had welcomed the Revolution because she believed it would improve the lot of the people. Without any bitterness she accepted the privations the Soviet state held in store for her. Like hundreds of thousands of other intellectuals she tried for years to explain away the rigors and injustices of the regime as diseases of infancy. "As a mother tries to cover up and interpret favorably everything her naughty child does, so we defended everything the Soviet state undertook," Irina said as we lay side by side on the boards of the cell.

She went on defending the regime until after she made a trip to the Ukraine. It was during the collectivization of the peasants. The misery, hunger, and starvation she saw there was something she could find no extenuation for. When she got back to Moscow she expressed her indignation to her tennis partner, a friend of long standing. She forgot about this conversation. But one day she gave him a sharp talking to when he told her he loved her. That was the end of their tennis games and their harmonious friendship. He never forgave her for rejecting him, although he knew that she was happily married.

Early in 1937 she was arrested. She was charged with Trotskyism.

"I have never belonged to the Party," she said naïvely to the examining judge, "so I can't very well be guilty of Trotskyist deviations from the Party line."

"You have agitated against Party policies. You spoke against the policy of collectivization, and in so doing you supported a Trotskyist opinion." As proof he showed her the denunciation of her tennis partner.

The verdict: guilty. The sentence: eight years of corrective labor camp, which she spent in Kolyma.

But the worst of it was that her husband, a young Communist engineer, was also arrested, charged with Trotskyism on her account and shipped to Vladivostok at the same time as she. There in the transit camp, separated from her only by barbed-wire fences, he died of spotted typhus. When I met Irina again in camp at Kolyma, her resemblance to a marquise was even more striking: snow-white hair framed her young, resigned face.

Semyonova was a simple woman who had never given much thought to political matters. When she heard that Marshal of the Soviet Union Tukhachevsky had been shot as a German spy, she dropped a remark among a group of neighboring women: "Oh, he was a handsome man. I once saw a picture of him."

She was arrested for that. There is always one malicious person in a group of women. She was indicted under Paragraph 58, Article 10: counterrevolutionary agitation and propaganda. The case went swiftly; she had said what she had said and there were witnesses against her. The sentence: ten years imprisonment for extolling an enemy of the people. And at home two motherless children remained alone with a father who drank—and did not wait for her. Ten years are a long time.

A wrinkled old peasant woman looks around the cell for convicted prisoners with eyes filled with horror. It is a tower cell with narrow high windows sunk in the thick walls and hardly admitting light or air. The little old woman does not know that she is in a historic place. In this cell the great rebel

Pugachov was held prisoner until Catherine the Great (who built Butyrka Prison) had him executed. The little old woman would scarcely be consoled to learn that poor Pugachov had the cell all to himself, while she is sharing it with sixty-five other convicted prisoners.

Shyly she raises the hems of her many wide petticoats, sits down in a corner, claps her hands over her face and rocks her gray head with its dark shawl back and forth, wailing softly under her breath.

"Well, grandmother, what did you get?"

"Five years," she sobs.

"What for, grandmother?"

"What for? I don't know. They say I am a Tr . . . a Trok . . . a Tractorist," she gets it out at last.

No, grandmother, not a tractorist. Not until we were called out for transhipment and the name and verdict of each prisoner was again read aloud did we learn for certain what your crime was. You were condemned for being a Trotskyist! Although you cannot even pronounce the word and do not know the difference between a tractor and a Trotsky.

A Communist Mother

In Vladivostok transit camp the story of Mother D came to its end. But I will tell it here because it throws some light on the motives that make parents and children, brothers and sisters, men and their wives, repudiate one another once either has been arrested. This is not always done out of cowardice; sometimes it is prompted by an unshakable faith in the justice and infallibility of the Party and the NKVD.

I heard the first part of this story from one of the participants, an elderly engineer who was at work building a bar-

49

rack for women in the transit camp of Vladivostok. The second half of the story I witnessed.

"Are you sure it was my mother?" the young prisoner asked a new arrival in his cell.

"I couldn't possibly be mistaken," the other said. He was an elderly man who made a strange contrast with the other inmates because he was still clean shaven and his suit was carefully pressed. "It was at my last Party meeting. Shortly afterwards I was expelled from the Party because of contact with an enemy of the people—an old schoolmate of mine with whom I exchanged letters once or twice a year. He was an army officer, and when Tukhachevsky fell he was ruined too. Unfortunately one of my letters was found in his possession when he was arrested. There was nothing incriminating in it, but as you see it was enough to send me to prison."

The younger man's haggard features lit up with a sympathetic smile.

"It happens every day," he answered. "If you stay around here any length of time you'll find out that about 90 per cent of the inmates were arrested for similar reasons. I worked as a secretary in our trade mission in Berlin. Kossior, the brother of the People's Commissar, recommended me for the job, and when he was charged with being a German spy, I was arrested too. But tell me about my mother."

"I've known your mother since the Revolution. She was always one of the most active Communists in the textile factory where I worked as an engineer. A person of extraordinary energy. Sometimes I wondered how she managed to do her work and attend so many meetings, and yet have time for a private life."

"She never did have much time to spare for me," the young man said bitterly.

"Recently," the engineer continued, "I'd been noticing how changed she was. She seemed to have aged overnight. We couldn't understand this slump until the day she made her statement at the Party meeting. Then we found out for the first time that her son had been arrested. She had made a point of informing the Party secretary at the factory, and I suppose he ordered her to make a statement at the Party meeting."

"And what did she say?" the son asked, trying to make his twitching features expressionless. He thrust his hands into his pockets to conceal their trembling.

"I'm sure she did not speak voluntarily," the engineer said apologetically. "Certainly not, because when she got up on the platform she was so pale that we all thought she was sick. And her voice had none of the warm, enthusiastic quality we were all used to; it could hardly be heard at the back of the room. It must have cost her a great deal to get up on that platform and announce to hundreds of comrades that she must repudiate her own son."

The son listened without a quiver. And for a moment he involuntarily squinted his sharp eyes, beneath which were dark rings from many sleepless nights—although the same naked bulb dangled as ever from the vaulted ceiling of the cell and the corner where the two men were leaning against the wall was in semidarkness as always.

"She said her son had been arrested six months earlier, that all through that time she had been hoping his innocence would be proved and that he would be rehabilitated and released. But he had not come back and she could therefore no longer doubt that he had been proved a traitor. For no innocent person would be kept under arrest in the Soviet Union, and the NKVD did not make mistakes. A Party mem-

ber who felt an intimate tie with an enemy of the people—
even her own son—could not remain a sincere Party member.
Therefore she was now publicly declaring that she no longer
considered herself related to her son, since he had fallen into
the snares of the enemies of the people."

"So she publicly repudiated me," the son murmured.

"How could we on the outside possibly know that there are
so many guiltless persons in prison?" the older man apologized, feeling that he had to say something in extenuation.
To his own surprise he wanted to justify himself for having
taken part in that meeting. Why had it never occurred to
him at the time that it was immoral to require a mother to
renounce her own child in the name of the Party? What mo-
rality remained in the Party when it made such cynical demands upon its members, and made the others applaud such a
spectacle?

But before he could fully formulate this startling new
thought, he heard the son whispering hoarsely:

"There were two things I formerly believed in: my mother
and the Party. I was never in the unhappy predicament of
having to choose between the two. When I was put behind
these bars it seemed to me a simple thing to prove my innocence. But nobody here is interested in proofs of innocence.
Guilty, guilty! the examining judges shout, and they think
their shouts are proof of the truth of their silly fabrications.
Their blows and kicks were not enough to destroy the image
of the Party that I still carried in my heart. I said to myself
that the Party and Stalin do not know what is going on here.
And in my simplicity I wrote to People's Commissar Yeshov,
to the State Prosecutor, to Stalin. I never received any answer. And I came to the conclusion that these intimate associates of Stalin, and Stalin himself, not only know what is

going on here, but want it to go on. After all, we are right in the middle of Moscow, a short walk from the Kremlin. And these things do not happen only to little people; they also happen to former close associates of Stalin, to his secretary, to people's commissars, to those who only recently were working on the Constitution with him, like Eiche, Kossior, Postyshev, Sulimov. People are brought to this prison from all parts of the Soviet Union—and in all the prisons in the whole country the scenes are the same. What interest could all these examining judges have in forcing obviously innocent men by extortion, threats and torture to make the most absurd confessions of guilt? These examining judges, or rather torturers, have been trained according to a carefully thought-out system. Only the People's Commissar for the Interior, the State Prosecutor, and Stalin himself could have developed and approved this system which is applied throughout the country.

"When I recognized this, I lost my faith in the Party. It did not happen when I was arrested and my Party book was taken away, but when I realized that the Party spits upon respect for individuals, that it poisons justice and truth with the blood of the innocent. 'You can't make an omelette without breaking eggs.' Human beings, thousands upon thousands of citizens, are not eggs. Yet their skulls are crushed as though they were. So it does not surprise me that the same rulers should demand such sacrifices from a mother. A spectacle as unnatural and repulsive as that characterizes the men who stage it.

"But—" his whisper became almost inaudible—"that my mother, my own mother, would betray me, would deny me for the sake of the Party—such a thought never occurred to

53

me, not even here where you learn to believe in nothing and in no one."

The engineer stared at the boy with incredulous horror and raised his arm as though to shake him. But at that moment the slot in the door opened, the military cap of the guard appeared, and a profound silence settled over the cell which a moment before had been buzzing with the whispers of its hundred inmates.

Slowly the soldier spelled out the name of the engineer, who uttered a loud, tense, "Here," and jumped from the boards down to the level of the door. The slot fell shut and with the typical rattle of prison keys the door was opened and the engineer let out. The murmurs and whispers resumed. Toward dawn, hours later, when the engineer staggered back from his interrogation, the younger man who lay sleepless between his neighbors, watching the bugs on the wall, had no need to ask questions. The man who returned was no longer a newcomer. That night he had found out what Soviet justice meant. With a suppressed groan the engineer sat down on the boards and stared at the small patch of stone floor by the door as though it were an open grave into which he had just laid his dearest love.

Although the mother had renounced her son, she remained under suspicion. A few weeks later her house was searched and two overlooked volumes by Bukharin confiscated. And Bukharin had meanwhile been classed as counterrevolutionary.

Here were grounds enough for issuing a warrant for her arrest. The two dust-covered books were proof enough that she was entitled to an eight-year sentence for counterrevolutionary activity. Such is the dictatorship of the proletariat. The woman who was condemned in the name of the proletariat was a textile worker, one of the many women of the people who had believed that the Party would bring light to the workers and carry out the socialist dream to which she had devoted her life. She had believed in this so thoroughly that she had given up any claim to a personal life. Her real life was her life in the factory. She was not ambitious, but she was proud of each promotion to a position of greater responsibility within the factory because it gave her the opportunity to share her knowledge and experience with more people. When she had been offered a better apartment—since her husband's early death she had lived in one tiny room with her son—she had indignantly refused, saying, "The time has not yet come for me to accept privileges when there are many workers' families larger than mine still living all in one room."

It was a real achievement for her when she managed painfully to work her way through a book on Marxist theory. She was always filled with secret awe when she saw her son gobbling book after book, and she felt intense gratitude to the regime which gave him the opportunity to study by daylight in libraries and universities, while she had always had to read at night, laboring through the pages by candlelight after a hard day's work. The mother and son were both proud of one another. But they had no time to give expression to their feelings. Moreover, such emotionality would have seemed improper to both.

Yet the boy knew that he would always give up tempting dates with friends his own age whenever he had a chance to spend an evening with this unassuming woman who wore old-fashioned dresses and a shawl around her plain face with its strong forehead, flat cheekbones, and wide, energetic mouth. "Mama," he would say to her, "when you laugh the little wrinkles around your eyes are like the corners of Lenin's eyes." Startled, she would protest his irreverence. For her there was nothing higher, nothing more sacred than Lenin. How could she possibly be compared with Lenin in any way? It was his voice that had called her to the Party and that had aroused in her her unshakable confidence in the Party, a trust to which she clung in spite of developments which were hard to understand. She needed only to remind herself of Lenin to brush away all doubt. Like her fellow members of the Party she did not notice that Lenin's successor had long misused his name to lead the Party away from Lenin's road. To her the Party was still the purest and most just of all parties; to her it had a copyright on all truth and wisdom. When the time came and she was told to testify for the Party against her son, she sacrificed even her child to the Party. Her mother's love, she assumed, must have blinded her—for the Party could not be mistaken.

It was not until after she was in prison that she realized what an injustice she had done her son. The monstrous fact of her own conviction as a counterrevolutionary paled before her despair over what she felt to be her failure as a mother. She who should have tried to defend him when all were against him had instead delivered the last blow with her own hands. And as she rode to the Far East in the cramped cattle car, the rattle of the train murmured incessantly in her ears: my son, my son, my lost child. . . .

Tens of thousands of prisoners passed through the transit camp in Vladivostok every month. The women's barracks are situated on a hill, surrounded by a small area of trodden ground behind the barbed wire. The barracks for the men are somewhat farther down the hill. Once a day a few men are let out of each barrack to fetch water. Then they go up the barren hill, whose only vegetation is barbed wire, and pass close by the women's zone.

Day after day the mother looked for her son, and at last he came. He came in tattered rags which hung upon an emaciated body; his sunken face was rough with whiskers, his shaved head drooped, his eyes were dull and apathetic. Only a mother would have recognized in this stooped shadow of a man her own son. She knelt at the fence, her hands gripping the wire, her face pressed so close to it that the barbs pierced her forehead like a crown of thorns.

"Son! Volodya! My son!" she sobbed.

The man turned. His lifeless eyes gazed indifferently at the tear-stained face of the old woman, and without a word he went on with his burden.

"My son, my son!" she cried when he came slowly back down the hill with the filled pails of water. "Forgive me, forgive your mother!"

For a moment he set down the pails, as though they were too heavy for him, and in a low, calm voice he said, "I have no mother any more. My mother repudiated me." Then he picked up the pails and vanished among the stooped figures at the bottom of the hill.

Convicted and Sentenced

When Anna entered our cell in the spring of 1938, scarcely one of the one hundred and thirty inmates so much as glanced at her. (I was in five different collective cells in Butyrka Prison. At the time, I was in a cell which had been the prison chapel during Tsarist days.) She was an unassuming, small, thin woman with straight, stringy hair, pale blue eyes and a wan, grief-stricken face which had the usual newcomer's expression of utter helplessness and great agitation.

When the cell orderly questioned her, she was able to answer with only a few words of broken Russian. She was German.

She placed her sneakers under the planks, climbed up on the platform, rolled up her shabby dark-blue mackintosh and put it under her head for a pillow, and stretched out in the place the cell orderly had assigned to her. At night she took off her skirt and blouse and used them for a pillow, covering herself with the raincoat. Most of the time she lay staring silently at the gloomy vault of gray stone ceiling above her. Although the food we were served scarcely stilled the worst of our hunger pangs, she always gave away part of it to her neighbors, who greedily devoured it. She did not bother about going out for the daily fifteen-minute walk in the yard; she did not bother about anything in this narrow world that surrounded her.

Once she was called out for a brief interrogation lasting no more than an hour. She came back somewhat more perturbed than she had been before. She lost weight with alarming rapidity; it was apparent that she was going downhill fast and was quite willing to die.

More than once I had watched her with acute discomfort. Discomfort, because I knew that I had to try to help this woman. And that was what I did not want to do. I was so filled with my own sorrows and the sufferings of others that I believed I could contain no more of the sort of unhappiness I read in her helpless eyes. Was I not just as helpless? Who tried to do anything for me? Had I not sat in my corner for months, my head pressed against the cold stone wall, letting the waves of the uncomprehended foreign language flow over me—hoarse, indifferent, curious, hostile or challenging whispers, but always words I could not understand. Now and then

I had been able to make out some meaning in the shallow stream of commonplaces, but I had become so fond of my solitude within the crowd that I exchanged words with my neighbors very rarely. Besides, my place was by now close to the window where I could see a bit of a tree—a branch with a few leaves. With that branch and the wind and the leaves I daily conducted endless conversations.

But then one night I saw her lying sleepless on the planks, squeezed in between her robust neighbors who were enjoying a brief, restless sleep—no one slept soundly, because we were in constant expectation of being called out for interrogation, which always took place at night. I saw her wrapped in her too-short raincoat. Her legs were uncovered and she was unable to draw them up against her body because then she would have taken up too much space. She lay there so submissively, so sunk in despair, without resistance, indignation or protest. It was like the dumb suffering of a dog who has been sold and sent far from his beloved master, and who is slowly dying from the separation.

I felt so ashamed that night that I could scarcely wait until morning to go to her and speak with her. And so I heard her story.

Anna came from Hamburg. She had been born there, grown up there, and married there. Until she was forty she had never once left the city. No opportunity or occasion for travel had come her way. But she was content with this. She had a good husband who worked as a chauffeur and they had always managed to get along in good times and bad. They had no children.

There was only one cause for disagreement between them —he was a Communist. Ordinarily this would not have disturbed her, for she knew nothing about politics and would not have wanted to interfere with him. But often he brought his comrades home and they sat around until the early hours of the morning, engaged in what they called discussions. They talked loudly and filled her kitchen with the smell of tobacco—what sort of housewife would she have been if she had not objected to that? Several times her husband came back from a demonstration with torn clothes and bruises, so that she was always worrying about him. But all in all theirs was a good life, until 1933. Then Hitler came and her husband had to go into hiding. The Nazis kept on his track, and eventually he had to flee the country.

For a long time she did not hear from him. Now and then one of his former friends would turn up and she would hide the man, forgetting how often in the past she had grumbled about these friends and thinking only that here was someone in danger.

At last a letter came from her husband. He was safe in Russia, had work, and was earning enough to support two. He wanted to know—it was just a question and she must not misunderstand him—whether she would be willing to come to him. He missed her very much, but he did not want to influence her because she might find it hard to get accustomed to conditions in Russia. He wanted very much to have her with him, but it was something she ought to think over very carefully. If she did make up her mind to come, he would take care of all the arrangements.

She decided to go, although she had never traveled anywhere in her whole life and although her family made a great fuss about it. An old friend of theirs, a retired sailor who was supposed to have a kind of sixth sense, advised against it. And the cards—she confessed with a shy smile that she was good at telling fortunes by the cards—predicted that great trouble would come out of the impending journey. But she went nevertheless, simply because she felt she should be with her husband. She always had been and there was no reason for her to be cut off from him now when he was living among strangers in a foreign country.

It turned out that he was living in Siberia. When he had crossed the Russian border without the necessary papers, he had been arrested and shipped to Siberia as a precautionary measure. Later on the Russians had found out that the German Communist Party had sanctioned his going into exile, and he was released. He had settled down and established a home where he was, if it could be called a home. She could not call it that. Nor could she get used to standing in line for hours every day for each little thing she wanted to buy. Nor could she accustom herself to the community kitchen, the language, and the cold. She could not become acclimated, no matter how hard she tried.

She saw less of her husband than she had in Hamburg. The official working hours were shorter than at home, but the pay was so low that most of the workers put in overtime. (Then the newspapers proclaimed: The workers of Factory X have volunteered to overfulfill the plan for the first quarter of the year by ten per cent. But she could not read the newspapers.) And although the Revolution was already won in this country, there were far more meetings here than there had been in Germany, where the frequency of meetings had been bothersome enough to her. Gradually she grew thinner and thinner. At first her husband thought she was physically ill. Then he realized that she was homesick, and at the first opportunity he moved to the Caucasus, where there were settlements of Germans.

He worked in a village as a mechanic, and she was able to

talk to the neighboring women in her own language. Here, too, it was not so cold as in Siberia. But these things still did not help; she was homesick and could not get over her homesickness. She could not live in Russia. At last her husband realized this and decided to send her back home.

But meanwhile a difficulty had come up. Both of them had become Soviet citizens. Her husband therefore wrote to the Comintern representative of the German Communist Party, explained the case and asked for help in sending his wife back to Germany. He received an answer that the case would be looked into.

By now it was 1937. Not even the Caucasian Mountains could stem the wave of arrests that flooded over the entire country. Communist refugees from Hitler Germany? To prison! German colonists who had settled in Russia three centuries earlier, at the invitation of Catherine the Great? They still spoke their old Swabian dialect—to prison with them! The villages were combed; in some scarcely a man was left. Screaming, the women ran after the trucks that carried off their fathers, husbands, brothers, and sons.

Anna was left behind, alone in the remote mountain village. She made every effort to find out what had happened to her husband, but she could not get any information. He had simply disappeared; she did not know what prison he had been taken to, and she was alone. There was now nothing to hold her in this country.

With the help of her neighbors she sold her possessions and set out for Moscow, all her remaining belongings in a small suitcase. She inquired her way to the Comintern building. After a long wait she was taken in to see a representative of the Communist Party of Germany. She told her story. But as soon as she mentioned the word "arrest," she was shown the door. No one here wanted to be associated with spies or their families. Once more she stood bewildered in the street.

She recalled that her husband had sometimes spoken of an organization called the Red Aid, and after a struggle with the unfamiliar language, she at last succeeded in getting directions. It was a long walk, and when she reached the proper authority the story was exactly the same. Since her husband had been arrested, he was an enemy of the people and nothing could be done for her. She knew her husband was not an enemy of the people and not a spy, but no one would listen to her protestations.

Once more she was out in the street with her suitcase, by now exhausted. She walked aimlessly around, and then it occurred to her to try the German consulate.

"You have become a Soviet citizen," the consular official told her. "We can get you home only if the Soviet authorities release you from your Soviet citizenship. Here is the address of the proper office."

She found the office and finally found an official who could understand her. "If you bring me a statement that the German consulate is willing to restore your German citizenship, we will release you from Soviet citizenship," she was told.

She took up her suitcase and walked back to the German consulate. There her name and the facts in the case were taken down and she was told to come back next day. She went out, wondering where she was going to spend the night. On the street she was arrested and taken to prison. She no longer needed to concern herself about shelter for the night, not for many years.

At her hearing she was told she was a spy like her husband. Then she was sent back to the cell.

I no longer had the unbroken leisure to lie near the window waiting for a bird to fly past. Often now a cloud tinted with pink floated past the window in the evening and faded without my watching it. I was busy. I had my hands full explaining to Anna that everything would turn out well. I didn't know whether my proofs—which I thought very clever —were especially convincing, but Anna came to trust me and to feel a quiet confidence in me. Perhaps what I said to her was not so important as how I said it and the fact that there was someone to tell her what she wanted to hear.

Although she was almost twenty years older than I, she clung to me like a frightened orphan who has at last found someone who cares for her. She forgot what was before her —trial and the threat of transportation. Her only fear was that we would be separated.

During my fourteen months of pretrial imprisonment I was called out for interrogation three times. The first time just personal data were taken. The second time a statement of my case was drawn up. Facts which anywhere else in the world would have seemed altogether harmless were to Soviet judges deeply incriminating. My record contained the suspicious item that I came from a bourgeois family, that I had lived in Holland and Switzerland as a child and had studied in Germany and Italy, and that I had lived in the house of a relative whose guests represented all sorts of political and intellectual positions. The record concluded with the statement: "I have never belonged to a counterrevolutionary organization," so I signed it. At the third hearing they read me the testimony of a prisoner who alleged that she had spoken with me in my hotel room concerning my counterrevolutionary activities, which were not otherwise defined. I asked to be confronted with the woman, but my request was not granted. Later on I learned from prisoners who had shared a cell with her that she had been on the "conveyor" and that after eighteen sleepless days and nights she had signed whatever they asked.

All these hearings took place in the eighth month after my arrest. In the fourteenth month I was informed of the charge against me. I was indicted under Paragraph 58, Article 4: support of a foreign state against the Soviet Union. They told me that this crime entailed the supreme penalty, death by firing squad, and that I would probably go before the military tribunal.

When I returned to my cell after receiving this information, most of the other inmates were asleep. My place on the floor was invisible; the bodies of the others had closed over it. I pushed aside a few legs and bedbugs and sat down on the edge of the platform. That night I did not feel any need for sleep.

"Military tribunal," the examining judge had said. "Death by firing squad." He had spoken the words as casually as a teacher might say to his students, "Examination" and "Failure."

It was not so long ago that I, too, had been a student, wearing an antifascist button on my lapel, distributing leaflets and holding the briefcases of my comrades when they had fights with Nazi students. And now, "death by firing squad." But the fear I had felt on my first ride to prison fourteen months before did not recur. I felt the same numbness that had overcome me when I was arrested, the same terrible helplessness and sense of abandonment. The loneliness of creature man, thrust out into a hostile, threatening, uncanny, uncomprehended world with nothing to hold to, nothing to hope for. Unreality had become reality. It was the primeval nakedness of humanity. But here was not the clean, open struggle of the prehistoric world; here was a corrupt, stinking chaos where people talked about Marxist truth when what they meant was that they would knock your teeth out.

"Death by firing squad. . . ." The words still remained incomprehensible. Such a death, so undeserved, inexplicable, meaningless, was too monstrous to be grasped, too impossible to cause fear.

And then, out of the loneliness around me, I heard the voice of the gray-haired woman lying beside me and felt her yellow hand with its arthritic swellings upon my arm. "Child, why are you crying?"

A few weeks later the slot in the door opened and a dozen names were called out. "Get ready with all your things," the guard growled, and closed the slot.

With trembling hands Anna packed her few clothes into a bundle and stood with the others at the door. Her face was colorless. They would all be going to trial, we guessed. But Anna was not thinking of that. She was looking at me in horror at the prospect of separation. And then the slot opened once more and a single additional name was called. It was my turn to tie up my little bundle with trembling hands.

For more than fourteen months I had waited for this moment to come. For fourteen months I had seen women pass through these cells, women who had hoped, wept, cursed and prayed, until finally after a few months the iron door opened for them again and they disappeared from sight. I alone was always left behind. Sometimes I thought I would stay in that cell the rest of my life. And now it was over. What was awaiting me on this fall day of 1938? I ached from all the good-by embraces when I finally took my place at the door beside

Anna. I looked at her with concern, but she was calm again. Whatever happened now, we were together.

Then we were let out into the corridor. Silently—we were strictly forbidden to say a word—we began moving. At last the soldier turned us over to another, who let us into a new cell. This was a kind of waiting room, for it was empty except for several stone benches against the walls. Some hundred women from various cells stood or sat around in it. Every now and then someone would recognize a friend and rush sobbing into her arms.

A waiting room exists for the purpose of waiting. We waited. One hour, two, three. Would we be going to trial now? Would we have a chance to defend ourselves? Would there be witnesses?

Then a guard opened the door a crack and shouted, "Quiet!"

There was no need; we had fallen into a numbed silence as soon as his face appeared. He told us to form a line at the door, in any order, and disappeared.

Every Soviet citizen is an expert at standing in line. In a moment there was a neat, orderly line going up to the door. But in this line there was no pushing or shoving or trying to sneak ahead. On the contrary, there were polite offers of, "Would you like to go first?" which were refused with equal politeness.

After a good long wait the door opened slightly again and the first woman was let out. She returned in three minutes and the next went. The procedure was marvelously efficient. Every three minutes a woman came and another went, and each one returned with her sentence. As the number of those who had gone grew, the sobbing in the room became louder. In all corners of the room little knots formed, but nothing could be heard but tearful, whispered phrases: "Ten years . . . eight years . . ." Rarely, someone said, "Five years."

We waited to see whether anyone would be set free—for example the old woman of seventy—but she too came back with a sentence of ten years. There were no exceptions; all were convicted.

Anna stood behind me in the line, her eyes widening and her thin figure shrinking. I heard her choked breathing and could feel her trembling. Perhaps I myself was trembling; I did not know.

Then a soldier led me down the corridor to another room where an NKVD officer sat at a long table. I was told to sit down in a chair facing him. (The chair was there because prisoners tended to faint when they received their sentence, and this would slow up the procedure.)

He asked my name, moistened the forefinger of his right hand and began running through a pile of small slips with the speed of a bank teller counting money. When he found the right one, he repeated my name, cleared his throat and intoned in a totally unemotional voice:

"Prisoner Elinor Lipper has been convicted by the special commission of judges of the NKVD in Moscow at the session of . . . for counterrevolutionary activity and has been sentenced to five years loss of freedom, to be served in a corrective labor camp. Sign here."

As I signed my name to the slip of paper I gritted my teeth so loudly that the officer looked up in surprise and amusement. Then he shouted, "Next."

The next was Anna. I had just time to give her an encouraging look as I returned with my five-year sentence.

Again a woman was let out, but Anna did not come back. I was so worried by her disappearance that I had no time to think about my five years. At last she came stumbling back into the cell, half dead from agitation. The officer had rattled out the sentence for her, but she had not understood a word. Then he had telephoned for an interpreter, and meanwhile she had been led off into one of the so-called "doghouses." She did not know what it was all about and was convinced that her last day had come. Since she was not being taken back to our cell like the others, she felt sure that an especially terrible sentence awaited her; she expected to be called out to face the firing squad at any moment. Instead she was led back to the same officer, who apparently had not succeeded in locating an interpreter. He put his elbow on the table, spread out the fingers of one hand and waved the hand several times in front of her nose. Then he asked whether she understood. She nodded. Five fingers—five years. She signed.

Such was our sentencing.

Of the hundred women in the cell that night, about ten received five-year sentences, about thirty, eight-year, and the other sixty, ten-year sentences. After all had been taken care of, we each received a sheet of paper on which to write the name of a relative who would be entrusted with our possessions during the years of imprisonment. I had no relatives in the Soviet Union and therefore requested that the NKVD take care of my things. My confidence was somewhat exaggerated, for I never saw any of my belongings again. Shortly before I was sent home I timidly asked an NKVD official about them. He looked at me with honest amazement, as though after ten years of imprisonment I were asking about fresh eggs I had left behind in my room.

Anna's total possessions were her wooden suitcase, which had been taken into custody when she entered the prison. She wept softly as we were walked slowly down various courtyards and through gateways piercing high walls, past watch towers and iron gates, to the round tower-cell for convicted prisoners. There everybody rushed madly to the planks to get a place. It was as though everybody thought his sole happiness in the coming ten years depended upon those sixteen inches of space; each woman defended hers with bitter desperation. Neither Anna nor I had grasped the situation in time, so that we were left sitting on the edge of the platform, surrounded by the feet of exhausted battlers who like us waited sleeplessly for morning. Next morning another plank was added to the platform, so that we too had our place.

Anna had stopped crying. Now and then she mumbled under her breath, "Five years? What for? Five years. . . ."

I choked back my own despair and tried to cheer her. "Five years or ten or twenty—what does it matter?" I said. "In any case we won't serve them. You must realize that. After all, we aren't among Hottentots. This is a civilized country (Oh, my simplicity!). There are so many cases that mistakes have been made, but they'll be righted in time. We will write petitions, prove our innocence; then our cases will be reviewed and we'll be released. It's just a matter of reaching the right person; then you'll see that everything will turn out all right." (In the course of the next ten years I wrote petitions to every imaginable bureau, but apparently the right person was not in any of them.)

I made such an effort to console her that in the end I began to believe my own words. Now and then she looked at me with timid confidence, and finally we were both smiling in our misery.

A few days later she fell ill. She had a high fever and nephritic hemmorhages. For a week she writhed in pain on the boards and there was nothing I could do for her but curse the nurses who handed pills for her in through the slot in the door and would not even come in to look at her. Once a month a prisoner was entitled to see the prison doctor, who ran through her sick-call in the corridor with miraculous speed. I went to her and explained—in a rage of indignation and in terrible Russian—what was the matter with Anna. She shouted at me to tend to my own affairs, but she examined Anna and had her transferred to the prison hospital that same day. Anna went against her will, for she was afraid that I would be shipped out in the meanwhile. In fact the day we were to be transported, she heard about it by chance and had herself discharged from the hospital, although she was still hardly strong enough to stand.

The Children's Organization

While Anna was in the hospital I had time to become acquainted with my other neighbor on the planks. All I knew about her was that she had received a five-year sentence in her home town of Kostroma and that she was now with us awaiting shipment to camp. Shortly before her arrest she had begun studying medicine. She looked like a Russian peasant girl with her auburn braids, her somewhat flat stub nose, her full mouth, and her powerful hands. Her high, white forehead above light blue eyes was creased by a deep furrow.

"Lydia, what are you thinking about?"

"My father."

"Is he free?"

"No, we were arrested the same day."

"Are you in on his account?"

"No, I was convicted of failure to denounce: Paragraph 58, Article 12. Five years."

"Whom did you . . . fail to denounce?"

"My kid brother."

Lydia stared silently down at the planks.

"Your only brother?"

She flicked a bedbug off her sleeve.

"Yes, I have only one. He was three years younger than me. At the time he was sixteen and going to school. One day I was looking for a pencil in his desk and I came across something that horrified me. It was a leaflet, an anti-Soviet leaflet. And the hectograph that had been used to run it off was in his closet.

"You see, that was the time the mass arrests were beginning, and so many children in school had lost their parents. They knew their parents were innocent, and when their fathers and mothers were not released, the children got together and issued a leaflet protesting the arrest of their parents."

"Yes," I interrupted, "I've heard that during 1937 and 1938 there was a children's organization in many of the big cities that called itself Revenge for Our Parents. But I imagine it was quickly liquidated by arrests and expulsions from school. One of the girls who belonged to the organization was in detention with me and told me a good deal about it."

"I don't know why my brother ever got into it," Lydia went on. "Nobody in our family had been arrested. But of course they must have needed to enlist help from among children who would not be suspected. Anyway, when he came home from school I spoke to him. At first he was scared to death about my discovery; then he became obstinate. 'Mind your own business,' he told me angrily. 'I'm old enough to know what I'm doing.'

" 'You're old enough to get us all into trouble,' I told him.

'Don't you realize that father and mother will be held responsible for your actions?'

"He had never thought of that. I suppose he had all sorts of romantic notions about dying heroically for a just cause, but it had never occurred to him that his mother whom he loved could be sent to prison on his account. Like my father and myself, he literally worshipped her. All our lives we'd done our best to keep all troubles and upsets from her, because she was sickly and suffered from spells of depression. His defiance evaporated and he pleaded with me, 'Lydia, Lydochka, don't tell anybody. I'll take all the things away today. And I promise I won't have any more to do with this business.'

"He kept his promise, and I said nothing about it at all. But it was already too late. One of his schoolmates must have betrayed him. A few months later he was arrested, just a week after his seventeenth birthday. At the door, with the two NKVD men on either side of him, he turned around once more to see his mother fall in a faint. That was the last he saw of us. Then he was taken off to prison.

"One day our doorbell rang. A bearded old droshky driver was standing at the door. In a whisper he asked for my father. I showed him in, but he would not sit down. He kept tugging at his fur cap; then he looked around for a scrap of newspaper, took out his tobacco pouch, and busied himself rolling a cigarette. He looked at my father and at me and down at his felt boots and finally blurted out, 'Do you have a boy in prison?'

" 'My son was arrested a month ago,' my father said in a choked voice.

" 'Do you have any news from him?' I asked.

" 'Ahem,' the driver growled, and then he fell silent for a

73

while. 'I sometimes drive prisoners from the city jail to the NKVD prison for hearings when the prison vans are overcrowded. This morning I took one of them, a young boy, and one guard. When we turned into this street he asked the soldier to stop for a minute, just a few seconds, because his parents lived here on the corner, on the second floor. He just wanted to run up to see his mother for a moment. But the soldier said no. Then he begged, "Just let me go up for a minute, just to look at my mother who's sick, and I'll be right down." But the soldier said, "Shut up. Forbidden." We were just riding past the house, and suddenly the boy jumped out of the carriage. Before I could say Whoa to stop my horses, the soldier shot him.'

" 'Dead?' my father cried out.

" 'Dead,' the driver nodded. Then he left.

"A few days later we had to take my mother to a sanatorium. So at least she was not there when my father and I were arrested. It wasn't enough for the NKVD that my brother was dead.

"At my hearing I told them everything just as it had happened. I hoped that at least they would release my father, who really knew nothing about the whole business with the leaflets. But they blamed it all on him, because he was in charge of our upbringing. He was given eight years for counterrevolutionary activity. A woman in my cell who was in the prison hospital at the same time as Father told me what his sentence was. And they gave me five years for not denouncing my dead brother."

3. En Route

The Transport

AFTER SEVERAL WEEKS in the cell the day came when we
were marched out of the prison gate, a silent, motley lot
of unhappy women, young and old, each of us still wearing
the clothes we had had on when we were arrested. The
clothes of some even showed traces of former smartness. But
all of us had the seats of our skirts worn through from moving
around on the rough boarding. The holes were there in spite
of all our efforts to patch them.

Filled with fear of the unknown, we crossed the threshold
of the prison. The first thing we saw was the prison van, the
Black Raven as the sinister vehicle is called in Russia. Down
a lane of fixed bayonets we walked to the Black Raven. Those
bayonets destroyed our last illusions. From that moment on
we were, for everyone who came in contact with us, convicted
counterrevolutionaries, the worst sort of criminals, far more
reprehensible than any murderer. When I signed the slip of
paper which stated my sentence, it had just been a piece of
paper to me. It was not until the following month, when I
was marched out of the prison, that those five years suddenly

75

became horribly meaningful. I hung my last hopes for justice on the points of those bayonets.

One after the other we clambered up into the Raven and disappeared into the black maw. Several of us half pulled, half pushed Anna up; that desperate criminal was too weak to climb in without help. Silently she sat down next to me and we listened to the sobs of the Moscow women who were saying good-by forever to their native city.

Towards evening we were loaded into a cattle car at the freight yards on the far outskirts of the city. Some of the older women remembered that during Tsarist times these cattle cars had been marked, "Twelve horses or forty-eight men." Now there were no inscriptions on them at all. But when our eyes became accustomed to the darkness in the interior of the car we saw that the Soviet authorities had heeded Stalin's slogan of "Catch up with and surpass the past." They had far surpassed it; our group of some twenty-five women raised the total number of women in the car to about a hundred. We then discovered that these other prisoners were all female criminals who greeted our entry with loud shouts of malicious enthusiasm, dubious compliments, and a rain of the filthiest swearwords.

We stood confronting them, a wretched, helpless little group, enduring this reception without protest. Our horizon was widening. We were getting our first insight into the fact that not only wardens, camp commandants, and all kinds of guards would be making our lives a hell during the years to come, but our own fellow prisoners as well.

They lay in three tiers on the familiar planks, beside, above, and on top of one another, peering at us, pointing us out with tattooed arms, giggling, jeering, grinning, and spitting contemptuously at our feet. Our arrival was an occasion significant enough for them to light one of their carefully hoarded stubs of candle, so that they could see our faces and take an inventory of our possessions, intending no doubt to relieve us of them as soon as the train started moving.

In the flickering candlelight their faces seemed even more sinister, vicious, and bestial than before. There was no trace of sympathy or mercy in those faces, nothing but a brash challenge to all the saints and devils in the world. Colored bits of rag bound tangled hair. We saw burning gypsy eyes in wasted, immature faces; a pair of white breasts barely covered by a ragged blouse; a creature dressed in man's clothes, with a cap pulled low down over a wide, dark-skinned, brutal face, its visor almost concealing sharp, mocking eyes. This person was the leader of the criminal group. She kept a chunk of chewing tobacco in her cheek, and she had a hoarse, masculine laugh. She was the spokesman and told us off when we civilly asked for a few free places on the planks. "Go to the devil, you bitches," she said deliberately, and her public grinned applause.

The bravest girl among us, a strong young railroad worker who for unknown reasons had been convicted of Trotskyism, tried to get up on the planks. But she thought better of it when the candle was blown out; it was scarcely wise to get into a brawl in pitch darkness.

So we remained awake all that night, pressed close together for warmth. The nights in cattle cars are long. The heavy iron sliding door is locked from outside and only the dimmest trace of light enters the car from two tiny barred windows.

I could not see Anna's face, but I could feel the slight movement of her arm now and then as she wiped away her

77

incessant tears. Once or twice I heard her whisper, "Oh my God, my God, what for, what for?"

I suppose that those who could pray, prayed that night. I stared steadily up at the place where the window must be, until finally at dawn the dark bars showed against a patch of brighter sky.

At first some of us had the idea of refusing to accept our rations until we were put into another car. But then it turned out that even in our little group of twenty-five it was impossible to agree on this question. Some refused to go along because they were hungry, some because they were afraid. It was too dangerous. It looked like a demonstration, and demonstrations other than those ordered by the state are not customary in the Soviet Union. Nor are they wise. They always end with a demonstration of how demonstrators are punished. So we abandoned that plan.

When the commander of the transport came for the morning count, we petitioned him to put us into another cattle car. We were lucky. The train was not leaving that day and another group of counterrevolutionaries like ourselves had arrived from Tula Prison, so that there were enough to fill a whole car. During the trip of several weeks, however, we often had the pleasure of sharing our car with criminals who were put on and taken off en route. All the other twenty-eight cars in the train were crammed with male prisoners.

Sometime during the second night the train began moving slowly. Where to? We traveled for days and weeks and none of us knew where we were going. It is not customary in Soviet judicial practice to inform prisoners what camp they are being sent to, although that is decided at the same time as the sentence. There are three kinds of camps:

1. Near—camps in European Russia.
2. Distant—camps in Siberia and Central Asia.
3. Remote—camps in the Arctic regions and the far northeast.

When our train began twisting its way through the Ural Mountains, we knew that the European camps were not for us. Anna and I lay silently on the top row of planks. We had forgotten how to talk. Words were superfluous now where facts spoke all too clearly. When we stretched out our hands, we could touch the ceiling of the car, which creaked every evening as the guards raced back and forth along the roofs. Accompanied by their barking wolfhounds, they examined the roofs of the cars to make sure that no attempts to escape were in progress.

We were given hard-frozen bread to eat and a daily teaspoon of sugar. Water was a precious luxury, although it was usually swamp water and handed around in filthy pails. Sometimes we were so thirsty we tried licking the round iron plates set in the wall, which were encrusted with hoarfrost because of the cold. The train ran only a few hours at a time—it rarely covered more than a hundred and fifty miles in twenty-four hours. But although it stood on sidings for half a day at a time and we often shouted, "Water, water, we want water," for hours at a time, nobody paid any attention. As a matter of fact our car—the women criminals had been unloaded before we reached the Urals—had the advantage over the men's cars. Every few days we received a supposedly warm soup, although it was usually cold by the time it reached us. After ten days of traveling almost every one of us suffered from diarrhea; the diet and unclean water made that inevitable.

We warmed ourselves most of the time by looking at the

friendly little round iron stove. It was very seldom that we asked this little black friend to work for us, for we received coal or coal dust at most once every three days. Then we eagerly filled the stove with our bare hands, since we had no shovel, and for an hour we crowded around the fire, excited and talkative. With solemn faces, as though we were going through a religious rite, we stretched out our emaciated, gray, unwashed hands to the warmth.

The fire lasted only an hour. Then we crawled silently back on our planks, each one of us alone, a helpless, abandoned creature with too few blankets, too few clothes, too thin blood to combat the icy Siberian winter wind that whistled through many cracks in the frame of the car. The last few embers would fall through the grating into the ashes and go out. Then there was only cold, darkness, and the rattle of the train. Where were we going, where, where?

Only one little old woman, a former nun, continued to sit on the floor in front of the stove. She had tasted the bread of many prisons and passed through all the camps in the country. But neither camps nor prisons had persuaded her that it would be better for her to renounce her religion. In her weary, resigned old voice she would say, "Now I've suffered almost as much as Jesus Christ. Now I will certainly be redeemed soon."

One night I was awakened by a movement beside me. Cautiously I crept out from under my coat into the cold, and at once I realized that something was wrong with Anna. I felt for her. She was not lying beside me; she was kneeling on the planks.

"Anna," I whispered, "Anna, what are you at?"

She gave a start.

"Anna," I whispered again, "why don't you answer me?"
She was silent. I felt for her hands to make her lie down.
In her hands she had a noose which she was trying to fasten
to the ceiling of the car. I pulled her over to me by force,
threw away the noose, which felt as though it were made
from a towel, and held her trembling body firmly while I
covered her with our coats.

"Anna, Anna, how could you do it?"

"Oh, why don't you let me die? Why not? Why should I
suffer for years in this country where life was impossible
even when I was at liberty? What for? Can you tell me
that?"

I could not. I could only hold her firmly in my arms and
give her a little warmth from my own freezing body.

We had been en route for three weeks when the train
stopped at the Siberian city of Mariinsk. The sliding door
was rolled open with a clatter and the commander of the
transport, with two soldiers, appeared. He read out a long
list of names and told the women whose names were called
to get off the train. When he was finished, only thirteen
women were left. I was among them. Anna was among those
who were called out.

That was how we parted, Anna and I. I stood at the door
and watched her trudging off through the deep Siberian
snow in her dark-blue raincoat and her sneakers. Then the
iron door was closed and locked again.

Arrival in Vladivostok

On the thirty-fifth day the train stopped, the door slid open
and the guards shouted, "All of you, get your things and get
out." Blinking because our eyes were unaccustomed to full
daylight, we stood on the tracks for a moment. Then the

guards with their dogs were all around us, shouting, "Get down. Squat. If anyone stands up, we will take it as an attempt to escape and shoot instantly." The twenty-eight hundred men and thirteen women who had been spewed forth by the train squatted down in rows of five, their heads bowed, their limbs stiff, keeping their balance with difficulty. The wolfhounds, trained to watch prisoners, tugged at their leashes and slavered, their long fangs showing and their pink tongues hanging out. The soldiers called out commands to one another, chased away several curious bystanders, and counted the rows again and again, their rifles with fixed bayonets held at ready. In the cold November wind the gray-green faces of the prisoners turned blue. The wind brought with it the smell of ocean. We had reached Vladivostok.

We saw little of the city. We were marched across the tracks and down a highway at a furious pace, with cursing soldiers and panting dogs in front, behind, and on both sides of us. After about an hour's march the first gate of our first camp opened—Vladivostok transit camp. Barren hills were dotted with wooden barracks and barbed-wire fences. After the transport guards and the camp commandants had counted us again and again, we were driven into a square within a wooden palisade, the small group of women a little to one side of the men. For the first time since the day of our arrest we saw men who were not examining judges or guards. And they saw women for the first time since their arrest. Conversation between male and female prisoners was forbidden. But the silent language of hungry, sorrowful eyes passed back and forth.

We spent the entire day out in the square, in the midst of a November gale. Again and again we were counted, registered, and called up. Later the men were led off to the bath in small groups. The bath could take care of only twenty people at a time, and the women had to wait until last. We were given nothing to eat. It was long after darkness before the group of women was taken to the bath. It consisted of an unheated shack partitioned into three rooms: undressing room, washing room, and dressing room. The undressing room and the dressing room were to one side of the washroom, and were connected by a disinfection chamber.

We had to strip naked and hang all our clothing on an iron ring which was then handed to the disinfector. The disinfector was a man, and not an old man. His arms, tattooed from wrist to shoulder, and his comments on the naked women who filed past him, indicated to us that he was a criminal prisoner. Then we waited, purple with cold, until two more criminals on camp duty appeared. They were a barber and a medical aid. The medical aid examined our heads for lice. Any woman who was so afflicted was shaved to the scalp. Then all the women had to line up before the barber to have their pubic and underarm hair shaved. He paid no attention to the sobs and protests. There was no woman barber in the camp, he said. When some of us refused, the attendant in charge of the bath—another criminal —came in, made some lewd remarks about our modesty, and threatened to call the commander of the guard. We decided that enough thugs had inspected our naked bodies and resigned ourselves to being shaved. It was done with a single dull razor which was neither washed nor disinfected between persons.

In the washroom we were each given ten grams of soap and a wooden tub which we were allowed to fill twice with lukewarm water. Then the water was turned off. In the dressing room our supposedly disinfected clothes lay in a heap on the dirty cement floor where before us twenty-eight hundred men from our train had dressed. Still trembling with cold, we got dressed. The heat in the disinfection room had sealed into our clothes the dirt of thirty-five days in the cattle car.

We were led along a path glaringly illuminated by flood-lights and edged with barbed wire, and up a hill to the special zone for counterrevolutionaries. The women's barrack was surrounded by several barbed-wire fences. The guard unlocked a wooden gate, opened the door of the barrack, announced that here were thirteen newcomers, and vanished. We stood in the doorway for a moment, looking at the light inside and listening to women's voices. Now, we thought, we would have our first peaceful night after thirty-five days of traveling. We no longer remembered that we were hungry; we could think of nothing but sleep.

It must have been about midnight when we squeezed our way in through the door. We got no further. The entire floor was strewn with sleeping bodies. The plank platforms, which were arranged in two tiers along both the long walls of the barracks, were bowed under the weight of the women who lay pressed together on them from wall to edge. The barrack orderly, a red-haired woman, made her way over the sleepers and told us she could not assign us places because there were none. Nevertheless, a few kindly women squeezed together on the floor to make a little room for the newcomers. I had been the last to come in, and as I was also more timid than the others, I found no place at all. The air in the barrack was stale and heated by the exhalations of some two hundred and fifty women. The building was sixty-five feet long and twenty-two feet wide. Now and then someone stepped gingerly among the bodies and went out to the latrine in the yard. Since I was standing by the door, I was in the way each time, and finally I went out into the yard also. For the first time in sixteen months I enjoyed the sensation of being able to open and shut a door.

The weather had cleared. The forces of nature always seem to be against prisoners, and it had been storming all the while when we had had to stand in the square. Now a brilliant starry sky, wonderfully tranquil, stretched above watch towers and barracks, guards and prisoners. The moonlight, however, was utterly superfluous; its gentle glow was outmatched by the blinding glare of the floodlights.

I walked back and forth in the yard, from one barbedwire wall to the other. Each time I passed the barrack I looked and felt for a protruding spike. There was no suitable nail anywhere, but each time I looked up along the wall I saw the glint of a bayonet in the watch tower. With a loud snort the soldier on guard blew his nose between his fingers. (The masses of the people consider handkerchiefs sheer luxury.) So I would get nowhere trying to hang myself. I continued wandering up and down a while until the cold drove me back into the barrack. I observed a tiny space on the lower platform where a sleeping woman had drawn up her legs. But as soon as I settled cautiously down on the edge of the planks, she stretched, encountered a foreign body where her feet should be, and without opening her eyes drew back her leg and gave me such a kick that I fell over the edge onto the floor. But as the Russian proverb has it, there is no good luck that hasn't had some bad in it. In this way I obtained a few inches of space on the floor. I leaned my head against a wooden post and fell asleep.

Vladivostok Transit Camp

Prisoners whose destination was Kolyma in northeastern Siberia were shipped to Vladivostok from prisons all over the country, and were kept in the transit camp until they could be sent on to Kolyma by freighter. But between December and May all communication by water with Kolyma is cut off by ice, and since every ship can carry "only" seven thousand prisoners, the prisoners often have to wait half a year and more at the transit camp. I spent six and a half months at Vladivostok.

The transit camp was a highly instructive place to be, especially for those who still held the illusion that the mad fury of the purges was only a local excess. Here, in this reservoir for prisoners from all over the country, was palpable proof that not a corner of the Soviet Union had been spared in the mass arrests. Everywhere the same methods of interrogation were being applied. Everywhere the same arbitrary procedure was followed: the first to be arrested were the erstwhile functionaries of governmental, economic, and military agencies, then everybody who had had official or friendly relationships with them, and finally everybody who was related to them by blood or marriage.

In the eyes of every prisoner you could read the question, Why? and none of them had the answer. In the Moscow prison the faces of people had worn a look of frightened astonishment, of incredulous amazement that men could so torment their fellow creatures, that men could be so cruel to one another and inflict such shame upon the innocent. Here in Vladivostok the characteristic expression was different; it was an expression of fear and bitterness.

It was not only my own fate that filled me with bitterness,

nor was it only shame at the recollection that but a year and a half ago I had praised and defended this Soviet system as progressing toward paradise on earth. More strongly than anything else I felt the gnawing pain of helpless pity for these patient Russian, Caucasian, Tartar, Central Asiatic, Mongolian, and Siberian villagers who accepted their uncomprehended fate with the dumb submissiveness of beaten animals. "No one is ever safe from prison or the beggar's bowl," was all they could say about it. That ancient Russian proverb has kept its tragic applicability to this day.

There were two zones in the Vladivostok transit camp, one for criminals and the other for counterrevolutionaries. The criminals were assigned to all types of labor, received better food, lived in heated barracks, and each one had a cot, a straw mattress, and blankets of his own. Some of them were given passes and could move about with relative freedom. The zone for the counterrevolutionaries was divided into several smaller zones, each of which was surrounded by a cluster of barbed-wire fences. The wooden gate was always shut and there were watch towers at the corners of the enclosure. At night brilliant floodlights illuminated the entire area and patrols of guards incessantly made the rounds with their trained dogs.

In the unheated and frequently unlighted barracks the counterrevolutionaries slept on two or three decks of unplaned planks and had no mattresses or blankets.

Hygiene was out of the question. The criminals had access to water at all times, but a far too small number of counterrevolutionaries were assigned to the water detail. Water was brought in pails from a distance of a hundred to a hundred and fifty yards, and only once a day. The tiny water ration for each prisoner was scarcely adequate for drinking, let alone for washing. Now and then the female prisoners were able to beg a few extra pails, and then furious battles for water broke out among them. Screaming hysterically, they fell upon the pails, snatched them from each other, pulled each other's hands, and wept. And always the same group would look on sadly, standing at a distance, gazing at the water with timid longing; and always the same tough customers were the ones who got it.

Two or three times a month we were sent to the bath, where again there was a battle for the insufficient tubs. Those who seized one first were again the strongest and most forward women. They were able to wash in peace, while the others waited cursing, for by the time their turn came the water had usually been turned off. Often we had to go out into the dressing room with our bodies still covered with soapsuds. Meanwhile our clothes were being deloused. But since the disinfection chambers were run by criminals, who have careless work standards, the temperature was never brought up to the hundred degrees centigrade which is necessary to kill the lice. Usually the heat in the disinfection chambers was just right to make the lice feel comfortable and stimulated.

In the end we became so louse-ridden that we gave up trying to kill the lice. Now and then we would reach under our blouses when we could no longer endure the itching, fish out a handful of the vermin, and throw them away. As often as not they landed not on the floor, but on other prisoners.

Since lice are carriers of spotted typhus, a frightful typhus epidemic broke out in the camp in 1938. It carried off thousands of prisoners. The camp infirmary was so crowded with the sick, who lay on every cot and along all the floors of the wards and corridors, that any kind of care was impossible.

Some of the women from our barrack were called in to act as nurses. Their chief occupation was counting the dead who had escaped the misery of the gold mines which awaited the others.

In silence we stared through the barbed wire at the hearses which drove out of the camp every night. Piled high with naked bodies, the load tied on with cord and covered with canvas, the trucks drove out, carrying the victims to eternal freedom. As usual there was a reaction from Moscow only after the epidemic in Vladivostok had cost tens of thousands of lives. Then the camp commandant was arrested. His successor carried through a thoroughgoing delousing program so that the epidemic gradually subsided in 1939.

Few Soviet citizens are fastidious as far as bedbugs are concerned. Their presence is taken to be in the order of nature, for there is scarcely any place in the country that is not overrun with them. But the bugs in Vladivostok transit camp became a legend which was told with vivid details to future groups of prisoners, who had never been through that camp.

The barracks were so overrun with the bedbugs that sleep was almost impossible at night, when the creatures are most active. From the walls and the planks, above and beneath us, they came crawling; they fell upon the tormented bodies of the prisoners, who twisted and writhed at the stinging bites and tried to catch them. But no matter how many were crushed, they were always replaced by new hordes and the struggle would last until dawn, when the exhausted victims were at last able to sleep. In spring, when it got warmer, the hordes of bedbugs attacking us increased steadily, until at last we decided to sleep on the ground outside the barrack. And then there took place a spectacle that we watched with speechless horror. From the empty building the hordes of bedbugs marched in close formation, a long, dark, crawling procession crossing the threshold after their sickened, incredulous victims.

Those were the bedbugs of Vladivostok; they multiplied without let or hindrance.

Ships

Everyone in the transit camp of Vladivostok had to resign himself to being shipped off to Kolyma sooner or later. Nobody knew anything about the place. "The end of the world," some said, "completely cut off from everything." Then one day a geography book found its way into our barrack and was passed from hand to hand. We skipped over the material on fisheries and the fur-bearing animals in which the Kolyma district was rich, and we paid little attention to the fact that there were gold and silver mines in the area. What was impressed upon our minds forever were the three sentences about the cold. "Even in summer the earth here thaws out only to a depth of eight and a half inches. The lowest temperatures on earth have been recorded in this region. In winter the temperature drops to minus seventy degrees centigrade (−94° F.) and even lower."

We became very quiet and thoughtful after reading that. Next morning I saw the girl who slept next to me, a young pianist from Moscow, busily searching through her suitcase. After a while she came up with a pair of thick woolen stockings which she offered to me. "You must take them," she said. "Last night I had a dream about you with frozen feet."

The following winter, when I tramped through the snow in Kolyma, I returned again and again to the gratifying thought that I still had Lillian's woolen stockings. I kept putting off the day for wearing them on the theory that I could still endure the present cold and it might get still colder. The presence of those stockings, the mere possibility of wearing them, comforted and warmed me. Finally the day came when I opened my knapsack—improvised out of a piece of blanket—to get the stockings. The stockings were gone; they had been stolen long ago. From that day on I felt the cold worse than before.

Lillian and I were separated in Vladivostok. One of her legs was shorter than the other, and she was among the group of invalids and cripples who were to be sent back to Mariinsk in Central Siberia, an invalid camp where such prisoners were permitted to die slowly. There is no camp drearier and more hopeless than an invalid camp, as I heard later on from many eyewitnesses. A medically certified invalid does not have to work, but he receives only fourteen ounces of bread a day. Mad with hunger, the cripples will battle over a fishhead in the garbage heap of the camp kitchen. Unlike all other prisoners whose only thought is how to get a day off from work, the invalids report to work again and again, hoping in this way to receive a little more bread. But they are always sent back by the foremen on the grounds that they are unable to do the work.

Transfer to an invalid camp does not mean that a prisoner serves the rest of his term there. Medical commissions regularly comb the invalid camps, declare some of the inmates fit for work, and send them to the general camps. These in their turn send their waste human material to the invalid camps, so that there is a constant interchange between the two types of camp.

I do not know what became of Lillian. She had an eight-year sentence for "counterrevolutionary Trotskyist activity" because she had been briefly acquainted with a young cellist, a German exile who had spent three years in Nazi camps for illegal Communist activity and had then escaped to the Soviet Union in 1936. In 1937 he was arrested and convicted as a Trotskyist. Lillian's husband, a resident of Moscow, had repudiated her. Nevertheless, she never doubted for a moment that he still loved her and she bore him no ill will for the repudiation. She knew what it would have meant had he refused to do it: the sacrifice of his artistic career as a composer and teacher of music at best, prison at worst. Lillian was one of the few prisoners who received a package from home during the winter of 1938 in Vladivostok. Among all the wonderful things her mother had solicitously packed was a tiny package wrapped in letter paper and marked "Vitamin C." That was all. But this tiny notation in her husband's handwriting, on his letter paper, meant as much to her as a long, ardent letter; it was a silent message from a suffering man that he still loved her.

When the invalids departed for Mariinsk, those of us who remained behind lost our last hope of escaping Kolyma. During the spring sowing a few hundred prisoners were sent to the near-by *sovkhoz* (state farm) of Dubininsk to plant potatoes, but they returned to the camp a few weeks later. They came back late at night, a queer, stumbling, groping procession of people all clinging to one another, for most of the women had been struck with night blindness. The doctors eventually located some cod-liver oil and this mass attack of night blindness was cleared up.

Early in May 1939 the first rumors of a ship waiting for us at the port trickled through. It was the steam freighter *Dalstroi,* and one bright, warm day we vanished into its hold. There were seven thousand prisoners, among them five hundred women in a separate, partitioned-off section.

During the entire voyage, which lasted a week, no member of the guard or the ship's crew ever entered the prisoners' hold. They were afraid to, especially when a large number of murderers and bandits were being transported, since they were an insignificant, though heavily armed, minority compared to the number of prisoners. They stood with raised guns, ready to fire, when the prisoners were let out on deck in small groups to use the toilet. None of them took any account of what went on below decks. As a result, during all such voyages the criminals put across a reign of terror. If they want the clothing of any of the counterrevolutionaries, they take it from him. If the counterrevolutionary offers any resistance, he is beaten up. The old and weak are robbed of their bread. On every transport ship a number of prisoners die as a result of such treatment.

In the course of every voyage some counterrevolutionaries attempt suicide by jumping overboard. Usually they drown quietly. Some of them attempt the leap while the ship is passing through the narrow Strait of Tartary, a few miles from Sakhalin Island. Here they may manage to swim to shore or be rescued by a fishing vessel. In such cases the ship is stopped, and if the fugitive cannot be picked up, he is shot.

In the fall of 1939 the freighter *Djurma* went to sea with a shipment of prisoners. The criminals succeeded in breaking through the wall of the hold and getting at the provisions. They robbed the stores and then, to wipe out the traces, set the storeroom on fire. There was a frightful panic among the prisoners who were locked in the hold of the burning ship. The fire was held in check, but the *Djurma* entered port still burning.

Early in December 1939 the freighter *Indigirka,* the last ship of the season, left the port of Magadan. There were a number of free citizens on board as well as prisoners who were being released from Kolyma. There was a Russian woman prisoner among them, and there was also a German Communist named Erna D, former secretary of Ernst Thälmann and Wilhelm Pieck, who had been sentenced by a Moscow military tribunal to fifteen years of penal servitude and who was now being turned over to the Nazis in honor of the Stalin-Hitler pact of friendship.

But the Soviet and the German police waited in vain for their victims. The *Indigirka* never arrived in the port of Vladivostok. Lashed by gales, it went off its course and was finally wrecked upon the underwater portion of an iceberg. A Japanese steamer saved two hundred of the passengers. Erna D was not among them; she had been washed overboard and drowned. But the workers in all countries have a short memory. Who wonders about the thousands of sincere antifascists who did not die in the war or in Nazi concentration camps, but in Soviet prisons and camps?

The people who were rescued by the Japanese were taken to Vladivostok and turned over to the Soviet authorities whose first action was to subject them to a severe interrogation concerning their stay aboard the Japanese vessel. The Russian woman prisoner told about the adventures of the *Indigirka* to the prisoners awaiting transportation from Vladivostok, and they in turn brought the story to us at Magadan.

In 1944 several hundred young girls came to Kolyma. They were the so-called *ukazniki,* sent out here for unauthorized absences from a war factory, or for some similar minor offense. During the war the number of guards was cut

94

down everywhere, and on the ships as well; moreover, the guards had to put on civilian clothes during the passage through Japanese waters, since the Japanese would allow no military personnel to pass. The criminals, who formed the greater part of the human freight aboard this ship, had an absolutely free hand in the hold. They broke through the wall into the room where the female prisoners were kept and raped all the women who took their fancy. A few male prisoners who tried to protect the women were stabbed to death. Several old men had their bread snatched from them day after day, and died of starvation. One of the criminals, who appropriated a woman whom the leader of the band had marked for his own, had his eyes put out with a needle. When the ship arrived in Magadan and the prisoners were driven out of the hold, fifteen were missing; they had been murdered by the criminals during the voyage and the guards had not lifted a finger. The upshot of this particularly glaring scandal was that after the facts became known in Magadan, the commander of the ship's guard was called on the carpet and arrested.

We lay squeezed together on the tarred floor of the hold because the criminals had taken possession of the plank platform. If one of us dared to raise her head, she was greeted by a rain of fishheads and entrails from above. When any of the seasick criminals threw up, the vomit came down upon us. At night, the men criminals bribed the guard, who was posted on the stairs to the hold, to send over a few women for them. They paid the guard in bread that they had stolen from their fellow prisoners.

4. Kolyma

*May Heaven preserve man from enduring
what man is able to endure!*

Arrival in Magadan

WE WERE ON LAND. We took our first steps across the
paved quay in the port of Magadan. Now we were in
Kolyma where I was to spend eight years of my life, eight
years of imprisonment. It took a while for us to convince
ourselves that the ground underfoot was no longer swaying.
The daze of seasickness was slowly dispelled under the lash-
ing cold of the wind that raged across the Sea of Okhotsk
and through this port on its shore. Around the bay blue-
tinted mountains rose up, their gentle, rounded curves clear
against the pale sky and melting into the steely gray sea at
their foot. At this season they were clothed in the spring-
green of larch forests, among which bright red and violet
patches of blooming *ivan-chai,* or fireweed, glowed. We
looked about, and on all sides the eye encountered cascades
of hills ranging out to the horizon. The tallest of them could
scarcely have been more than three thousand feet. A high-

way, in part blasted out of the cliffs, wound for some four miles toward the as-yet-invisible city. On the seaward side we were accompanied by darting gulls, screeching silvery creatures—and free. We were not free. We were reminded of that by the wooden watch towers along the road, outposts of the realm of imprisonment.

The first frame houses of the town rose before us. We marched along a named street, although the houses were still scattered, widely separated by large empty lots overgrown with brush and strewn with debris. Stalin Street, one of the main streets of the growing town, was at that time rough and unpaved. The town itself was only beginning to thrust back the forest. At the end of Stalin Street we came to the *Sanpropusknik*, Magadan's baths, which were the pride of the town. Here the populace kept clean in large shower rooms which were used on alternate days for free citizens and prisoners. We newcomers entered the baths in our various civilian clothes and left them as Kolyma convicts, all dressed in the same wadded dark jacket and with kerchiefs of black-and-white checked cotton.

We turned off Stalin Street and walked about a hundred yards down another flanked by two-story frame dwellings. Then, about twenty yards beyond the road on our left, we saw the women's camp (*Zhen-Olp*). There were the barbed wire, the unmistakable palisades, the guards and the watch tower. Through the slats of the wide gate we saw figures in the camp yard wearing the same jackets and the same headgear as ourselves.

Soon we mingled with them, shared the planks with them, shared their hunger and labor and the fierce embrace of frightful cold, shared hopelessness and stubborn silence.

The Development of Kolyma:
Berzin—Garanin—Vyshnyevetsky—Nikishov

Kolyma, a region in the northeastern part of Siberia, is named after the Kolyma River. It is bounded on the north by the Arctic Ocean, on the east by the Sea of Okhotsk, an arm of the Pacific, on the south and west by impenetrable virgin forests (*taiga*). There is no railroad into the area. Administratively, it belongs to the Khabarovsk district. On Russian maps it is marked as being directly under the jurisdiction of the Executive Committee of the Ministry of the Interior (NKVD). There is no civil authority; there are no local elections. The region's candidate for the Supreme Soviet, however, is confirmed by a general election.

In 1932 a large group of geologists concluded their researches in this area. The region had been known earlier, of course, to sailors, explorers and fur trappers, and at one time the Japanese had held some fishing concessions along the shore of the Sea of Okhotsk. But the interior of the country was the undisputed territory of the Yakuts, Chuktos and Evens, who lived in scattered settlements and hunted, fished, and raised herds of reindeer. The natives are probably dying out, for they are the prey of tuberculosis, syphilis, and alcoholism.

No matter how far the geologists forged into the interior of this country, the landscape remained the same, though never monotonous. It is a region of vast forests, tremendous marshes, round hills of volcanic origin (*sopki*), the entire area intersected by great rivers with an extensive network of torrential tributaries. Two weeks of spring are followed by three hot summer months during which stinging gnats (*komari* and *moshkara*) are present in clouds, then two weeks of fall and eight months of winter with its terrible cold. Eight months during which snow and ice cover the forests, marshes, rivers and hills. The Sea of Okhotsk, too, is frozen hard.

In this country the geologists found immeasurable wealth in gold. To mine the vast treasure would require hordes of workers. But who would go voluntarily to this inaccessible, inhospitable country? The solution was found swiftly, for there is an inexhaustible supply of one kind of human material in the Soviet Union—prisoners.

In 1934 for the first time they were loaded by the thousands into the holds of freighters at Vladivostok and unloaded at the place on the shore of the Sea of Okhotsk where the port of Magadan now stands. The bay there bears the pretty name of Bukhta Vesyolaya or "Cheerful Bay." Another bay which forms part of the port of Magadan is called Bukhta Nogayevo. At the time of the arrival of the first prisoners, three tiny wooden huts amid the forest were all there was to see.

A member of the People's Commissariat of the Interior (NKVD) was placed in charge of Kolyma. He was a Latvian by birth and an old-time Communist named Berzin. His task was to produce gold out of the void, out of the virgin forest and the ice. The early years took a frightful toll of life, and he realized that the army of prisoners—at that time it consisted mainly of criminals—could do productive work only if it were well fed, warmly dressed, and adequately paid. During the last years of his administration Berzin managed to establish the necessary preconditions, in spite of being cut off entirely from all sources of supplies during six months of the year.

Woods were cleared and an excellent broad highway was begun; it now runs for hundreds of miles through the entire country. This highway, which is called a *tros,* was built upon the bones of thousands of prisoners. It runs from Magadan across the northwestern gold territory to the gold mines further west in Indigirka; from there it runs southwest across the Aldan, a tributary of the Lena, to Yakutsk on the Lena, the capital of the Yakut Soviet Socialist Republic. As yet it is passable only in winter. A railroad is also planned which will rescue the country from its utter isolation. Magadan, the capital of the area, was built, and all through the region, in the vicinity of the large gold mines, there sprang up small settlements of free citizens in addition to the large prison camps. The forest was cleared for five large state farms with pasture and tillage. These were:

1. Dukcha, six miles northwest of Magadan.
2. Ola, fifteen miles northwest of Magadan.
3. Talon, one hundred and fifteen miles south of Magadan.
4. Elgen, three hundred and fifty-five miles northwest of Magadan.
5. Zuzuman, four hundred and fifty miles northwest of Magadan.

The names recall former Yakut settlements. The main crop of these state farms, which are worked entirely by women prisoners, is cabbage. It is raised under very difficult conditions. This cabbage forms a large part of the prisoners' fare. The coarse outer leaves are used for prisoners; the cabbage heads are for the free citizens. The brew that is made out of the leaves is called by the prisoners "khaki soup" because of its greenish-brown color. Some potatoes are also planted, although in much smaller quantities; the crop is always imperiled by the early frosts and is intended solely for the free populace. In addition, turnips are grown and oats are sown; the oats do not ripen but are prized as green fodder (*selyonka*) for the cattle.

Because of the shortage of free labor, hunting and fishing are largely left to the native population, who cannot approach anything like full exploitation of the tremendous wealth of fish that abounds in the country. There are, however, five large fisheries; the fish are caught by men and cleaned, salted, and packed mostly by women prisoners. These fish factories are in Nogayevo, near Magadan, Ola, Balagannoye, a hundred and ten miles south of Magadan, Yana, sixty miles south of Magadan in the Yana Government, and Armany, thirty-seven miles south of Magadan.

The fish consist of herring and various types of salmon; whales and walruses are also caught. Salt herring and salted fish form an essential part of the prison fare. Under Berzin's administration the prison food was adequate when the arrival of supplies was not hampered by transportation difficulties, and prisoners who worked well were entitled to additional food bought at the camp commissary. At that time it was thought right in view of the murderous climate to include vodka in the regular rations—or rather pure alcohol mixed with water. In winter the prisoners were given fur coats, fur caps, and warm felt boots. Even in those days, however, the treatment of criminals was considerably better than that of counterrevolutionaries. And for the most part only criminals were given time off their sentences for satisfactory work, which was a great incentive to their working well. This general policy toward the prisoners lasted until 1937 and had the desired results; gold from Kolyma poured into Moscow.

Most of the gold mining in Kolyma is done underground. But some of it is done by a simple panning process, each man working by himself or with a single partner. The average production is twenty grams (.7 oz.) of pure gold per man per day. The season for panning gold is about a hundred days. But months before, the preliminary work is done; this consists in removing the layers of peat which cover the ground everywhere in Kolyma. In the underground mines machine drills and explosive cartridges filled with ammonal are used. The pace of the work is so furious that the use of explosives occasions frequent accidents and prisoners are crippled or killed. There are also many tales of despairing workers who blow themselves up.

At the end of each day's labor the workers, free men as well as prisoners, are searched with extreme care, although there would be little point in smuggling out gold, since there is nowhere to sell it. All the gold that is dug belongs to the state and anyone who offered it for sale would be convicting himself of theft. It is somewhat amusing that in this rich gold country there is not a single individual who is allowed to have a cap for his teeth made of gold. In the Soviet Union steel is used instead.

But although they have no personal share in the product, the prisoners are nevertheless overcome by a kind of gold fever, especially those who wash the gold directly out of the river sands. Many of them have told me how they trembled when they saw the pure metal glittering in their hands. These *lotochniki* as they are called (after the pan they use for washing the gold, the *lotok*) enjoy considerable freedom of movement, since they are sent out to scout gold-bearing locations for themselves. If they make a rich find, they keep it secret so that they can pan out their daily quota of about twenty grams undisturbed. If they should deliver a considerably larger amount of gold over a period of several days they will receive more tobacco, but they will also attract the production supervisor's attention and he will send a larger number of workers to the location—enough so that each has to work hard to meet the quota—or in the case of really big finds he will install a machine for washing out the gold.

The streams of Kolyma and Indigirka are so rich in gold that for the present no attempt is being made to exploit the gold mines systematically. New mining camps are opened constantly, and the prisoners fear them because the living conditions are so primitive. Usually the only shelters are tents and there are no straw pallets or any other equipment; the prisoners are lucky if they can lay hold of a blanket, and day and night shifts alternate in sleeping on the same narrow planks, which are like box lids arranged in three tiers.

The more gold there is, the more prisoners—and the more lice.

Such new camps are usually off the highway and have inadequate access roads. During the thaws in May, when everything turns to mud and marsh, they are often completely cut off and the bread ration may be held up for days. This is what happened in the gold camp called "Spokoiny" which was opened in 1944 in the northern mining district. *Spokoiny* means "rest" and it was a good name, for many prisoners swiftly found eternal rest there.

In traveling through this region of virgin forests and steep ravines, in which torrential streams noisily celebrate their brief release from the ice, you constantly come across ugly gray mounds of earth near abandoned hoisting towers. The earth is washed-out gold ore.

During the hundred-day season for panning gold some

two hundred thousand men are employed and the extraction of gold amounts to about four hundred tons annually, in value some $460,000,000.

The 1937 wave of terror also overwhelmed the rulers of the Kolyma gold mines. When Yagoda, head of the NKVD, fell, his whole organization fell with him. Berzin was arrested, taken to Moscow and shot, although he had achieved great triumphs in gold mining and laid the foundation for his successors' work. His wife also was arrested; she was a pale, fragile woman with whom I shared a collective cell in Butyrka Prison in 1938. Yagoda's successor, Yeshov, in collaboration with the then Chief Prosecutor of the Soviet Union, ground down millions of human beings in his thousands of prisons. It was the first flush of the NKVD purge which Stalin had inaugurated.

During the years 1937 and 1938 the élite of Russian intellectual life were annihilated. All who were still capable of independent thinking and independent decisions, all those who still knew what the word socialism meant, who still had some idealism, all those whose vision of freedom was not yet distorted, were to be robbed of their influence and liquidated.

The penal code was made far more stringent in 1937. Hitherto the longest sentence had been ten years; it was now raised to twenty-five years. The death penalty was retained —until 1948. The former practice of curtailing prison terms as a reward for good work was now rescinded. The treatment, diet, and clothing of the prisoners deteriorated immeasurably.

Berzin's successor in Kolyma was Garanin, a worthy associate of the men now in authority in Moscow. At that time the Kolyma "population" rose tremendously; about a hundred thousand prisoners were now brought in annually. These new prisoners were preponderantly counterrevolutionary elements; that is, mostly people who had never done any physical work. Scientists, artists, politicians, educators, leaders of industry, trade, and government, set out every morning on the horror march to the gold mines.

In 1938 Garanin undertook to liquidate thousands of intellectuals. Henceforth there was no more fur clothing for the prisoners. The standard equipment became wadded jackets and trousers which soon hung like torn rags upon the bodies of the gaunt prisoners. The felt boots were replaced by shoes made of canvas, and practically every mine worker suffered from frozen feet. But as the Russian proverb puts it: If you lose your head, you don't weep over your hair. And here the head was at stake. The wretched rations of the prisoners were deficient in fats; the major component was bread. But the quantity of bread in all Soviet camps is governed by the amount of work the prisoner performs. He gets more bread or less according to whether he fulfills, overfulfills, or fails to meet his quota. Each worker's performance is listed by free "brigadiers" (foremen) or by criminals, who are favored for such supervisory posts. It is common practice for the brigadiers to assign part of the work performed by counterrevolutionaries to the criminals who "grease" the brigadiers in various ways, while the counterrevolutionaries are without the means to practice bribery. But even if the work performed is listed honestly, it is impossible for a person unaccustomed to physical labor to fulfill the quota. He quickly falls into a vicious circle. Since he cannot do his full quota of work, he does not receive the full bread ration; his undernourished body is still less able to meet the demands, and so he gets less and less bread, and in the end is so weakened that only clubbings can force him to drag himself from camp to gold mine. Once he reaches the shaft he is too weak to hold the wheelbarrow, let alone to run the drill; he is too weak to defend himself when a criminal punches him in the face and takes away his day's ration of bread. He employs his last remaining strength to creep off to an out-of-the-way corner where neither the curses of the guards, the fists of the brigadiers, nor their eternal cry of, *"Davai, davai!"* (Get going!) can reach him. Only the fearful cold finds him out and mercifully gives him his sole desire: peace, sleep, death.

But Garanin was not satisfied with this sort of liquidation of the "enemies of the people." It was too slow for him. Therefore he traveled about from camp to camp examining the list of counterrevolutionaries. He took special note of those who were convicted of KRTD (counterrevolutionary Trotskyist activity).

"Which of these have not met their quota?" he would ask.

Most had not, could not. At evening roll call, when they returned from the mines, he would call out these unfortunates, revile them as saboteurs who were trying to continue their criminal counterrevolutionary Trotskyist activities even in camp, and he would have them driven in a herd out of the gate. At a short distance from the camp they would be shot en masse under his personal supervision.

This was still not enough. At night he would have thousands of enemies of the people taken out of all the Kolyma camps, loaded on to trucks and driven off to a prison. This prison, called Serpantinka, is about three hundred and seventy-five miles west of Magadan, in the midst of the forest, and it is probably one of the most ghastly institutions in the Soviet Union. Only ice and snow, mountains and forests, were the witnesses of the death-rattle of those tortured men who uttered their last scream of terror before they were shot. Only a few fortunate prisoners, who were sentenced merely to a ten-year addition to their term, came back from this prison to the labor camps. Years later they were so gripped by the horror of it that they did not dare to tell their fellow prisoners of the inhumanity they had seen and experienced. When they at last brought themselves to speak of it, they looked anxiously around to make sure that no informer was near by. In terse whispers they told of how Garanin, the Communist, had ordered thousands of innocent persons to be tortured and shot to death at Serpantinka during 1938.

It was estimated that Garanin had the deaths of some twenty-six thousand persons on his conscience. Twenty-six thousand people were killed in one year before the alarming reports of some of Garanin's assistants forced Moscow to intervene. He was finally recalled. According to one rumor, he was given fifteen years of penal labor; according to another, he was shot. Most of the additional sentences he had imposed were rescinded, but a certain percentage of the prisoners—in spite of all their written protests and petitions— were held without explanation to the extra ten-year sentence —if they could survive it.

Along with Garanin, his chief in Moscow, Yeshov, also vanished. Yeshov was responsible, with the knowledge of the chief of state, for the conviction of millions of innocent persons. Officially he was transferred at the end of 1938 to the People's Commissariat for Water Transportation; afterwards he disappeared from view. Thus the man who had knowledge as executor and accomplice of untold crimes was eliminated. His assistant Vyshinsky, the then Chief Prosecutor of the Soviet Union, soon afterwards began a new career in the People's Commissariat (now Ministry) for Foreign Affairs.

Vyshnyevetsky (not to be confused with Vyshinsky) succeeded Garanin and served as chief of Kolyma from 1938 to 1941. No change was made in the treatment, clothing, or food of the prisoners. But the summary trials and the shootings of prisoners without trial ceased. The mortality among the miners remained at a constant 30 per cent, to which no one objected. Vyshnyevetsky fell not because of that, but because of the expedition to Pyostraya Dresva Bay.

In this region too the geologists had discovered great reserves of nonferrous and noble metals. In the spring of 1940 a ship was outfitted for an expedition. Several thousand prisoners and some eight hundred free citizens went on board. In the summer of 1940 the ship sailed northwards from Magadan. There were some warnings that the ship was departing too late, but Vyshnyevetsky insisted on going through with the expedition that year.

After the first few weeks of its voyage the ship ran into icy storms at sea. The prisoners had been sent out in their summer dress, that is without wadded trousers, without mittens, and with thin shoes. When their winter clothing was looked for it was discovered that the needed articles were at the very bottom of the hold where they could not be got out during the voyage. Even before the ship reached its destination many of the prisoners had frostbitten hands and feet.

When they arrived at the bay they set about building the camp. One group of prisoners erected blockhouses for the free men and stables for the horses—the prisoners themselves lived in tents. Others busied themselves setting the first posts for the tall palisade, for how could prisoners possibly be kept in this wasteland without palisades and barbed wire?

Kolyma

In spite of the icy sea wind, they sweated under the weight of the beams for the palisades. The wind swelled to a gale, but they went on ramming one post after the next into the unwilling earth. For these were Soviet prisoners who build their own prisons, and the guards were standing near by with fixed bayonets.

For thousands of years this land had remained unsettled, plaything of the sea winds. Now men came to grace it with the marks of their civilization: watch towers and barbed wire. The gale rose to a hurricane. And the hurricane did not distinguish between free men and prisoners. It snatched them up in its roaring arms and tossed them into the sea. Guards and guarded vanished beneath the waves. Their property was scattered or torn to bits. Scraps of tents fluttered through space. Horses were picked up, whirled around, and thrown into the sea which they had feared throughout the whole long journey. There they drowned along with the men.

The only men who were saved were those who at the last minute tied themselves to the posts rammed into the ground. They had done their work well—the palisades held even in the hurricane. But not one failed to pay for his life with frozen hands or feet, frozen ears, nose, or cheeks.

In the spring of 1941 the remnant of the expedition was unloaded in the port of Magadan: two hundred free men and a hundred and fifty prisoners. In the prison hospital at Magadan, where I was working as a nurse at this time, these hundred and fifty were laid side by side on cots in three barracks. They were hollow-eyed relics of humanity, but they kept silent about the horrors they had endured; only those in the delirium of pneumonia screamed out their memories.

The frightful stench of rotting human flesh filled the barracks.

The morning after their arrival the surgeon came with his assistants and his instruments and went down the line. With the aid of the nurses the sick were sat up and their arms stretched out at right angles to their chests, palms down. Then the surgeon cut off the frozen, suppurating fingers. Twenty-five cots along one wall, twenty-five cots along the opposite wall. The bits of flesh in the kidney-shaped bowl piled up. After the fingers came the toes.

Those were the light cases. Others were left with stumps of arms and legs. A good many survived the pneumonia, and when they awoke for the first time after long days of fever and coma they looked for their limbs, but the limbs were gone. For many, medical care came too late and they died of blood poisoning. Unknown Soviet heroes. No newspapers mention them. There is only a number on their nameless graves.

Vyshnyevetsky had thought that this hastily and ill-prepared expedition would win him a new decoration. Instead he was recalled to Moscow, not because of the few thousand prisoners who had lost their lives, but because of the not-so-expendable free citizens. When he stepped aboard the ship for Vladivostok, NKVD officers informed him that he was a prisoner. In Moscow he was sentenced to fifteen years imprisonment.

Vyshnyevetsky was succeeded by Lieutenant General Ivan Fyodorovitch Nikishov, who was commander of Kolyma throughout the war and afterwards. A tall, handsome man, he is icily, mercilessly cruel. By cruelty he pushed through the fulfillment and overfulfillment of the gold plan; by cruelty he won decorations and large money bonuses. In

1942, at the age of fifty, he divorced his first wife, a woman of some culture who had never taken advantage of her husband's position of power to live expensively. He placed her and her grown son, who was state's attorney at Magadan, aboard a ship headed for Vladivostok, and married a Young Communist girl of twenty-nine named Gridassova, a primitive, crude, avaricious creature, who was only too well known to myself and to other female prisoners, for she functioned as the harsh commander of the Magadan women's camp. Thanks to her husband's position she has risen in the military hierarchy and has been decorated. She is the head of Maglag, the camp district of Magadan and the surrounding region, and rules the lives of tens of thousands of prisoners.

The couple's country house is located on the highway forty-five miles northwest of Magadan. It is furnished and equipped in the greatest comfort and is surrounded by Nikishov's private hunting preserve. Near by the prisoners of the invalid camp called "Seventy-second Kilometer" work in a glass factory which is under the special protection of Gridassova and consequently always registers a marvelous production record. During the war burnt-out electric bulbs were repaired there, since new bulbs were almost unobtainable and even tiny bulbs were sold at a hundred and fifty rubles.

Henry A. Wallace on Kolyma

Henry A. Wallace's book, *Soviet Asia Mission*, is typical of the superficial and unprincipled reports made by foreign visitors who, after a brief stay, think they are equipped to tell the truth about the Soviet Union. He speaks with admiration of the mushroom growth of Magadan whose first houses were built "twelve years ago." "Today," Wallace says, "Magadan has forty thousand inhabitants." He does not mention, or does not know, that this city was built solely by prisoners working under inhuman conditions. He also admires the three-hundred-and-fifty-mile Kolyma Road that runs from the port northward over the mountains, and he calls it "an all-weather highway." He does not say—or does not know—that this highway was built entirely by prisoners and that tens of thousands gave their lives in building it. His statement that "in the Kolyma area the Russians have about 1000 men engaged on road construction" is false, and ridiculous in view of the tremendous natural obstacles to road building. In fact thousands of prisoners are kept busy merely keeping the existing highway open to traffic amid the continual snowstorms.

Wallace says: Commander "Nikishov gamboled about, enjoying the wonderful air immensely." It is too bad that Wallace never saw him "gamboling about" on one of his drunken rages around the prison camps, raining filthy, savage language upon the heads of the exhausted, starving prisoners, having them locked up in solitary confinement for no offense whatsoever, and sending them into the gold mines to work fourteen and sixteen hours a day, at no matter what human cost.

According to Wallace the gold miners of Kolyma are "big, husky young men who came out to the Far East from European Russia." He also reports that "about three hundred thousand people" now live in the Kolyma district. The figure is amazingly close to the true one. But Wallace fails to say—or does not know—that most of these three hundred thousand persons are prisoners.

"Such is the return of the exiles to Siberia—they are pioneers of the machine age, builders of cities." Can Wallace possibly be aware of the grotesque irony of his words? For like their fathers and grandfathers, the children and grandchildren are also exiles, prisoners. But the conditions under which they live are far more inhuman now than they ever were in Tsarist times. In those days the prisoners' families could accompany them into exile; today prisoners are buried alive, cut off from everyone. No one who has a relative in a Kolyma camp is permitted to enter the district.

Wallace also has a touching story to tell about Gridassova, the head of the women's camp. He speaks of her efficiency, maternal solicitude, and little unostentatious attentions. All these traits he found united in the wife of Ivan Nikishov "whom we first met in Magadan at an extraordinary exhibit of paintings in embroidery, copies of famous Russian landscapes. The landscapes were made by a group of local women who gathered regularly during the severe winter to study needlework, an art in which Russian peasants have long excelled. . . ." Nikishov presented Wallace with two "wall pictures." "Who did them?" Wallace asked. Nikishov replied that he couldn't possibly know all the sewing women in a city of forty thousand. Later Wallace learned from the exhibit director "who that sewing woman was. She was 'one of the art teachers'; Ivan's wife."

In fact, Gridassova was no art teacher and never took up a needle. "The group of local women" were female prisoners, most of them former nuns, who were employed to do needlework for such highly placed ladies as Nikishov's wife. The whole insipid tale fits very well into the general picture that Wallace paints of Nikishov and his wife, those exploiters of slaves who cared as little for the thousands of prisoners whose lives were in their hands as they did for the excellent fish with which they plied Wallace.

Wallace's visit aroused a great deal of excitement among

the prisoners of Kolyma. I shall come back to that after I have described camp life in more detail.

In the party accompanying Vice President Wallace was Dr. Owen Lattimore, Professor at Johns Hopkins University, who represented the Office of War Information. This opportunity offered to an American scholar was unique: no free foreigner had set foot in this NKVD country before, and no one has done so since, but Dr. Lattimore had the privilege, after his return, of printing, without worry of censorship, whatever he liked about his impressions of Soviet Asia. Unlike the unhappy Soviet scientists, he did not have to be afraid of losing his job and his freedom if he spoke honestly and objectively.

Owen Lattimore's Report

An article, "New Road to Asia," written by Dr. Lattimore was published several months after his return in the *National Geographic Magazine* (LXXXVI [December 1944], 641–76). If his report to the Office of War Information was in substance the same as this article, the Office could scarcely have profited by his work. Since it cannot be assumed that Lattimore is naturally a poor observer, he must on this trip have voluntarily refrained from making use of his talent for observation. Instead of telling us what he has seen, he hands out unexamined Soviet propaganda.

"Political oppression under the Tsars was so harsh that the mildest liberals were often sent into distant exile. For this reason university professors, doctors, and scientists and intellectuals of all kinds were among the earliest exile pioneers of Siberia" (p. 646). If Dr. Lattimore was really interested in political oppression, why didn't he inspect the hundreds of camps in Kolyma where contemporary "pioneers of Siberia" are starving to death? Why didn't he ask the present-day "intellectuals of all kinds" why they are being physically and mentally crushed in the gold mines of Kolyma? Nowhere on the face of the earth is there a country like Kolyma, where the *entire* population is made up of victims of political oppression.

Now, however, there is no more oppression. "The scientific tradition continues, with the difference that the scientist no longer works as a lonely exile but with the organized support of the government" (p. 646). How true! There are no more "lonely exiles" in Siberia; they have thousands and tens of thousands of companions. "The organized support of the government" could possibly mean the splendidly organized mass arrests by the NKVD and the transportation of prisoners in cattle cars to the Far Northeast of Siberia.

"There has probably never been a more orderly phase of pioneering than the opening up of Russia's Far North under the Soviet" (p. 646). This is absolutely true. What other government would send hundreds of thousands of its own citizens every year to forced labor in new territories?

"From the air we could see that prospecting shafts had been sunk at intervals in long lines across the country" (p. 646). It is remarkable that Dr. Lattimore did not see, near these prospecting shafts, either the wooden watchtowers or the high palisades of the concentration camps.

"Magadan is also part of the domain of a remarkable concern, the Dalstroi (Far Northern Construction Company), which can be roughly compared to a combination Hudson's Bay Company and TVA" (p. 657). But the Hudson's Bay Company is not run by the police nor does it make use of forced labor. Furthermore, neither the Hudson's Bay Company nor the TVA shoots its workers if they refuse to go to work.

"Mr. Nikishov, the head of Dalstroi, had just been decorated with the Order of Hero of the Soviet Union for his extraordinary achievements. Both he and his wife have a trained and sensitive interest in art and music and also a deep sense of civic responsibility" (p. 657). What would Dr. Lattimore think of a man who, having visited the Nazi camps of Dachau and Auschwitz, afterwards reported only that the SS commandant of the camp had "a sensitive interest in art and music"?

". . . high grade entertainment just naturally seems to go with gold. . ." (p. 657).

Who would be willing to take the responsibility for such statements as this if someday the camps of Kolyma are thrown open to the inspection of the whole world, as the camps of Dachau and Auschwitz were opened? Would these words bear repetition when the mounds of frozen corpses under the snow are one day disinterred to testify to what the Soviet Union really is?

5. Women's Camps

Into the Taiga

ᴇACH MORNING at the Magadan women's camp the labor brigades set out. Slowly they moved forward toward the open gate of the camp. Today the search at the gate was unusually strict and a few women were kept back out of every brigade. They would not have to march out to work, but they were by no means happy about it. Pale and disturbed, they stepped aside and waited while the ranks marched past them, until the gate was shut behind the last woman. For weeks and months they had waited fearfully for this moment. They were to be sent into the virgin forests. Taiga! The very word was fraught with horror.

They were told to hand in all camp properties and to pack up their own few possessions. They asked where they were to be sent, but received no answer as usual; no prisoner is ever told what he is being called out for. But these women knew nevertheless. They knew each other, and more than half of them were pregnant. The latest medical commission several weeks before had exposed their carefully guarded secrets. Now they were to be sent to Elgen, the punishment camp for women. How far away was it? Three hundred miles? Four hundred?

"About three hundred and fifty," said a little snub-nosed blonde girl, shaking out of her mattress sack the woodshavings that are used because there is no straw. "I know, because my Grisha is a truck driver and he's been there often."

"You're lucky," one of the others sighed. "He'll be able to visit you there."

The snub-nosed girl had few illusions. "Do you think the men are going to wait for us when we do time for years in the taiga? That's over with. We'll have to find someone else, if there are any men at all in those damned woods."

"I never want to see a man again," another woman said grimly; she was a dour person who looked to be about fifty and was in reality thirty-eight. "The woman always gets the worst of it. The men get off scot-free. And it's just as Katya says, as soon as we're gone they have another on their line. These women lay right down if they catch sight of a slice of white bread. They're all like that, these white-handed little ladies, these intellectual bitches." She glared viciously at a young woman who was vainly trying to hold back her tears. Silently the young woman carried her empty mattress sack into the barrack. Was it possible to explain to these creatures that even in camp an emotion like love could occasionally exist? She threw herself down on the planks, pressed her face against the sack, which was now filled with her possessions, and held it tightly while she sobbed. A short distance away the dour woman with the piercing eyes and wrinkled, yellowed skin was packing her own things. "I'd rather have got myself syphilis than a brat," she said.

The truck was ready. Its body was a rectangular box made of thin boards. In the center was a tiny iron stove and a still tinier supply of firewood. "You won't freeze," the guard remarked. "You'll keep each other warm."

It was crowded enough, certainly. Thirty women with their belongings stumbled over one another. After the door was shut the inside of the truck body was dark as a coffin. The only light came from cracks around the opening for the stovepipe in the roof of the van.

The truck rolled along the packed snow of the highway at a moderate speed, averaging no more than fifteen miles an hour. At three o'clock in the morning they reached Strelka where they were given warm soup in the *dispecherskaya* (waiting room and customs office for travelers on overland busses). In no time word went around that a shipment of women had arrived. Every man in the place sauntered into the waiting room to have a look at them. A glance or a smile was enough; tobacco pouches were opened and generously offered around. The men from all districts looked for women from their own parts, and always found them, for these women criminals had been everywhere. Katya, the snubnosed girl, was in her element; laughing loudly she disappeared into an adjoining room with a young masher and returned after a while with the various remunerations customary in such cases: butter, sugar, and white bread. The guard did not care, so long as none of his charges left the low frame building. And he too received his reward from the happy lovers.

Then the women went back to their rumbling black box and kicked, cursed, and pushed each other to keep their places. On the afternoon of the second day they arrived in Elgen. Valentina Mikhailovna Zimmermann, for many years the dreaded commander of the camp, was personally present and watched with silent, critical coldness as each woman stepped out. Katya's fate was sealed at once, for she was pretty even in her rough prison garb. Valentina Zimmermann, whose prominent canine teeth had prompted the prisoners to nickname her "the Pike" could not endure pretty women. She would do everything in her power to send Katya off to work where no men with white bread were anywhere in the vicinity.

The new prisoners would not be sent to chop wood. That was not allowed from the sixth month of pregnancy on. In winter they could do snow shoveling and in the spring field work. During the last month of pregnancy the women would be relieved of work and placed in the highest ration category (twenty-one ounces of bread daily).

The Children's Combine

The children come into the world in the prison hospital. For a week mother and child stay together. Then the mother is dismissed from the hospital and the child taken to the children's house, or "combine," as it is called. The mother is not obliged to work for the first month after the birth of the child. Then she is sent to work at a place fairly near the children's combine, for it is Russian custom that the mother has the right to nurse her baby for nine months. At certain times the nursing mothers, who are called *mamki,* are assembled and taken under guard to the combine.

The mothers are not admitted into the children's room. The babies are brought to them in an empty room called the "nursing room." Here, sitting on wooden benches, they nurse the babies seven times, five times or twice a day, according to the age of the infants. Afterwards the mothers return to their work under guard. After nine months of nursing are over the mother has the right to see the baby for two hours once a month, if she remains in Camp Elgen or nearby. Commander Zimmermann had a savage hatred for these mothers. It infuriated her that in spite of threats and punishments prisoners went on bringing children into the world. Besides, the mothers were a liability to the camp owing to their shorter hours of work. And so she eliminated these limited visiting hours during the months from May to September on the grounds that the prisoners could not be released from field work.

As soon as the mother's sentence is complete, it is her duty as well as her right to take the child from the children's combine. Since alimony for children born out of wedlock has been legally abolished in the Soviet Union, the mother has to provide for the baby alone.

The children's combine at Elgen shelters on the average between two hundred and fifty and three hundred children. They remain there until the end of their seventh year. They are then transferred to the boarding school at Talon (on the Tauy River, twenty-two miles upstream from Balagannoye). Here they go to school with the Yakut children. They no longer see their mothers.

The children's combine includes several large barracks where the children are divided into groups according to age. Heading it is a free woman doctor who is assisted by a convict woman doctor. In every group there is one free supervisor and one convict, both women, for the day and night shifts; one supervisor is in charge of twenty to twenty-five children. Infants are cared for exclusively by prisoners, and prisoners alone work in the kitchen, laundry, and sewing room.

Chiefly criminals are selected for work in the children's combine. But since they are altogether unsuited for their tasks, there is a constant struggle between the head of the combine and the commandant of the camp, who does not want to send counterrevolutionaries to such preferred work. Even a good supervisor, however, does not have the time to pay the slightest attention to any individual child. She just about manages to place the children one after another on the insufficient potties, to clean their faces hastily with the small trickle of water at her disposal, to dry the little creatures, all of whose heads are shaved, with the same towel, and to stuff their food into them as fast as possible. These children rarely have toys; they rarely smile. They learn to talk late and they never experience affection.

The smaller children forget their mothers from one visiting day to the next. Just when they are beginning to thaw out a little, a guard comes along and calls the mothers. "Come on now, get going, it's time." Out in the yard they still hear the children crying. Children are always crying in the combine, and it always seems to each mother that the one crying is her own. The larger children put their noses to the window and watch knowingly as their convict mothers are marched off in rows of five—behind them the soldier with the fixed bayonet.

The Boarding School of Talon

The NKVD officers were frequently very tactful. They learned not to say to a woman, "You are under arrest." That always produced unpleasant scenes—hysteria, sobbing children. Therefore they said instead: "We need information from you; it will take only half an hour. We have a car downstairs to take you to the office."

The unsuspecting women sometimes took their children

along. These were usually taken from them as soon as they arrived at prison. But sometimes, especially in small prisons in the provinces, the children would stay with their mothers for months and would, after the mothers' conviction, go along with them through all the stages of their journeys. Only after they arrived at their destined camp would the children be taken away, not to be given back until the day of the mothers' release.

At Kolyma the separation of mother and child was very strict during the years from 1936 through 1940. A mother was never allowed to stay anywhere near the children's home in which her child was placed.

In 1938 a young mother was brought to the women's camp at Talon. Her four-and-a-half-year-old boy was taken from her and she herself was sent on to another camp in the taiga. It is the usual thing for prisoners to be shifted constantly from one camp to another so that the free people whom they meet in the course of their work will not grow too habituated to these "enemies of the people" and get into the pernicious habit of considering them as merely unfortunate fellow human beings. So it happened that the mother of this boy was sent, several years later, back to Talon, where her child was being kept. The camp administration had forgotten about this, and the mother kept the matter secret. She succeeded in getting assigned as a cleaning woman to the children's home where her little boy lived. She saw him every day, but he no longer recognized her. And the mother did not reveal herself to him because she was afraid the child would expose the secret and then she would be separated from him again. She washed the floors and was able to see her child, and that was a source of tremendous happiness to her.

Elgen Women's Camp

Three hundred and fifty-five miles northwest of the port of Magadan is the women's regimen camp of Elgen. "Regimen" is a Soviet euphemism, and in this case means a stricter regimen, or disciplinary camp. Magadan is a day and a half by truck from this camp. That is theoretical, of course. For prisoners who are sent into the virgin forest, return to the port city is very rare indeed. There is something so attractive about this forest that most prisoners never leave it at all. Another attraction is the number of snug, hidden cemeteries in the taiga; with their small tablets, marked only by a number, they blend beautifully into the landscape. So many prisoners cannot resist the appeal of such a grave.

I had already passed through the women's camps in Magadan, Balagannoye, Talon, and the invalid camp near Magadan. In the fourth year of my imprisonment in Kolyma I was shipped off to Elgen. This was not a punishment for anything I had done, but because I was a foreigner. And foreigners or people of German extraction, even though they may have been Soviet citizens all their lives, were during the war removed as far as possible from the port of Magadan; they were sent deep into the taiga. Balagannoye and Talon are small camps where ordinarily there are no more than a few hundred women. The two largest women's camps in Kolyma are in Magadan and Elgen; they averaged a thousand or more inmates. I am anticipating here in describing Elgen because I want to give a picture of typical camp life, before I go into my experiences in Magadan, which were connected mostly with my work in the prisoners' hospital there.

At the entrance to the small settlement of Elgen we are

greeted by a wooden, green-painted arch, a kind of arch of triumph, on which in huge red letters is the inscription: "Long live the great Stalin." That makes us feel at home immediately. We may be ragged, hungry, lousy and frozen, but the great Stalin is with us wherever we go.

Then comes another arch, a large wooden one with a gate beneath, which is adorned with another inscription, one slightly less edifying but equally to the point:

ELGEN MAIN CAMP
Women's Camp of the Administration for Northeast Corrective Labor Camps of the NKVD

All around is a high palisade crowned by barbed wire; there are two rows of barbed wire outside the palisade, ringing the entire camp except for the entrance. Within the camp there are also two rows of barbed wire; if prisoners approach closer than a yard to them, the guards may shoot without warning. At the corners of the camp are wooden watch towers, each with its guard. The gate is so wide that the customary rows of five prisoners can be admitted easily. Next to the gate is a narrow door meant only for one person. It is connected with the guardroom and can be opened only by the commander of the guard.

The guardroom is a small wooden structure in which the commander of the guard and the guards stay. It has a small window that looks out on the road, so that the commander can see from a distance whether anyone is approaching the camp. A second window looks out on a narrow hallway that leads to the door. On the commander's desk is a book listing all the names of the camp prisoners by brigades and by their places of work. No prisoner may enter or leave the camp without permission from the commander.

After passing the guardroom, you are in the assembly ground where the prisoners gather to march out to work. This assembly ground continues on and becomes the main street of the camp. On the left, opposite the guard, is the lockup. Then, on both sides of the street, are the barracks, five on each side. The first barrack on the left is the dining room; then come three living barracks; then the club. On the right side is a living barrack, then a barrack that is half infirmary, half living barrack for prisoners on camp duty, then two more living barracks, and finally the disciplinary barrack.

On the left side, about forty yards from the barracks and running parallel to the barbed-wire fence, are two latrines. On the right side, fifty yards away, is a toilet marked "For free citizens only"; the prisoners are strictly forbidden to use it.

Parallel to the living barracks on the right are the administrative shed, with offices for the camp commandant and the chief of statistics and labor assignments (URTsh); a barrack with rooms for seamstresses and cobblers who patch up clothes and shoes for camp use; a shed where prisoners apply for clothing and receive changes; a shed which contains the camp food supplies, and an attached store, or commissary, for prisoners. In addition, there is a woodshed and a stable for the oxen that haul the water barrels to camp. There is no plumbing, of course, and the water is fetched from a small stream several hundred yards away from the camp. When the stream is frozen over, as it is eight months of the year, the ice is pierced with an iron rod, and the hole has to be reopened every day when water is fetched.

Behind the dining room is the water kitchen (*kipyatilka*) where the drinking water is boiled in a large iron kettle. The prisoners commonly call this hot water "tea."

On the right side of the camp, beyond the guardroom, there is the economic department and a dayroom for the guards; the guards' barrack is outside the camp. There are no trees, shrubs, or any other greenery inside the camp. Not that we missed them. Living as close to nature as we prisoners did, spending, for example, twelve hours a day chopping wood in the forest, quite satiated our desire for the beauties of nature, and our need for fresh air as well. It did not disturb us at all that the windows in the barracks were fixed, so that they could not be opened. During the three short summer months an open window would only admit the mosquitoes; enough of them got in anyway through the door. And in winter we were always hunting for rags, tow, bits of board and paper to stuff the holes and the cracks in the panes; for storm windows were not used, although the winter temperature dropped to seventy and eighty below zero.

The living barracks are about sixty-five to seventy feet long, twenty-two to twenty-five feet wide, and contain approximately one hundred inmates. They are one-story structures made of planks, the spaces between the boards filled by peat. The outer door leads into a tiny hall called the *tambour* where smoking is permitted; then comes a second door which opens into the barrack proper. On the left is the washroom, partitioned off by a few boards. It has an iron stove with an arrangement of cords strung over it for hanging the prisoners' wet mittens, foot-rags and shoes. These things can be hung overnight; drying clothes by day is not allowed. It is just too bad about the night shift.

If a prisoner does not develop ulcers from the diet, he develops them from the daily irritation over drying his clothes. The general principle of the camp is first come, first served. If you come back to camp with your labor brigade at night, rush into the barrack just ahead of another brigade, and get to the stove first with your sopping foot-rags, you are lucky and can get a good place to dry your things. However there is another working principle: toughness is next best to good luck. So if you have not been fortunate enough to get there first, you push someone else's foot-rags off to a cold corner, or just throw them on the floor, and hang your own in the warmest place. If someone protests indignantly, you answer with a torrent of curses and blows of your elbows. This is the favorite practice of the criminals who share the barracks with the so-called counterrevolutionaries. You must be thankful if you find your foot-rags at all in the morning, since these criminals have the pleasant habit of appropriating the foot-rags of others if they like them better than their own. It is impossible to realize what foot-rags mean until you have worked twelve hours in the rain, snow, and frost, in fields, swamps, and woods, wearing shoes that scarcely deserve the name.

When you return to the barrack at night, exhausted from work, the first sound that meets your ears is the squabbling in the washroom. That is as natural and inescapable as the buzz of mosquitoes in summer or the howl of snowstorms in fall. It is as inevitable as the nocturnal groans and cries of the prisoners in their sleep.

The washing arrangements are wonderfully ingenious. The water is in a tin container. It trickles out through three holes. Underneath the container is a narrow tin basin with a drain in the center. The dirty water flows into a pail underneath this drain. If the pail is not there you are not allowed to

wash. The water in the pail is also used for washing the floor
and for illegal laundering. If anyone has set his heart on a
luxury like a footbath, he must leave that for the night when
the demands on the pail are not so heavy.

In order that the water will flow from the container only
when needed, small iron rods with iron discs at both ends can
be moved over the holes. You push up the iron rod, catch
a little water in your other hand, and soap your hands; then
you let a little more water trickle down, soap your face, and
raise and lower the rod ten times without getting any significant amount of water. Meanwhile the soap is burning
your eyes, and behind you the woman next in line snaps,
"How long do you intend to go on making up? We want to
get finished today too." And so you resignedly wipe the soap
off into your towel, which is made of a piece of sacking.

The towel you received from the camp administration has
either become tattered long ago, or you have cut it up for a
foot-rag, since neither stockings nor foot-rags were given out
by the camp after the beginning of the war. Consequently,
everyone was constantly searching for something with which
to wrap her feet. How we blessed the Americans for deliver-
ing their flour in such splendid white bags. I don't imagine
the American flour manufacturers had any idea what luxury
articles were made out of those bags—from brassieres to embroidered blouses. We still went on wearing brassieres out of
a silly sort of habit, and for the sake of the additional warmth
they provided, although we were so emaciated that there was
not much for them to support. We had a difficult time getting the American bags from the free women of the area,
who also prized them for making all sorts of embroidered
coverlets. In addition, there was the risk that during the daily
shakedown at the guardroom we might be caught with such

a bag, which would have meant confinement in the lockup, since the bag would be stolen property. . . . While I am speaking of American goods I should mention that all our drinking cups and eating bowls were made out of American tin cans, the contents of which, naturally, had been eaten by the free citizens. While we gulped our cabbage soup with salted fishheads, we would thoughtfully spell out: "Chopped pork, to be served with. . . ."

Along the left and right walls of the barracks were two tiers of cots; in the center, between two rows of wooden posts which supported the roof, were one or two brick stoves whose fires were always feeble, a narrow table with two benches, and overhead an electric bulb which the prisoners themselves had purchased. Electricity in Elgen was highly capricious, so that usually only a faint reddish glow indicated where the bulb hung; you were rarely troubled by any glaring light from it. At midnight the electricity was turned off entirely, except for the circuit that supplied current to the camp floodlights and the guardroom.

Each bedstead was double, made of planks and four feet wide, with an upper berth about three feet above it. This made room for four persons, so that each had about two feet to herself. The one in the lower berth could just sit upright without banging her head on the upper bed. Whether the person in the upper tier could sit up at all depended upon the height of the barrack; in a low-ceilinged barrack she could not enjoy the luxury of sitting. This, by the way, pleased the person underneath, because a woman sitting up in the top deck would have to dangle her feet over the side and into the face of her fellow prisoner below—and in a woman's camp there was little enthusiasm for female legs, especially when the feet had been washed only two or three times a month in the course of the obligatory bath. Between each bedstead was a space of a foot and a half where, when they were dressing in the morning, four women twisted, stooped, pushed, and scolded.

Upper and lower berths each had their advantages and disadvantages. The lower berths were easily reached and slightly less afflicted with bedbugs; on the other hand they were colder and darker, while dust, crumbs and now and then larger objects fell on your head. To reach the upper berths you had to take off your shoes and clamber up; on the other hand, they were warmer and lighter, and except for bedbugs nothing got in your hair. It was rare for anyone to fall out of the upper bed, except when two criminals got into a fight and threw each other down. Then, too, the group orderlies—prisoners in charge of camp duties—were accustomed to pull you down by one leg if you didn't report quickly enough for a spell of extra duty inside the camp at, say, ten o'clock at night.

A so-called straw mattress went with each prisoner's bed. There was no straw in it and rarely hay, because there was not enough hay for the cattle; instead it contained wood shavings or extra clothes, if a prisoner still owned any extra clothes. In addition there was a woolen blanket and a pillowcase which you could stuff with whatever you had, for there were no pillows. Then you also received two sheets: one for use and the second to be put aside and used to dress up the barracks on orders from above. This second sheet was spread over the woolen blanket so that an innocent stranger or one of the numerous and well-paid Soviet inspection commissions would be greeted with the sight of pleasant white beds.

The barracks were divided up among the labor brigades, so that there was a barrack for field workers, one for construction workers, one for cattle tenders, and so on. Thus the prisoners had the opportunity to continue in the barracks the quarrels that began at work. Moreover, this method of housing was in accord with the policy of mingling criminals with counterrevolutionaries; they had a profound mutual hatred for one another and their greatest pleasure was to denounce each other to the camp administration for all sorts of infringements of the camp regulations. I should say that the criminals were more keen on denunciation than the others. And the administration put more trust in their word, despite their pathological tendency to lie.

Two barracks were excepted from the principle of housing by labor brigade. The first was the disciplinary barrack. This was the worst-constructed, lowest-ceilinged and most bug-ridden barrack in the camp. After evening roll call it was locked up. A larger squad of guards, accompanied by dogs, supervised the inmates when they went out to work, and the brigade as a whole was assigned the hardest tasks. The prisoners of the disciplinary barrack were usually the toughest and stubbornest type of criminals who were being punished for refusal to work, attempted escape, theft, stabbing, drinking bouts, or card-playing. God help the *contriki* (counterrevolutionaries) who fell in among them, for sometimes you could be sent to the disciplinary barrack for a minor offense. The outlook for the inmates of the disciplinary barrack was usually shipment to Camp Mylga, which is about eighteen miles from Elgen. The conditions at Mylga are so ghastly that Elgen seems a paradise by comparison. But even Mylga is not the last stage, for disciplinary camp Mylga has its own disciplinary camp called Izvyestkovoye, where women work in gypsum quarries. A woman who swings the pickax there does not have to reckon out how many more years of imprisonment she faces. She can be quite certain that within a year she will be released from all earthly sorrows.

The second exception to the principle of housing by labor brigades was the so-called German barrack, which was started during the war. In it were concentrated Germans from Germany and from the Volga Republic, from Siberian and Caucasion villages, Jews from Germany, Austrians, Russians, Hungarians, Finns and Latvians—all "enemy aliens" in other words, although almost every one of them was a Soviet citizen. They too were employed for heavy "general" tasks and were the first to be routed out of their beds for nocturnal shock-troop work; otherwise their fate was the same as that of the other prisoners. Only occasionally were they isolated completely in specially remote camps under reinforced guard. Although the idea of this barrack was that Russians, even though prisoners, should not be forced to live with Germans (for all that, they were mainly long-since-Russified Volga Germans), the Russian prisoners had a disconcerting habit of wanting to move into this barrack because it was relatively clean, quiet and disciplined, and there was less stealing and swearing in it.

In every barrack an elderly woman, medically certified as an invalid, was on barrack duty. She swept and washed the floor, fetched drinking water and water for washing, carried out used water and refuse, kept the stoves burning and, with the aid of inmates who took turns helping her, sawed and split the firewood. She brought food to the sick who were temporarily excused from work, collected dirty wash once a month and took it to the prison laundry outside the camp, brought back the laundry and distributed it. Her bread ration was seventeen and a half ounces when the top ration for prisoners was twenty-one ounces; when the top ration was reduced to seventeen and a half ounces in 1941–43, she received fourteen ounces, and no pay at all from the camp. But it was customary for the other inmates of the barrack to make a voluntary collection every month, so that she usually received more money than any of the other prisoners. All knew that what few decencies of life they had in the camp depended upon this old woman. Everyone was grateful to her. When we came back to the barrack, soaking wet, frozen, and exhausted, she was there to welcome us with a friendly, maternal smile. She contrived to steal a little extra firewood somewhere in the camp—the official ration of wood was always ridiculously small; she saw to it that the "tea" was hot and in adequate quantity; and she did not fuss overmuch about the snow that everyone tracked into the barrack. And it was she who awoke us in the morning when we stubbornly refused to hear the bell for rising.

The clothing of female prisoners consisted of:

1. Undershirt (of thin linen).
2. Short underpants (also of linen).
3. Cotton print blouse.
4. Cotton shirt in summer or wadded long trousers in the winter.
5. Gray checked cotton kerchief for the head in summer, or dark flannel shawl in the winter.
6. Quilted khaki jacket in summer or lined and padded sailor-type jacket in winter, the so-called *bushlat*.
7. Mosquito netting to protect the face in summer; wadded mittens in winter.
8. For summer wear, men's shoes of artificial leather; for winter wear, canvas boots commonly called *burki*.

Burki is the local name for warm, soft top-boots. But our special prisoners' burki were a Kolyma invention. They were made of lightly padded and quilted sacking with high, wide tops that reach to the knee, the shoe itself being strengthened by oilcloth or artificial leather at the toe and heel. The sole is made of three cross sections of rubber from worn-out automobile tires. The whole thing is fastened to the foot with strings and tied with string below the knee so that the snow does not get in. These burki are so roomy that you can wrap three footrags around each foot. After a day's use they become all twisted, and the flabby soles turn every which way. They absorb moisture with incredible speed, especially when the sacks of which they are made were used for bagging salt, and hold the moisture obstinately. During the eight months of winter, drying the burki is the prisoner's principal problem. They are so heavy that after a march of several miles from the camp to the place of work you can scarcely lift your feet, although your day's work is just beginning. Heavy nailed mountaineering shoes are like elegant dancing pumps compared to these Che-te-se, as the prisoners call them; it is the abbreviation for Chelyabinsk Tractor Factory.

The clothing of male prisoners consists of:

1. Shorts (of thin linen).
2. Long underwear (of the same material).
3. Military tunic.
4. Light cotton trousers in summer or wadded trousers in winter.
5. Heavy cloth cap in summer, with earflaps for winter.
6. Quilted khaki jacket in summer, *bushlat* in winter.
7. Mosquito netting in summer, wadded mittens in winter.
8. Artificial leather shoes in summer, sackcloth burki in winter.

These articles remain the property of the camp; selling or exchanging clothes or blankets is punished with confinement in the lockup and a fine. The fine amounts to five times the price of the traded article; it is deducted from the prisoners' earnings on the grounds of *promot,* that is, waste of camp inventory.

Snowstorm

Balagannoye is a small port with a single main street of one-story wooden houses and huts. The other dwellings are distributed in a semicircle at both ends of the main street. The camp is situated about a mile or a mile and a half from the shore; it consists of long, dark wooden barracks which are not, like most of the other little houses, plastered with mud and whitewashed. Balagannoye was actually the second camp I was sent to in Kolyma. It is considered by the prisoners one of the most tolerable camps in the region, but I was there only a short time. The camp is divided into two parts by a high wooden palisade and by barbed wire; one part is for women, the other for the men prisoners who are crippled, too weak, or too ill to work in the gold mines, and who therefore are employed as porters and drivers, woodsmen, and craftsmen.

Beyond the camp are the fields which stretch out to the edge of the forest. There is always a fresh wind from the sea, and when the prisoners work in the fields or the fisheries in the summer, the mosquitoes are not so bad as in other places in Kolyma. Here the women prisoners dress in short cotton skirts in summer, whereas elsewhere they go to great lengths not to expose the smallest patch of skin to the mosquitoes and therefore make themselves long pants out of sacks; they tie the pants carefully around their ankles before they put on the heavy prison shoes with their thick wooden soles.

At this camp you even hear a few women singing now and then as they cut up the shining red meat of the big salmon, drop the red caviar, the heart, and the liver into their separate containers, and swiftly toss the fish with their bellies slit open onto the long wooden table where they are salted. Another group packs them into high barrels for shipment. The fish packing plant is right along the shore. Among the tables brigadiers walk up and down, all of them excited, all caught up in the driving tempo, for the fish spoil quickly and the catch at this bay of the Sea of Okhotsk is always very large.

For twelve and fourteen hours the women stand stooping over the tables, their knives flashing into the next fish and the next, repeating again and again the same swift, practiced movements. Everything reeks of fish—the air, knives, clothing, hair. The hands of the women at the tables are red and swollen; the skin on the back of their hands is cracked and the salt burns in the cuts. And yet none of the hundreds of prisoners would exchange this work for any other, for during the brief noon pause a wood fire is quickly started and pails of fish are cooked over it. Under the fish the prisoners have hidden salmon hearts and livers, which are great delicacies. Others meanwhile are busy secreting small packages of caviar which they will smuggle back to camp with them—precious additions to the thin evening soup, something to exchange for bread, or to give as a present to the hungry women who work in the fields and the woods.

In winter when the huts are buried deep in snow, almost all the prisoners work in the woods. In winter the sea breeze becomes a hurricane, a freezing blizzard in which you cannot see a step before you, and the whole world becomes one white mass of snow whirling in the howling wind. Then the inhabitants of the village stretch heavy ropes between one house and the next, and they cling to these ropes with all their might when they go out, lest they be swept away into the snow and certain death.

All day long the storm howled, drowning out the screech of saws in the woods. On this day the guards themselves urged getting back to camp early. As the drivers, men as well as women, tied the last load of wood on the low sleds, their curses were inaudible above the howl of the wind. Running along beside the small, skinny horses, the drivers continually lashed them with the knout upon the protruding bones of their hindquarters and upon their thick, woolly pelts in which the snow settled and melted.

The sky darkened swiftly and the storm raged. Two sleds fought their way through the woods. Two little horses tugged at the traces, stood still and lowered their heads. Their skin twitched under each blow of the knout, but they did not move. The drivers, a man and a woman, untied the ropes with numb fingers, kicked and shoved the wood off the sled, and pulled the resisting horses forward by the bridle. The animals moved slower and slower, placing one leg deliberately after the other; then they quivered and stood still again. By the time the two panting drivers had unhitched the horses from the sleds, darkness had fallen. The animals groped on a few steps; then, snorting, they bent their knees and lay down side by side in the snow.

The woman squeezed in between the horses, so that she received a little warmth and shelter from their bodies. The wind tore at the horses' heads and at the shawl of the woman who lay there in the shrieking darkness waiting for the end.

A profound weariness overpowered her; less and less often did she shake off the snow that kept piling up on top of her.

The man had disappeared. He had shouted into her ear that the camp could not be far; he was going to try to make his way to it for help.

He stumbled, fell, got up, took another few steps, was thrown against a tree by the wind, and groped on until he fell again and continued to crawl forward on all fours for a while. Then he struggled to his feet again and stumbled on. Around him was nothing but darkness, snow, and the fearful howling of the storm. He felt terribly alone, afraid and exhausted. Tossed about by the storm, he struggled for his life, for his wretched, shameful prisoner's life, against all the roaring forces of the hostile north.

He kept going somehow until he stumbled into the group of prisoners who had volunteered to go out and search for their missing comrades. The two unfortunates had actually been only a few hundred yards from camp; otherwise they would never have been found on such a night. The group went on and found the woman, covered with snow, still lying between the two snow-covered horses.

When the two were carried into the brightly lighted, warm infirmary of the camp, the rescuers saw two tears frozen to the lashes of the woman's closed eyes. She was given a little alcohol and a large amount of hot tea; her body was rubbed and she received an injection to stimulate the heart. Gradually life and warmth returned to the numbed body, and when she began to complain of the painful pricking in her hands and feet, they knew she was recovering.

When the doctor gripped her right foot, she cried out in pain. There was a large blister on her big toe. "Frozen," the doctor murmured. She took her scalpel and pincers and

139

swiftly removed the dead skin of the blister, placed a gauze pad soaked in yellow antiseptic on the wound, and bandaged it. Then the woman was carried to her cot and covered with blankets, jackets, and wadded trousers. She fell asleep at once. Meanwhile the doctor wrote out the certification required in cases of frostbite, a statement that the prisoner Krylova, Anna Vassilyevna, thirty-four years old, KRD (counterrevolutionary activity), term: 10 years, had suffered frostbite as a consequence of an accident at work and through no fault of her own. In other words, the case was not one of self-mutilation. Self-mutilation occurred frequently, especially among male prisoners, and was punishable.

Toward morning, when the blizzard began dying down, the two horses were fetched and taken to their stalls.

Krylova was released from work that day and was able to rest. But at dawn the next day she was again standing in line, shivering, her shoulders hunched, her face so swathed that only her eyes with their hoarfrosted lashes showed, waiting to go out to work with her freezing and equally swathed comrades. With wadded trousers and jackets which they had patched and repatched, with a piece of cord around their waists to keep the jackets close against their bodies, so that the wind would not blow in, with bare feet wrapped in filthy, tattered rags and covered by the huge sackcloth burki, they looked like shapeless, fat creatures, although in reality they were but skin and bones.

When Krylova turned into the barnyard with her group, a male prisoner waved to her. He had already hitched his horse to the sled. It was the man who had been lost in the woods with her.

"Well, so you're still alive," he called to her across the yard.

"Nichevo," she called back indifferently. "I froze off a toe."

"Is the bone all right?" the man called back.

She nodded.

"Then don't worry," he shouted encouragingly, getting up on the board between the sled runners and taking the reins in his shapeless mittens. "If the bone is left, the flesh will grow back over it."

She went into the stable to fetch her usual horse. But the stableman gave her another.

"What's the matter with my Laska?" she asked, examining the new horse.

"Your Laska needs a rest," the stableman said. "Her forelegs keep trembling. The veterinary says she has nervous shock from the night in the woods."

"Well, well," the woman said, "nervous shock, eh? And she's getting a rest? Oh well, she's a horse, not a prisoner."

6. Nuns, Thieves, Speculators and Lovers

Article 124 of the Constitution of the USSR

"FOR THE PURPOSE of assuring freedom of conscience to the citizens of the USSR the church is separated from the state and the schools from the church. The freedom to practice religious rituals and the freedom of antireligious propaganda is extended to all citizens."

During the war, in the hour of need, the rulers of the USSR bethought themselves of God. Everything had to be done to inspire the very least of Soviet citizens with absolute devotion to his country. In spite of all the Communist propaganda the Russian villages, and not alone the villages, had remained religious. That was true even of a generation who were born and educated after the Revolution.

In the ten different Soviet prisons and the fourteen Soviet camps in which I was confined, I met a great many people. During the eleven years of my imprisonment constant streams of new people poured into the camps. Only an infinitesimal minority of these people were convicted of a "religious

crime." But contrary to my original conception, I learned
that the majority of my fellow prisoners, apart from former
Party members and Young Communists, had not lost their
faith, although they scarcely ever practiced the rituals of
religion. And many former Party members who had lost faith
in their ideal because of their unjust imprisonment sought to
fill the void within them with something else—and that something was God.

During the war high church dignitaries—those who were
still alive—were released from their camps in the far north
and restored to office. They were by then willing to do anything, for decades of imprisonment had not failed to leave a
mark upon their souls. They prayed for the Little Father
Stalin as they had formerly prayed for the Tsar. They uttered
prayers of thanksgiving to God for His goodness in sending
the nation Stalin, the "leader of the peoples, the genius of
the twentieth century, the benefactor and liberator of the
Soviet people." The rulers of the Soviet state, with a great
show of sincerity, pinned the Order of the Red Flag to the
breasts of these church dignitaries.

But all the lesser people who were rotting in the forced
labor camps on account of their religion were not affected by
this religious renaissance. Not one of them had his term
shortened. And they continued to cling to their view that
everything done by the Soviets was an act of the Antichrist.
They were the hardiest and most stoical people in camp.
Among them were members of sects whose forefathers had
been persecuted under the Tsar, but who still adhered steadfastly to their customs and beliefs.

Among them were nuns whose convents had been destroyed
thirty years before, but who still felt themselves and called
themselves nuns. The prisoners in the women's camps called

all those who were serving a sentence for religious reasons *monashki*, little nuns.

On all Sundays and church holy days they would go to the lockup. Neither persuasion, threats, mockery nor physical punishment could force them to work on the Lord's days. They ate their slender punishment rations and sang their songs. They were beaten. Their skirts were tied over their heads, and sometimes they were tied together by the hair. It did not help. On the following Sunday they allowed themselves to be pushed into the lockup as patiently, submissively, and unflinchingly as ever.

There were sectaries whose religion forbade them even to give their names to the Antichrist. Matushka Seizeva was one of these. Every night when she passed through the guardroom she looked with silent contempt at the commander of the guard, who had to register each prisoner in his book. Other prisoners who knew her quickly called over her shoulder, "Seizeva," and she was allowed to pass. If no one else was there at the time the commander roared once or twice, "Name?" and when he received no answer, Matushka was promptly sent to the lockup without her supper, to spend the night there.

In many sects there were tenets against accepting any official documents. Contact with any such devices of the Antichrist was sin. Lack of papers was the cause of the arrest and conviction of many sectarians. After serving their five years they were taken to the camp office to receive their discharge papers. But they refused to accept them. Without papers no one can live in the Soviet Union. Therefore they were soon brought to trial again, and vanished once more into the camps.

Nadya, a dark-complexioned, dark-eyed peasant woman

with shining black hair, who always radiated cheerfulness
and kindness, whose strong, beautiful body not even camp
life could afflict, came from some sect in the Ukraine. She
was about thirty-eight years old.

Her release and her husband's occurred during the war.
It had been a rare piece of good fortune that the two had
met again, for usually husband and wife are not only sent to
different camps, but also to regions very far from each other.

It was impossible at this time, of course, to return to the
Ukraine where their orphaned children had been left behind.
And so they went to work on the Elgen state farm, she as a
field worker and her bearded husband—for shaving too is sin-
ful to this sect—as a cabinetmaker. At forty-eight he was a
broken old man. But they were at last together after so many
painful years of separation.

Then came the Easter holidays. Nadya did not go to work.
Absence from work without a medical certificate is punishable, and during the war there were few days of rest even for
free Soviet citizens. There was always some "shock-troop
work" that was urgent and had to be done on Sundays. And
the rare official rest days did not coincide with the church
holidays.

Her husband submitted to the state power, but Nadya remained at home and spent the holidays in praying and singing hymns. This first time she got away with a public rebuke.
Then came Ascension Day. Again Nadya stayed at home in
their tiny room and prayed and sang. Her husband pleaded in
vain with her to go to work and not to bring fresh misfor-
tunes down upon them. This second time she was rebuked
sharply and told that a third such absence from work would
be punished to the full extent of the law.

Then came Pentecost. Sobbing, her husband went on his

knees and pleaded with her. "Nadya, I implore you, Nadya, give in. This sin cannot be counted against us because we are not committing it voluntarily; we do it only out of bitter necessity. Nadya, have mercy on yourself, on me. Nadya, I no longer have the strength to go through all that horror again. Nadya, listen to me, Nadya. . . ."

But Nadya would not listen.

"You do what God has given you the strength to do," she said softly in her melodious Ukrainian dialect, "as I must do what my conscience tells me to do."

And she stayed home for the third time, devoting herself to prayer, accepting martyrdom.

Three weeks later we were sitting, hungry and exhausted, around the stove with its dying fire. A woman entered and softly closed the barrack door behind her.

"Nadya, where have you come from? Greetings, Nadya."

Her powerful arms embraced us; her large eyes examined our wasted faces with sorrowful affection.

"Nadya, what did you get?"

"Five years," she said in a calm, indifferent voice, putting her bundle down on the boards of a bedstead.

Criminals and Politicals

The free population of Kolyma consists mostly of former prisoners, the majority of these being former criminals. One of the chief traits of the criminal is his drive to lead a better life than his work can ever yield him. If he does not have as much liquor as he can drink, if he has no presents to give his mistress, and cannot play cards for high stakes, life has no zest for him. What he cannot get legally he takes illegally. All these thieves, bandits, and murderers carry on their trades from the moment they are released until they are taken back behind the barbed wire. They know that they will never again be permitted to leave Kolyma, whether they are prisoners or freemen. They have connections everywhere, and everywhere in Kolyma there is stealing, profiteering, speculation, and bribery. A more corrupt society than that of Kolyma cannot be imagined. Even those free citizens from other parts of the country who are recruited for work in Kolyma and go there because money can be made there more quickly and easily than anywhere else in the Soviet Union, are soon infected by the local customs of cheating and profiteering. And all around are prisoners, usually the criminals also, who are ready to act as go-betweens for anything, so long as they get some eatables as their share in the deal.

Our attitude toward the criminals was highly ambivalent. On the one hand we considered them products of social injustice combined with hereditary degeneration and feeble-mindedness—people whose fault lay not in themselves but in their stars. On the other hand we had to share our days and nights with these heirs of social misery and parental alcoholism. And while we lived with them, charitable theories did not help; we could feel for them only hatred.

Nothing contributed so much to the wretchedness of our camp life as the criminals. Most of them were dull creatures with low, receding foreheads, who could neither read nor write; but they had grasped the fact that the camp administration was deliberately playing them off against the "counterrevolutionaries." A more or less morally unified mass of prisoners in Kolyma, where the free population was far outnumbered by the prisoners and where strong bodies of troops were not stationed, might have become dangerous. But even the contriki were a highly heterogeneous group who were not welded together by any common principle. "You die today and I'll live tomorrow," was the motto. All were pitted against all. The criminals, however, were always told: You have broken the law and must pay the penalty for it, but you are not enemies of the people. The enemies of the people are the counterrevolutionaries. The contriki and they alone are responsible for everything that goes wrong in our country. They must be annihilated.

This propaganda served as an outlet for the criminals. Their worst instincts were given free rein, and were covered up with a cloak of loyalty. The criminals knew how to make use of their opportunities. They were not punished for physical abuse, theft, false accusations, and rapes committed against contriki. In addition, not only the criminals but a considerable part of the so-called counterrevolutionaries were filled with hatred and contempt for their intellectual superiors, the intelligentsia. "Intellectual" was the most contemptuous epithet in the camp—and outside camp also.

In every country the language, ideals, and aims of the best thinkers are incomprehensible to the masses of the people. The gulf created by differences in education and the conditions of life and work is not bridged. In Russia this gulf between intellectuals and the broad masses is a chasm. In despising the intellectual, the person who is weak-muscled or awkward at physical labor, the man who has always worked with his body not only vents his unconscious inferiority feelings, but also expresses his suspicion and rejection of the state, which the intellectual seems to personify. In camp he at last has an opportunity to take it out on these intellectuals. And everyone takes advantage of the opportunity. The small number of intellectuals who were able to adjust to the demands of physical labor even tried to wipe out the traces of their class; they began watching with a mocking smile the fruitless efforts of their fellows who could never learn to use a saw and pickax successfully.

Rozochki, that is, "little roses," is the contemptuous name that the criminals have given to all noncriminal female prisoners; female criminals call themselves *fiyalochki,* "violets." The first epithet has been picked up by the contriki and is leveled tauntingly at the intellectual women in the camp. Back of the poetic word "rose" lies a rich complex of hatreds for those who differ from the masses.

Another word in Russian criminal cant is *frayer,* feminine form *frayersha.* It is another appellation for the noncriminal as a victim to be exploited, robbed, and cheated, for he is completely at the mercy of the criminals. Since there is no solidarity among the contriki and since the administration supports the criminals against them, they are quite helpless and defenseless. Their only course is to try by bribery, by humility, by performing all sorts of services, and above all by disgusting toadying, to win the favor of their vicious tormentors.

Blat, mat and *tufta* are criminal jargon for the internal laws of the camps. *Blat* means connection, acquaintanceship, protection, forbidden favors—all things that are available only to those who belong to the *blatnoy mir,* the criminal world. But noncriminals, too, quickly adjust to these methods, and anyone who tries to get along by acting decently is an object of ridicule and a doomed soul.

Mat is the collective noun for the vilest and filthiest swearwords, which are used not only by the prisoners, but by the highest executives of the camp administration on every suitable and unsuitable occasion.

Tufta is faking of all kinds. It is an art that has been developed by many generations of criminals over long years of imprisonment. There is tufta in all kinds of work. A man who understands the art of tufta can always turn out satisfactory work, although in reality his work should not pass. In the evening, for example, two wood choppers show their pile of wood to the free brigadier. He checks it and notes down: twelve cubic yards. That is a respectable performance. Nevertheless, the two wood choppers are not noticeably tired. In actuality they have felled just enough wood to camouflage artfully a pile of brush. That is tufta.

A Soviet camp is an incubator for all the vilest human instincts. Its name, "corrective labor camp," is a mockery. The only things that are corrected in such camps are the methods of petty occasional criminals, who leave the camp trained professional thugs. Not only does the camp provide no educational work; it gives the criminals the finest opportunities to practice their profession. The thief steals, the speculator speculates, the prostitute sells herself. Not only that. The normal person is perverted, the honest man becomes a hypocrite, the brave man a coward, and all have their spirits and bodies broken. Can tuberculosis patients be cured by shutting up all the sick, light cases and severe cases, in the closest quarters and under conditions that favor disease, in fact breed it? Can criminals of all types and shades be lumped together in the hope that their criminality will cure itself? If there is any chance to correct a criminal, or one who has strayed into wrongdoing, the basic requirement is to separate him completely from his criminal environment. The Soviet camp, on the contrary, is a university of crime; it has become a place of both physical and moral destruction.

The word "political prisoner" has been expunged from Soviet speech. Officially this category of prisoners does not exist, and consequently no one is eligible for the milder conditions of punishment which are granted to political prisoners in other countries (and which were standard in Tsarist Russia). Persons convicted on the basis of their real or alleged political views are counterrevolutionaries, who are far beneath common criminals in the Soviet hierarchy of values. The concept of the persecuted political prisoner is still too well known in Russia. In the past the political prisoner was a martyr for freedom, so the very term might awaken inconvenient associations. The martyrs, multiplied a thousandfold, have remained. The name has been erased.

Corruption

All property in the Soviet Union is state property. If there were reasonably adequate production and a just distribution of the boundless wealth of the country, the Soviet Union could provide a decent life for its citizens. But the rate of production is wretched, thanks to the unhealthy conditions in which the mass of the people live, and it is not reasonable because the main stress is laid upon the production of war goods, which will neither feed nor clothe people. A vast army must be maintained; it must have a cadre of officers who have a high standard of living compared with the rest of the people—though not high compared with the standard of living in capitalist countries—and who do no productive work. The troops of the Ministry of the Interior (the NKVD, now MVD), which are used for the suppression of the Soviet people, make up a tremendous apparatus with branches that extend into the tiniest villages. This police force is far larger than that of any other state on the globe. All its members enjoy considerable privileges which brings down still further the low level of the working people who have to support this army of parasites. The third totally unproductive group which reclines upon the patient shoulders of the people is the tremendous bureaucracy that has shot up out of Soviet administration. This officialdom would be grotesque if its existence were not so tragic for the people. The most flourishing kind of industry and agriculture would not permanently support such a threefold weight of parasites. And the Soviet economy is by no means flourishing.

Since the masses of the people continue to feel that they are cheated in the distribution of the goods they create, they try to compensate themselves. This has resulted in the development of a regrettable attitude toward state property. Only a decent standard of living could induce the masses to look upon state property as the basis for their own prosperity. Since they have no prosperity, each is interested only in securing a tiny part of this state property for his own personal use, no matter what the consequences upon the economy as a whole. Theft of state property on a small or large scale has become a matter of course.

When a worker's family is freezing in a cold room because there is no wood for sale, he steals fuel from the state factory. When no glass is obtainable, the peasant uses the pane of glass intended for the state hothouse to fix his own broken window. When the shops have no material for curtains, the nurse steals gauze from the state hospital and drapes it over her own window. What Soviet citizen would consider such actions as crimes? The masses of the people have lost all sense of honesty with regard to state property, just as the representatives of the Soviet state have lost all sense of justice, humanity, and responsibility toward the laboring masses.

What is true of Soviet life in general is doubly true with regard to the goods intended for prisoners. Everyone who has anything to do with supplies tries to make a profit out of them. In the carpenter shops which are supposed to take care of camp buildings, furnishings, and so forth, the administrators have their personal furniture made free. Cloth and even woolen blankets, which during the war were imported from America for the use of the prisoners, never came the prisoners' way. Any lady who had the slightest connection with the camp administration would have her coats made free in the prisoners' tailor shops. For their private benefit camp commanders freely made use of prisoners as cobblers, tailors, painters, artisans, fishermen, doctors, and so on. With the cooperation of prisoners in charge of food supplies and prisoners in charge of bookkeeping all sorts of manipulations were carried on. The prisoners had every incentive to cooperate. It insured their hold on the comfortable jobs, and they made a little profit besides; the mass of the prisoners in the camp suffered.

After the free citizens had taken the best pickings, it was the prisoners' turn. Camp duty is usually assigned to some of the criminal prisoners, whose consciences are not too keen. Thus, in every camp kitchen the cooks steal unscrupulously for themselves and their particular clique. If there are too many protests from the prisoners, the cook is replaced by another thief.

Every few years a solemn commission comes from Moscow. The commissioners are wrapped in heavy furs to the tips of their noses. They have had several vodkas and are surrounded by a swarm of officers of the guard. On such days a few fat globules are to be seen floating on the surface of the prisoners' soup, and the gruel is not quite so watery. The well-fed commissioners, with their decorations and their epaulettes, go through the camp, accompanied by the commandant, of course, so that no one will get the idea that he can accost the commissioners and make a complaint. As soon as the commission departs everything returns to normal. The few courageous prisoners who nevertheless dared to complain about the intolerable conditions in the camp will regret it later on. Moscow is far away; the camp commandant is near. Nothing has ever been changed after the departure of a commission. Liberally plied with liquor by the commandant during their stay, the visitors ride off in their black limousines feeling very pleased with themselves. The tattletales are sent off to the most notorious of the gold mines or to the remotest forest camps, where they lose forever all desire to seek justice in the Soviet Union.

Shurup

Shurup was a young thief, a chubby-faced, cheerful girl bursting with health. Camp life was her element. She had known nothing else since childhood, for she had fallen in with a band of thieves when she was a little girl and had since enjoyed only the briefest periods of freedom between the end of one sentence and her next arrest for theft.

By Soviet law every citizen who has reached his twelfth year is legally responsible for his acts, and in every prison in the country there are dozens of twelve-, thirteen-, and fourteen-year-old thieves who complete their schooling in camps and prisons where they live with adult criminals. It is true that near Moscow there still exists the model colony Bolshovo, inhabited by former delinquents who have returned to normal life; but this colony is a relic from times past when fine people were still willing to devote their lives, their sensitivity, and their infinite patience to leading unfortunate children away from criminality. The principle of re-education has long since been abandoned, and instead child criminals are punished, and punished severely. Three years of imprisonment for a few pounds of stolen flour is commonplace.

After a thirteen-year-old boy has spent these three years in the company of bandits, prostitutes, speculators, swindlers, murderers, and other criminals of all kinds, there is no longer any turning back for him. Ugly swearwords, filthy jokes, criminal cant, women, vodka, cards, and tobacco—such is the sum total of his education during those years. At sixteen he no longer has any illusions. After his release the only thing that attracts him is a life of crime.

The *urka*, as the Russian criminals call themselves, have their own moral code, their own organization, and their own system of justice. Shurup, the cheerful little thief, had to learn all this the hard way. She did not overwork herself in camp and she did not have to manage on the meager camp rations. For she always had half a dozen friends, with whom she had more or less intimate relations, who supplied her with bread, sugar, butter, and alcohol. The guards received their share and turned away their eyes. And now and then Shurup favored them too with the pleasures of her plump body. So Shurup did not have to strain to meet her labor quota. Her way of life was no different from that of her fellows among the women criminals. They had no particular grievances against her for that. But Shurup frequently took away their "steady" men friends, and they did not like this. They fought with her; but Shurup did not mind going around with a black eye, and she gave as good as she got. She did not take their jealousy to heart. But one day she went too far.

Then what was left of Shurup was carried to the hospital. Her whole back was one huge burn. The skin was gone completely, and the layer of fat beneath was largely burned away. Shurup lay on her belly on her cot and moaned softly, but she did not die. When her wound was treated, she fainted from the pain several times, but she never cried out. No one ever heard a word of complaint from her.

When she had recovered somewhat, the camp commandant came to find out what had happened to her. She said she had been sitting by a wood fire—the prisoners make fires wherever they work, in winter for warmth and in summer to drive away the mosquitoes—and that she had fallen asleep; her clothes had caught fire and she had managed to roll into a brook just in time.

The commandant knew, of course, that this was a fable. But he also knew that he would never get the truth out of her, and so he dropped the matter. Only a few of the prisoners knew the true story. I happened to learn it because I was Shurup's nurse. Shurup had been sitting at a brush fire with some of her rivals. They got into a quarrel, and she answered back in her usual challenging and mocking manner. Suddenly the group of women seized her by her hands and feet and roasted her over the fire. When they thought she had had enough they threw her to the ground and ran away. Shurup had just strength enough to crawl to the brook and put out the fire in the remnants of her clothes.

She never said a word about this to any of the authorities. She knew that if she betrayed her assailants, others would "knock her off." The criminals' justice always functioned. The NKVD was well aware of this and never intervened in such affairs. Shurup's fable about falling asleep was duly recorded, and that was the end of the affair.

Love in Kolyma

When I was transported to Kolyma, one of my neighbors in the hold of the ship was a girl of twenty-one. Toward the end of 1937 she had been on the point of taking her examina-

tions for the post of elementary school teacher when she was
arrested on account of her Polish descent, although she herself had been born and raised in Russia. At that time all
Poles were suspected of espionage, and she received a ten-
year sentence for alleged counterrevolutionary activity. Her
real interest was romantic glamour; she herself had never
had any taste of it. She wanted to know whether there were
really balls in foreign countries, whether people really wore
evening dress to the theater, and what such evening dresses
looked like. Her appearance was in no way remarkable except for her beautiful green eyes, which peered under her
long black lashes with the expression of a sulky child.

After our arrival in Magadan we were sent to the same
women's camp. She went to work in a near-by men's camp,
washing the floors in the guardrooms and the administration
offices. During the day the men prisoners were outside the
camp at work.

One day she had just finished her scrubbing when a
brigade of men returned to the camp. The guard who was
supposed to take her back to the women's camp had not
yet come. The men, of course, hastened to pay her compliments, and invited her to have a cigarette with them in their
barrack. She should have realized that they were criminals,
but she was as foolish as she was inexperienced; laughing,
she went with them to the barrack.

A few men stood as lookouts at the door of the barrack;
the others fell upon her. There were about twenty of them,
one after another. Then they let her go.

After a while she learned that she had contracted both
syphilis and gonorrhea. Her experience was not unique in
Kolyma. There was even a common expression for it: "She
fell under the trolley."

Approximately eighty to a hundred thousand men prisoners are delivered to Kolyma every year, but only about five hundred women prisoners. The prisoners are forbidden to have any relations with the opposite sex. Their camps are completely separate. Thus the prisoners in the gold mines often do not see a woman, even from a distance, for as long as six or seven years.

Near the large women's camp at Elgen, with almost a thousand inmates, there is a small men's camp of about eighty prisoners whom the medical commissions have declared unfit for work in the gold mines. These men are employed as artisans and field workers. Thus men and women prisoners meet at their places of work. There have been cases where female criminals attempted to rape these disabled men.

The average male prisoner at Kolyma has no great sexual problem. His whole organism is exhausted by the severe physical labor, and his emaciated body desires only one thing —bread. When a person is exposed to merciless cold all day long, his passions freeze. Partly for these reasons and partly also because of the relatively innocent character of Russians, there is no homosexuality to speak of in the camps. Most women prisoners had never even heard of the existence of sexual relations between two women. They learned about it for the first time as prisoners; for it is relatively frequent among female criminals.

The problem becomes important for a male prisoner only after he has secured a comfortable post which enables him to fill his belly. But even if there are women prisoners working in the vicinity, he has little chance at them. Women prisoners, if they have the slightest opportunity to take up relations with men, choose their partners from among the free citizens. A law does exist which provides up to ten years imprisonment for Soviet citizens who have sexual relations with prisoners, but in Kolyma this law has sunk into oblivion. Free citizens are desirable because they can provide prisoners with food. "Butter, sugar, white bread," is the formula the criminals use in place of "I love you." During the war and postwar years not only criminals, but former honest women, could be bought for a pound of black bread. And the honest men of Kolyma snapped up the entire supply.

The woman was always the one who suffered for it. If a camp guard reported that he had caught one of the prisoners with a man, she would be given several days in solitary confinement and then transported to another camp with the first outgoing shipment.

There are thousands of free citizens in Kolyma who have been persuaded or ordered to work there as geologists, engineers, doctors, economists, camp administrators, guards, and so on. Most of these men are without women. Husbands rarely venture to take their wives into this inhospitable country where there is nothing but cold, scurvy, barrenness, and vodka. Moreover, young unmarried men are usually picked for jobs in Kolyma.

In addition to this aristocracy of genuine free citizens there are the plebeians, former prisoners who have finished their terms and who are automatically settled in Kolyma. These two groups live quite separately and rarely mingle. But all of them are avidly in search of a woman. No social stigma attaches to women who were former prisoners. Every woman, no matter whether she did time as a counterrevolutionary or as a criminal, is married within a month after her release, at the very latest.

Usually there are several horse-drawn sleds waiting in front of the office where the women receive their release papers.

The men in the sleds have found out weeks beforehand when women are again to be released from the camp. They come from far away, thoughtfully bringing along a fur coat, fur cap, and felt boots, and immediately surround the newly hatched free citizenesses. Each outbids the other in describing the tempting post he supposedly holds somewhere in the forest or at a distant gold mine, either in the camp administration or in the management of the mine. The men's positions determine the choice, not their age, appearance, or character. Obviously there is no question of love. Usually the woman is twenty or twenty-five years older than her prospective husband. This does not bother him. The chief thing is that she is a woman and that he will no longer be alone with the blizzards and vodka, with his detached buttons and wretchedly cooked cabbage soup.

For the woman, on the other hand, the chief motive is to find shelter and protection. A woman cannot live alone in Kolyma. She will be molested everywhere she goes. Every man with whom she has anything to do will try to get her for himself. If she refuses, she will be persecuted. She will receive no slips entitling her to buy essential clothing; her employer will treat her badly; and at dark she will hasten trembling to her community barrack for free women, always terrified that she will be attacked and kidnapped. She will be incessantly importuned. In addition, the woman prisoner, like every other former prisoner, is afraid of life during the first period after her release. She no longer feels able to cope with life, and not because of her physical exhaustion alone. She is afraid of independence, of having to make decisions again after having had others determine every minute of her life for so many years.

So she gets into some stranger's sled and rides off with the unknown man into the unknown. If it works out, the marriage will be officially registered when the opportunity arises. In most cases it does not work out for very long. The woman allows herself to be fed back to health, to be clothed decently, and to rest. Gradually she becomes aware of her value, that is, of the exaggerated value she possesses in Kolyma on account of the shortage of women.

And so one day the husband comes home and finds his room empty and unheated. Cursing, he takes the bottle of vodka out of the cupboard. Later, in a drunken haze, he envisions his wife sitting in a sled and gliding away, pressing close to her seducer, just as she rode with him a short time ago, while the hoofs of the small, shaggy Yakut pony clatter on the hard, frozen snow.

Shortly after the war an appeal went out to Young Communist girls (*Komsomolki*) to devote their energies to construction in Kolyma. Attracted by the prospect of going to a region where there is no surplus of women, as there is in European Russia, several hundred girls volunteered. They were received in Magadan with great honor, feted and provided with the best of clothes. The newspapers waxed enthusiastic about these heroic girls. Naturally they were "sold out" in no time. But the stories of their heroic actions soon could be used only in newspapers outside of Kolyma; in Kolyma itself such stories were a source of amusement. For the girls' principal sphere of action became only too well known. After their arrival the rate of venereal disease shot up so sharply that some girls had to be forcibly locked up in hospitals.

The women of Kolyma are utterly faithless. The criminals have a phrase for it:

"Kolyma is the land where the sun is without warmth, the flowers without scent, and the women without hearts."

7. The Stages of Terror

Fear

FEAR IS the foremost factor in the life of the Soviet Union. The free Soviet citizen is afraid of incurring suspicion by, for example, a thoughtless remark. Political conversations are avoided. The name of Stalin is used only at public meetings; in private life circumlocutions are used so that a casual listener will not get the impression that a derogatory remark has been made about Stalin. If the name does come up, the form used is generally Joseph Vissarionovich.

Prisoners are afraid of discussing politics because such conversations might incur an addition to their sentences, or even worse punishment. Stool-pigeoning flourishes in camp. Discipline is maintained by fear: fear of starvation, fear of disciplinary camp, fear of the lockup. And released prisoners are even more fearful; they spend every day of their lives in dread of rearrest.

There is a popular joke that the Soviet Union is made up of three classes: prisoners, former prisoners, and future prisoners. That is not so funny; there is scarcely a family in the country which hasn't some relative, whether close or distant, in prison or camp.

During a shipment of prisoners across Siberia, a shipment of which I was one, when I was sent from Kolyma to Central Asia at the end of 1946, a sergeant who was unusually nasty and cruel particularly infuriated the criminals. At last one of the criminals shouted from behind his bars to the sergeant in the corridor: "Just wait, the warrant [for arrest] is out for you too." To which the sergeant replied equably, "Not yet, anyway."

No Soviet citizen ever expresses his real thoughts, not even to his closest friends or the members of his immediate family. Children are raised to look upon the Party, not their parents, as their highest ideal. No one dares to defend a counterrevolutionary prisoner; even to show the slightest sympathy for the unfortunate victim might mean ruin. The Soviet people keep their mouths shut, not because they approve of their government's policies, but because they are afraid.

How fear works both ways is illustrated by a story from the so-called *polit-izolator,* the prison for counterrevolutionaries. As I have already indicated, prison terms are usually altered to terms in corrective labor camps after a few years, so that I met a good many people who had done time in a polit-izolator.

Each cell of the polit-izolator of Yaroslavl holds two convicts. They are put in prison uniform, and the women's hair is cut short, while the men's is shaved. The prisoners are never addressed by name, but only as Cell 14, bed 1 or bed 2. In the cell they are permitted to talk only in whispers; all gymnastic exercises are forbidden. All work is forbidden. They may read the books in the prison library.

They are allowed to have a notebook with numbered pages in which they can write in pencil; at the end of the month these notebooks must be delivered to the prison administration. Once a month the prisoner may write a letter to his closest relative. He is allowed to receive one letter a month. His relatives may send him fifty rubles a month, which he can use to buy tooth powder, bread, sugar, and tobacco at the prison commissary. If he is sent no money, he cannot smoke. There is a twenty-minute daily walk in the yard. Every cell is separate. A man who serves a ten-year sentence sees no one but his cellmate for ten years. Under no circumstances is the prisoner allowed to draw his blanket up over his head; even when asleep he must lie so that the guard can see his face through the peephole. Otherwise he is awakened.

Twice a day the inmates of the cell are taken to the lavatory. For hygienic purposes inmates receive a piece of newspaper. After use this newspaper must be thrown into a special basket. The prisoners are taken back to their cell and then the guard must count the papers before flushing them away. If the paper has not been used, it must be returned to the guard. This is done to prevent the prisoners from getting in touch with the inmates of other cells or with the outside world.

There are good guards and bad guards. Some never interrupt the prisoners' sleep and others wake them three times every night. One morning a guard of the latter type handed the inmates of Cell 14 their papers for the lavatory. After the prescribed period was up he took them back to their cells and locked them in. A few minutes later he came back, a look of alarm on his face, and opened the door again.

"One paper is missing," he snapped.

Cell 14, bed 2 stepped forward.

"Yes," he said, "one paper is missing. Because I am outraged at the paper you gave me. You, who plague the life out of us because we're supposed to be counterrevolutionaries. You belong in this cell in my place. And, by God, this is just where you would be if I gave the warden the paper I received from you—for such a purpose! Here it is."

The guard snatched the scrap of newspaper, looked at it, and turned white. His hands trembled so violently that he could scarcely lock the door.

The scrap of newspaper showed a picture of Stalin. The guard never again awakened prisoners at night.

The System

All camps are governed by the Central Camp Administration in Moscow (Russian abbreviation: GULAG). There are two types of camp:

1. Corrective labor camps (ITL).
2. Forced labor camps (*Katorga*).

The corrective labor camps are located in all parts of the Soviet Union and are divided into three categories: near, distant and remote. The camp category to which a prisoner is assigned is determined at the same time as his sentence, but the prisoner is not told. The hardest camps are the remote ones, of course.

The corrective labor camps of Kolyma are remote camps, and these in turn are of different degrees of severity. There are general camps where the inmates are put to all types of work, and which are situated near or within settlements of free citizens. In such camps the inmates are permitted to correspond with their families. There are also closed camps whose inmates are used only for the heaviest physical labor;

they have no correspondence rights and are completely cut off from the world.

Inmates of these closed camps are:

1. Prisoners whose sentences contain the instruction: "To be used only for hard labor."
2. Prisoners who were originally sentenced to prison and have subsequently been transferred to camp.
3. Prisoners sentenced under "severe articles," which are all the articles of Paragraph 58 except Articles 7, 10, 12, and 14 (Article 14, counterrevolutionary sabotage, is usually thrown in on the indictment of criminals who have refused to work several times. Nevertheless, the camp administration continues to treat these prisoners as criminals rather than as counterrevolutionaries.)
4. Prisoners convicted as "Trotskyists."
5. Foreigners.
6. Recidivist criminals.
7. Prisoners who in any way have aroused the displeasure of the administration in another camp.

In addition there are disciplinary camps to which all prisoners who have broken camp regulations are assigned for a definite or indefinite term. These camps, like the closed camps, are characterized by heavy physical labor, deprivation of correspondence, the absence of all sanitary and hygienic facilities, and the roughest treatment of prisoners. The disciplinary camps of these disciplinary camps are virtually death camps; there the prisoners are completely exposed to the cruelty of specially selected guards.

In addition, every general camp has a disciplinary brigade which goes out to work under extra guard. Every general camp has a disciplinary barrack which is barred and locked at night. Every general camp also has a lockup which is equivalent to a small prison within the camp.

A Russian camp commander has defined the corrective labor camp as "a prison of the open type."

In actuality the same sentence—to corrective labor camp—means very different things to different prisoners. Conditions vary enormously from camp to camp. First of all, the fate of the two principal groups, criminals and counterrevolutionaries, is vastly different, as I have already mentioned. Among criminals, only one group is treated on a par with the counterrevolutionaries: those who are sentenced under Paragraph 59, Article 3: banditry.

The most leniently treated group among the counterrevolutionaries are those who were not sentenced by a court, but by the invisible commission of judges. The lightest charge is SOE (socially dangerous element), which sounds very similar to the SWE (socially harmful element) which is meted out to criminals. SOE's have almost as good chances as criminals of being assigned to the better jobs. KRTD (counterrevolutionary Trotskyist activity) is considered equivalent to the severest articles of Paragraph 58, and those convicted under that formula are often given the worst treatment.

Article 10 of Paragraph 58 (agitation and propaganda) applies to the most harmless and trivial acts. Of persons convicted under that article it was said: "He must have said something without thinking." In fact, a popular joke in which the name of Stalin figured was frequently the cause of a ten-year camp sentence under Paragraph 58, Article 10. Prisoners convicted under this article would have an easier time of it.

All this gives a rough idea of the way the Soviet camp system fitted the punishment to the crime. Naturally, there are always exceptions. It is the same as it was with the Nazis: Every Nazi knew a certain Jew whom he thought was a Jew by sheer accident. Similarly, every camp commandant and every production chief knows certain counterrevolutionaries whom he recognizes as useful people and good workers, and he protects them with all the means at his disposal. These means are not very extensive, for the free citizens are constantly checking up on one another, and favoring a counterrevolutionary is a dangerous business. But to the prisoner, every day that he does not have to perform killing physical labor is so much gained.

The free citizens of Kolyma have to remember what kind of people they are dealing with. It is hammered into them at every Party meeting that counterrevolutionaries are the scum of humanity. It is open to doubt whether the citizens of Kolyma really believe this. Every citizen, administrator or technician who depends upon prisoners' labor in his field, whether it be a gold mine, farm, or factory, knows perfectly well that he can hope to meet his production quota only through the work of the counterrevolutionaries; he can never count on the criminals.

In the official reports neither criminals nor counterrevolutionaries are mentioned. The reports invariably speak of "our glorious Young Communists who in honor of the Stalin Five Year Plan have again exceeded the annual quota for gold production."

Katorga was the severest form of forced labor in Siberian mines under the Tsars. It was abolished by the victorious Revolution, but reintroduced during the war, along with death by hanging for war criminals and collaborators with

the Germans. Those who were spared death were sentenced
to from twenty to twenty-five years katorga.

Katorga convicts, both men and women, were shipped to
Kolyma to serve their sentences. The differences between
ordinary prisoners and katorga prisoners are as follows:

Katorga prisoners are transported in chains.

They have no names, but only numbers which they wear
on their backs.

They live in barracks on bare boards in three tiers, without straw mattresses or blankets, so that they never dare to
take off any of their wet work clothes. They are granted a
blanket only after three years of good conduct.

Their camp is totally isolated from all other prison camps.

All contact with the outside world, all correspondence, is
forbidden to them.

In 1944 three thousand katorga prisoners were delivered
to the Maxim Gorky gold-mine camp. Sickness became such
a problem that a special hospital had to be set up at the
camp, for these prisoners could not be sent to an ordinary
camp hospital. Since katorga prisoners may be used only for
the hardest physical labor and there were not enough free
citizens on hand to staff the hospital, the hospital personnel
was drawn from ordinary prisoners. With the help of one of
the hospital attendants a katorga prisoner contrived to smuggle out a letter to his family, who foolishly sent him an answer addressed to the Maxim Gorky Gold Mine. When it
was discovered that the addressee was a katorga convict,
there was a grand investigation and it was decided to send
these prisoners to an even more remote mine called Laso,
where total isolation would be easier. The transfer took
place in 1945. Of the three thousand convicts, five hundred
were healthy enough to be shipped; another eight hundred

were in the hospital with dysentery, in a hopeless condition; the other seventeen hundred had died. (I was given these details by the head of the medical division who was in charge of both the Maxim Gorky hospital and the camp hospital where I was working as a nurse.)

The female katorga prisoners were put to road building on the *tros* from Tyenki, to clearing land, or sent to the gypsum quarries. The trials of these prisoners had been wholly careless and summary procedures. How much so is evident from the fact that a commission was sent to Tyenki in 1946, because of protests and petitions from members of the prisoners' families. As a result of this commission's work, five hundred female katorga prisoners who had been sentenced to twenty and twenty-five years had their terms reduced to ten years of corrective labor camp, and were transferred to the ordinary camps. They told us about the case of one *katorzhanka* (female katorga convict) who was discovered to be pregnant. Since the only men these prisoners had had any contact with were guards, the guilty soldier was soon found out. An abortion was performed upon the woman—ordinarily this is illegal in the Soviet Union—and the soldier was arrested.

Even before katorga was officially established, conditions in the closed camps approximated those of the katorga camps. There are closed camps at the mouth of the Yenisey near the Arctic Circle in Narylsk (Krasnoyarsk Territory). In Kolyma the notorious gold-mine camp of Yelgala was of this type. These camps also have their own infirmary; it is very rare for prisoners from there to be transferred to the general prison hospital.

Yelgala has spur camps, and in one of these, at the Zolotist gold mine, prisoners of German, Austrian, Finnish, Lithuanian, Latvian, Esthonian, Rumanian, Hungarian, and Czech nationalities were concentrated during the war. There they labored under incredible conditions. The mortality rate was so high that only a very small percentage of the prisoners survived the camp. Yelgala, together with its various spur camps, held on the average from ten to twelve thousand prisoners.

Elgen, too, had its foreigners' camp during the war. It was seven kilometers from the main camp, on the right side of the road—a road passable only in winter, since in summer stretches of it disappeared into the swamp. The camp consisted only of a few barracks. Called the Seventh Kilometer, it was one of the oldest of the disciplinary camps for women. Hundreds of women passed through this camp; hundreds had gone out into the woods with their saws and axes before the winter of 1944, when the camp burned down—to the great joy of the prisoners. But new camps ten, twelve, and fourteen kilometers from the main camp of Elgen were built, where all winter long the mournful screech of saws broke the silence of the virgin forest.

Some forty women were in the Seventh Kilometer isolation camp. They were guarded by four men and one wolfhound. All of them were nationals of countries at war with the Soviet Union; almost all of them had Soviet citizenship. The youngest prisoner was twenty, the oldest about sixty. The barrack orderly at the time I was there was Ida W, an old Hungarian revolutionary who had been thrown into a Hungarian prison in 1919 after the abortive Communist revolution in Hungary. After a while the Soviet government effected an exchange of prisoners and she was liberated. She lived in the Soviet Union until 1937. Then she was sent to camp on "suspicion of espionage." This sick woman—she suffered from angina pectoris—with her warm, dark eyes and thick black hair framing a high forehead and sunken cheeks, would swing the axe with her thin, strengthless arms in order to split the daily supply of firewood for the barrack stove. She would have attacks of dizziness and shortness of breath, and when we returned from work we usually found her lying white and gasping on the boards.

It was night when we went out to work in the morning. But in that region the endless winter nights are never quite dark because everything is wrapped in blinding white snow. Hills, fields, roads, and trees are all covered with snow. We set out into the milky mist produced by the frost; it surrounded us like walls of icy white linen. In pairs we tramped over the frozen forest road, one of us with the axe hung from the cord around her waist, while the other carried the long narrow saw alternately on her right and left shoulder, for the hand holding it froze painfully inside the wadded mitten.

Our brigadier was a good-natured Ukrainian peasant, a former convict himself. He assigned each pair of us a place in the woods, far enough apart so that the trees we felled would not come crashing down upon another couple. First of all we set about finding dry wood. Carefully, because matches were precious, I lit the little heap of silvery twigs we had assembled on the snow, until the friendly flame shot up. We fed it with larger and larger twigs, and finally with big dry tree trunks. Then we rolled a suitable log up to the fire, sat down on it and stretched our legs out to the warmth while we waited for dawn. In a circle around the fire the snow melted; the fire itself sank deeper and deeper into the hollow it created, until our legs were dangling over a patch of bare forest soil. Now it was time. We placed two fresh logs across the fire to keep it going and tramped through the breast-high snow to the first of the six trees we had to fell. I and my partner, a surly peasant girl from the Volga region, had to deliver six cubic yards of wood a day. With our hands and feet we cleared a firm place to stand in the snow and used the axe to cut a notch a few inches deep in the side of the thirty-foot larch. Then we started sawing from the other side. Now and then we glanced up at the trunk which rose straight into the air. With our left knee on the snow, our left arm braced against the trunk of the tree, our right arms bent and straightened out at an even pace. When our arms grew tired we let them dangle for a moment, breathing heavily, without changing our position. The saw ate through the trunk until louder and louder creaking announced the imminent fall of the tree. We stopped more and more frequently to glance up at it; we tested it by kicking it, but it still held. Peering up warily, ready to jump, we drew the saw back and forth a few more times, then wrenched it out and threw ourselves sideways into the snow. A last crack, and with a rain of falling twigs the tree thudded to the ground. With expressionless faces and a secret sigh of relief, we glanced for a moment at the delicately marbleized surface of the fresh stump, sprinkled with sawdust; then we crawled out into the deep snow again to remove all the limbs from the tree. Four or five cuts divided it into six-foot lengths, and then we set to work on the next tree. When the sixth tree lay on the ground, we turned back to our fire, which had meanwhile burned down to embers. We fed it again, took hard-frozen pieces of bread from our pockets and stuck them on sticks so that we could thaw them over the fire. The last rays of the icy winter sun bled away on the horizon. We tramped a path through the snow to a place where the sled could come in, loaded the logs on our shoulders, and struggled out with them to make a woodpile. Sometimes the weight on my shoulders forced me to my knees two or three times, and each time I remembered a movie I had seen many years before in another life. It had shown Indian elephants at work, kneeling on their forelegs and winding their trunks around a tree, then slowly swaying to their feet. Would I not have been better off if I had been born an elephant?

Then we sat silently side by side at the fire, poking peripheral pieces of wood into the flames and listening to the stillness of the frozen forest crowd tangibly around us. At last the brigadier would appear silently beside us on his snowshoes and call out a loud, genial, "Home, girls," as he measured our pile of wod. "Home," we would repeat bitterly as, accompanied by a single guard, we marched back to camp with the others.

Provocateurs and Their Victims

Fomenko, the chief physician at the Magadan hospital, was a worse than mediocre surgeon. Among the prisoners, however, there was a distinguished surgeon, Professor Koch. Doctor Koch, who was nearly sixty in 1939, had been sentenced to ten years in camp for alleged counterrevolutionary activity because he was a Volga German. He never talked about politics; he had never been interested in anything but medicine. When a free citizen in Magadan needed a serious operation, he asked for the prisoner Doctor Koch instead of Fomenko. The top administrators in Kolyma did the same. (Later, after Fomenko was replaced, the city hospital was placed in charge of a highly competent surgeon named Serebryannikov who was not ashamed to call in qualified prisoner physicians to consult with him on difficult cases.) But

Fomenko seethed with envy and inferiority feelings over these slights, although poor Koch could not have refused an operation if he had wanted to. Fomenko finally had Koch investigated for alleged counterrevolutionary activity.

Once a man is branded as a contrik he is more than ever at the mercy of malice. Everybody knew that Fomenko's charges were invented, that the kindly old man's sole passion was curing the sick, and that in all other respects he reacted with childlike innocence. But Fomenko was a free citizen and a member of the Communist Party. The result was that Koch was sent four hundred and fifty miles deeper into the forest, to the gold mines of Byoryolyakh. Here, too, he was soon employed in the prisoners' hospital and practiced his profession under the most unfavorable conditions. Hundreds of sick prisoners counted themselves lucky for having met up with such a surgeon in this wasteland. But the end was not yet.

Camp commanders are generally poor specimens of humanity who combine incompetence with frenzied ambition. During the war they made use of the rise of hatred for Germans to distinguish themselves by their "revolutionary alertness." Anyone of German descent was sure to be convicted of any charges against him.

Koch was a tempting victim for such careerists. He was triply suspicious, first as a Volga German, then as a convicted counterrevolutionary, then for having been sent into the taiga for new counterrevolutionary utterances. In 1943 he was accused of having made pro-Hitler, profascist speeches to a group of prisoners. The shameful witness at this trial was the despicable Krivitsky, former Deputy People's Commissar for Heavy Industry, who himself had been sentenced in 1937 to fifteen years imprisonment as a counterrevolutionary. A slimy, fawning, cunning creature, he hoped to buy his freedom by acting as a provocateur. Old Koch, whose sole fault was that he had saved the lives of thousands of people, was shot.

From 1939 to 1941 I had worked as a nurse in the prisoners' hospital in Magadan under Fomenko, and knew Koch then as head of the surgical department. Krivitsky was there too at this time; he had managed to worm his way into a job at the hospital on the basis of a superficial knowledge of Latin, a quick mind and, probably, because he had already begun working as an informer.

At the beginning of the war Magadan was cleared of all prisoners convicted under the "severe articles"—articles of Paragraph 58 dealing with counterrevolutionaries. Among them, Krivitsky was shipped to Byoryolyakh, where he again met Koch, and here the unscrupulous informer brought about Koch's death.

In 1945, when I was working in the prisoners' hospital in the northern gold-mine region, Krivitsky was in the hospital from a stroke of paralysis. I noticed how some of the patients from Byoryolyakh watched him with mingled hatred and fear, and refused to have anything to do with him. I did not understand until they told me of the numerous victims of Krivitsky's informing activities.

Just once a group of intellectuals attempted to collect systematic and factual evidence of the horrors that are everywhere obvious in Kolyma. Although they could not hope ever to publish this material, they thought they might at least preserve it for posterity. They added nothing, made no commentary, but simply set down the things that happened every day. All the participants were former members of the

Communist Party. One of them was the talented poetess J.W. Another was Anna Israilovna Ponisovskaya, a doctor serving a ten-year sentence for counterrevolutionary activities.

Those who had belonged to the Communist Party out of genuine revolutionary idealism broke inwardly with the Party after living in Soviet prisons and camps for a while. During the first period after their arrest they made every effort to prove that they had really never stopped being good, humble Communists ready to sacrifice everything for the Party. But later on they realized that it was ignominious to belong to a Party which had changed from an instrument of liberation to an instrument for torturing its own people.

On the other hand, those Communists who had joined the Party out of opportunism, like Dr. Ponisovskaya, simply because it was the government party, were not impressed at all by the cruelty of the prisons or the terrors of the camps, so long as they themselves were not affected. They were willing to use any means to obtain some amelioration of their own conditions and to prove at the same time that even in camp they had remained steadfast Communists. These people were the chief tools of the NKVD and were to some extent even employed to check up on the free citizens.

Anna Ponisovskaya worked in the Twenty-third Kilometer (from Magadan) hospital, where the poetess W was also employed as a nurse. At the time a number of intellectuals in the group were patients in various wards of this hospital.

One evening a sizable company of guards from Magadan appeared, occupied all the wards, drove the patients from their beds and cots, and began a search. They opened up the straw mattresses, tapped all the walls, tore up the floorboards, searched patients and attendants, and did not overlook a single corner. Dr. Ponisovskaya's ward, however, was gone over with amazing casualness.

A number of intellectuals were arrested and transferred to Magadan prison, among them the poetess. The alleged ringleader of the group, an old man who had been an agronomist, was shot. The poetess had ten years added to her ten-year sentence; the others also received additional sentences of ten years. All were charged with treason, although they had done nothing but draw up a chronicle of the things that happened every day with the knowledge and consent of the government.

N.A. was a first-rate pediatrician, who had often treated Radek's children. When Radek was arrested, N.A., who was a member of the Communist Party, went to his Party secretary and reported to him that he had entered Radek's house several times in his capacity as a doctor. The Party secretary thanked N.A. for honesty becoming to a Party member, and a month later N.A. was arrested. He was convicted of counterrevolutionary Trotskyist activity, which consisted in treating a Trotskyist's sick children, and was sentenced to eight years in camp.

In Magadan he worked in the prisoners' hospital, and since he was a doctor of great gifts, he was now and then asked to examine highly placed personages or their children. He was none too happy about this, for he had had experience with the dangers of contact with the high and mighty. What was more, his colleagues among the prisoners envied him for this distinction. They could not rival his medical abilities, but they were great intriguers. Among them was a doctor named Zazonov who had already made a name for himself in other camps as a provocateur. Zazonov apparently was determined to "get" N.A.

The doctors and medical attendants lived in a barrack within the hospital camp. The man in the cot next to N.A.'s was a medical attendant in Zazonov's section, a fairly good-natured fellow, but an alcoholic who would do anything for a few drinks. The commander of the camp for some reason disliked N.A. and had a weakness for the provocateur, even to the point of sharing a glass with him now and then.

All the preparations were made, and one morning a company of guards from town came to the hospital. They went straight to the living barrack and began a thorough search of it. Before long they found a bottle and a smaller flask under a straw mattress. No one was in the barrack at the time, since all the inmates were supposed to be at work. But Zazonov "happened" along just then; supposedly he had forgotten something and had come back for it.

The soldiers, after establishing the fact that he was a doctor, asked him whether he could tell them the contents of the two vessels. He was quite willing and gave the opinion that the bottle contained alcohol, and that the thirty-odd pink tablets in the flask were obviously corrosive sublimate. Thirty grams of corrosive sublimate are poison enough to kill hundreds of people.

N.A. was instantly fetched from the ward where he was unsuspectingly treating his patients. For the two vessels had been found on his cot and under his paillasse. Bewildered, the doctor swore that he knew nothing about it all and could not understand how the things could have been there under his mattress. Nevertheless, he was at once placed in a solitary cell in the lockup.

Then the investigation began. The rumor was spread

through the hospital camp that a terrorist Trotskyist organization had been discovered; it had already spread a network throughout Kolyma and had been planning to poison prisoners en masse. Prisoner doctors and medical attendants hurried to break relations with the colleague whom they had respected only the day before, and all of them suddenly recollected that he had behaved suspiciously or made suspicious remarks. The camp commander conducted the investigation. He could already see his name blazoned in big type in all the newspapers; he saw himself praised for saving thousands from poisoning, for being a pillar of revolutionary alertness. In order to assume the mantle of a hero as quickly as possible, he rushed the investigation along. At first everything went smoothly. The witnesses, who were prisoners, were intimidated partly by threats, partly by beatings. But the chief witness failed them. He was a young Ukrainian who worked as a medical attendant in N.A.'s hospital section. Nothing could persuade him to testify against his chief. This medical attendant knew better than anyone else that N.A., in spite of all the opportunities he naturally had as a doctor, never drank so much as a drop of alcohol. He knew that N.A. repeatedly checked the contents of the alcohol jug, which stood in a special cupboard along with the poisons, to make sure that the highly desirable liquid was used only for medical purposes and not for drinking. If N.A. had wanted alcohol he had plenty of opportunity to take it in the hospital, where he stayed uninterruptedly from eight in the morning until ten at night. There he could have drunk undisturbed in his office, while in the living barrack there would always be envious watchers.

This testimony made no impression on the commander. The fact that N.A. did not drink increased his antipathy toward the doctor. If that was the case, he concluded, then N.A. was using the alcohol to bribe his accomplices.

The medical attendant also had a great deal to say about the use of corrosive sublimate and the quantities requisitioned from the pharmacy by N.A.'s section. The commander worked on this medical attendant in person, but it was no use. Ukrainians can be extremely stubborn, especially when they are serving a ten-year sentence anyway.

At this point in the investigation an NKVD examining judge took over. The judge knew the camp commander as an unscrupulous drunkard. Above all, he recognized that the whole affair had been, as the Russian phrase has it, "stitched with white thread." He saw that the frame-up was so crude and haphazard that no political capital could be made of it. At this time N.A.'s friends and enemies both were convinced that he was as good as dead; but the examining judge found out a trivial fact which was devastating to the whole case. Each section of the prison hospital prided itself on having a neatly arranged supply of pharmaceuticals. In the interest of neatness each section tried to build up an array of uniform bottles. The medical attendants in charge of the pharmaceuticals had exchanged bottles with each other over a long period of time, until they had built up a collection of similar bottles and flasks. Since there was a shortage of all types of vessels in Kolyma, each section of the hospital ended up with flasks of a different type. The flask of sublimate was not of the type used in N.A.'s section; it was of the type used in Zazonov's pharmacy. After this discovery it was a simple matter to check up and discover that N.A.'s section had never requisitioned more than two tablets of corrosive sublimate at a time, while Zazonov's prescription list showed that he had ordered twenty tablets at one time. Finally the man whose cot was next to N.A.'s confessed that on orders from Zazonov he had placed the bottle and the flask under N.A.'s mattress.

N.A. was released from the lockup and returned to his work in the hospital. All the people who had testified against him rushed to congratulate him heartily. Zazonov was transferred to the town jail, where he spent a year in detention simulating religious madness. It did him no good, for he was sentenced to an additional ten years, and soon turned up in another camp. The camp commander disappeared.

The incident was one of the very rare triumphs of justice in the Soviet Union, and deserves to be remembered for that reason.

The Lockup

The lockup, a kind of miniature prison, is an absolute essential of every camp. It is usually without windows, without illumination, and unheated or very inadequately heated. Frozen toes among the prisoners are frequently due to a stay in the lockup. It contains a biggish common cell and a few tiny solitary cells, the usual planks and the usual bedbugs and lice. The daily ration in the lockup is ten and a half ounces of bread and a warm soup. The camp commanders hand out lockup sentences of from one to ten days for a great variety of infractions of camp discipline; only in very severe cases is the sentence for twenty days. You can be sentenced to the lockup with or without permission to work; the latter type is the harsher sentence. If the prisoner is let out to work he can usually manage to get a little more food than he is allotted, and above all, by moving around at work he can warm up more easily than he can in the lockup.

Lockup sentences are given for the following misdemeanors:

Lateness in leaving camp for work; talking while going out to work; impertinence to the guards, camp administrators, or other free citizens; smoking in the barracks; smoking while going out to work; wearing unauthorized clothing (say, private coats or shoes); leaving the place of work without permission; being found with a man, even though it is in a harmless conversation, which it usually is not; entering a house or store in a free settlement; drunkenness; bringing food back into camp; disorder in the barracks; disorderly cot; refusal to work; theft in camp; theft at the place of work; failure to meet labor quota; use of unauthorized places as a latrine; fighting among prisoners (guards who beat prisoners receive no punishment); refusal to take part in extra duty or shock-troop work (*udarniki*) for the camp, that is, work which must be done after the end of the official twelve-hour working day; leaving the barracks, except to go to the latrine, after the evening roll call; washing laundry in the barracks; washing hair in the barracks; burning holes in clothing, and so forth.

In a camp with several hundred inmates, not a day passes without some sentences to the lockup. At one time or another every prisoner receives a lockup sentence.

My fate caught up with me in the potato fields. It was sowing time. The potatoes had been held over the winter in boxes, between layers of peat, and were now sprouting. We worked in pairs planting them. Now and then we would pause and gobble up one or two potatoes raw. They tasted bitter and scratched the throat, but they gave us the illusion of having something in our stomachs. Besides, raw potatoes were good against scurvy, and all of us had bleeding gums and loose teeth.

The brigadier came along and ordered us to a new job. One of the small wooden bridges across the trench on the edge of the fields had collapsed and would have to be repaired. "The new stringers are lying there already," he said. "Hurry up." Naturally, neither of us had the slightest idea how to build a bridge, but we picked up our jackets and set out.

At my partner's suggestion I quickly stuffed five small potatoes into the sleeve of my jacket, since we had little prospect of being in the potato field again for the rest of the day, and were still hungry for more raw potatoes. When I straightened up I saw standing before me the well-known figure of the administration chief. Even if he had not noticed me pick up the potatoes, my flustered face would have made him suspicious. He said nothing, but I heard his heavy military boots tramping along behind me. My partner reached the fallen bridge first and casually tossed her jacket to the ground. With an elegant flip I threw mine beside it, and at the same time I heard a voice at my side ask, "What have you got in that jacket?" So he had seen after all. There was no point in denying it. "Potatoes," I said.

"Throw them out." My five miserable little potatoes rolled to the ground. Then he began to rage. For about twenty minutes he skillfully rang the changes on all imaginable and unimaginable curses. He swore he would leave me to rot in the forest where I could eat tree trunks; that at least would do no harm to Soviet agriculture. Not enough that we counterrevolutionaries had committed crimes while we were at liberty; even in camp we were determined to

184

undermine socialist agriculture. He would show me. I would remember him.

He kept his word. I remembered him.

During the next few days nothing happened, and I was beginning to hope that his tantrum in the field had been the end of the matter. Then an auxiliary brigade from the main Elgen camp came out to our auxiliary camp. With this brigade was my friend J.W., a German communist girl whose brother died in a Nazi concentration camp.

"Have you been in the lockup?" she asked me excitedly.

"I? Why? Not at all." But I felt a sinking sensation in the pit of my stomach.

"It was announced at evening roll call that you'd been given three days in lockup for stealing potatoes."

Lockup sentences for all prisoners were read out in the main camp as well as in the spur camps. The commandant of our spur camp, a young Russian who tried not to make our lives harder than they already were, knew I was a disciplined worker, and he was aware because of the evening "shake-downs" (searches) that I had never attempted to smuggle so much as a potato into the camp, although this was generally done by the prisoners. And so he had played the part of Providence; since he didn't want me sitting in the lockup he had not read the sentence at roll call. It is hard to imagine what a tremendous feeling of gratitude such evidences of humaneness call forth in a prisoner; years afterward prisoners would talk about such a commandant. Unfortunately they were rare enough. It is not that all of them are inhuman, but they are all afraid of one another.

I breathed a sigh of relief, thinking that the potato affair was over and done with. It was not.

It was the last day of sowing. Brigadiers, guards, agronomists, and camp commanders swarmed incessantly around us to spur us on to a last outburst of effort. Reeling with weariness, we returned to camp in the evening and threw ourselves down on the planks without washing or undressing. We felt as though we had not the strength to line up for our soup.

I was just dozing off when the group orderly came into the dim barrack with a list of names. Ordinarily, after the sowing incompetent workers were sent by the brigadiers back to the main camp, where they were switched from one job to the other and continually plagued. I had no reason to fear a transfer, and after blinking indifferently once or twice I closed my eyes again. Then I started up in fright as my name was suddenly called.

I had every reason to be frightened, for all the other names on the list were those of notorious criminals who were well known as work shirkers and who had all been caught several times with large quantities of potatoes. I was certainly not in very good company. A great many of the other prisoners had been caught with a few potatoes, of course. But when you have the bad luck to be reported by the administrative chief in person, when in addition it is wartime and you are a foreigner, there is likely to be a big fuss about it.

I packed my mattress sack and went out to join the incredibly ragged group, who greeted me with loud whoops and the amazed, flattering question, "What is the 'rose' doing with us?" The rose silently swung her sack to her shoulder. With a lump in my throat I answered the calls of, "Don't worry about it," from my friends who were staying behind, and for a second I saw the kindly commandant looking at me. Then he turned us over to the guards who were to conduct us the three miles back to the main camp. The guards had dogs, which meant that this was a disciplinary brigade. On the way we met the administrative chief, whose pale gray eyes flickered with satisfaction when he saw me in the company. I answered with a look of hate.

The commandant of the main camp took the list with our names, looked over the human scarecrows with their elbows, shoulders and toes protruding through their rags, and ordered in a loud, contented voice: "Put the whole pack into the disciplinary barrack."

The barrack was low, dark, and crawling with bedbugs. The inmates were all of the same type as those who had marched here with me. The newcomers made themselves at home at once; they were greeted joyfully with filthy curses, and they pointed out with a smirk what a queer bird they had brought along—namely, myself. They made it quite clear from the start that I had no business there. Some of them were lesbians; they lay on the planks, couples sharing one blanket, their faces ashen, dark circles under their eyes, and watched with malicious grins as I tried to find a place. It was hopeless from the start. Wherever I put down my sack someone said, "This place is taken. These planks are broken. Keep out of here. Get going." Or they simply tossed my things back to the floor, and from all corners of the room they hissed, howled and screeched at me, "Rose, rose. . . ."

They might have stripped me and taken away all my things, down to the last foot-rag; I would have been completely defenseless, and they knew it. That was the usual procedure when a solitary contrik fell into the hands of criminals. But they did not do it. They merely made it quite clear to me that I had better get out of here as fast as possible. The reason they did not touch me was that I was after all a foreigner. Toward foreigners Russians feel a certain respect, and this feeling comes out quite clearly in the more primitive and unspoiled of the people. There is in this attitude an element of innate hospitality, the consciousness of their own inadequacies, and the enchantment of the exotic, the fairy-tale quality of the unknown. Every day these people are given their antiforeign inoculation at meetings, over the radio, and in their newspapers. The words "spy" and "fascist" are on everyone's lips—but it is all lip service. Alongside of this artificially created suspicion of foreigners there is an altogether different attitude buried deep inside these people, an attitude passed down from their forefathers; it is an almost childish reverence for people from another world, a world that seems to them as strange and resplendent as the world of the Arabian Nights to us.

A trace of this lingered still in the unconscious minds of this utterly depraved band, and protected me from their fists that night.

The barrack was not yet locked, and I rushed out and sought refuge in the "German" barrack, which was after all also a barrack of outcasts. I cried out to the camp orderly, "Do what you like with me, but you won't get me back into the disciplinary barrack unless you carry me in." Apparently my desperation impressed her, for such outbursts were not usual with me. She quietly legalized the status quo and nothing more was said about the disciplinary barrack.

Next morning, however, I was called out to work as a member of the disciplinary brigade. The scum of the camp were in this brigade; when they marched out to work the strong convoy of guards had wolfhounds with them. Our place of work was five miles from the camp. The road led across the cemetery for free citizens where instead of crosses wooden pyramids, painted red and tilted by the wind, with Soviet stars on top of them, were slowly decaying. Sometimes a skeletal hand or a well-preserved foot protruded from the grave; it had been heaved to the surface by the thaw, for in winter it was impossible to break through the frozen earth to make a sufficiently deep grave. At the sight, the hardened criminals who were my companions today broke ranks, uttering piercing screams—for all criminals are intensely superstitious. All of them also make a great to-do over their religion, which does not stop them from committing horrible crimes. For that reason they are generally somewhat restrained in their behavior toward the nun prisoners, the *monashki*.

After a march of about two hours we reached the swamps where we were to work. Clouds of mosquitoes instantly fell upon us with enthusiastic buzzing. We could protect our faces against them with the *nakomarnik*, but not our arms, legs, and the backs of our necks. I often wondered what they lived on before prisoners were brought in to feed them.

In July the sparse swamp grass is mowed. We were supposed to chop out whatever brush might interfere with the scythes and throw it into the pools of water. It was unnecessary work which had been thought up specially for the disciplinary brigade. Lighting smudge fires to drive away the mosquitoes was strictly forbidden. It was impossible to munch so much as a piece of bread throughout the day, for the moment you lifted your netting a horde of mosquitoes settled on your face. The constant pricking and itching of mosquito bites drove you crazy after a short time, but what good was it to run around in a circle like a mad dog—you could not break through the line of guards.

The guards suffered only from boredom, since their good

uniforms and top-boots shielded them from the mosquitoes. Now and then one of them would kick a sleeping prisoner; then a furious blob of face, swollen by sleep and mosquito bites, would emerge from under the jacket that covered it. The prisoner would wait until the soldier turned his back; then she would promptly huddle under the jacket again. Hardly anybody worked. Why should they? The labor product was reckoned for the whole brigade together, and the majority of the members of the brigade were inveterate work-shirkers. Besides, who was going to count the number of twigs thrown into the water? We were already sure of the lowest bread ration, fourteen ounces. The prospect before this brigade was transfer to Mylga, the disciplinary camp of Elgen disciplinary camp.

The hours crawled by. The day stretched out endlessly. Had the earth forgotten to rotate? Would the sun remain forever in the same spot? The mosquitoes bit, stung, crawled, itched, and burned. No slow darkening of the sky promised the coming of night; the one feature that marked the approach of evening was that the buzzing of the gnats became louder and more threatening. Bright days, ghostly bright nights. Days filled with mosquitoes, nights with bedbugs.

At first I rejected the thought of begging the camp commander for another job. She might sometimes relent if you piteously crawled and confessed your sins to her. I was resolved not to do that. But after several weeks in the swamp I was desperate, and went to her. Several times I turned back at the door of the administrative barrack. Finally I went in. I stood for half an hour in the waiting room, biting my lips, until I was at last called in.

Behind the desk sat Valentina Mikhailovna Zimmermann,

known as "the Pike." When I entered and stood waiting at a suitable distance, facing the portrait of Stalin which hung on the wall above her head, she threw me a brief, icy glance and bent over her papers again. I stood and waited. I stood looking at the narrow, set face with its hard, unfeminine features, the ugly mouth and the finely shaped brow under smooth dark hair, the trim body in the neat, well-fitting uniform. I was standing there in my oversized shoes and my baggy, stained man's jacket, looking down at the cracked skin of my hands, which were puffy and hideous from mosquito bites. When I looked up again she caught my eye.

"What do you wish?" she asked with cold politeness.

I made my request for transfer to another brigade.

"Where are you working?" She knew perfectly well, since she herself had put me in the disciplinary brigade.

"Clearing the meadows," I answered.

"Oh. Then there's nothing I can do. The other brigades are already full." She maintained the pretense of sticking to regulations, although she knew that I knew that there were daily changes among the personnel of the labor brigades.

"How long must I suffer over a few wretched potatoes?" I said.

She lifted her eyebrows and replied with the complacent contempt of the well-fed: "You might have thought of that before you committed theft."

I turned and left the office.

Nevertheless, after another week she transferred me from the swamps to another brigade.

Afterwards, whenever anyone mentioned the word "potatoes" in my presence, I felt sick.

8. The Life of Slaves

Money

WHEN HE IS first taken into detention a prisoner is relieved of all the money he has with him. He is given a receipt for it, which he can use to draw food and tobacco twice a month from the prison commissary, to the amount of fifty rubles a month. If his relatives find out what prison he is in—a matter of considerable difficulty—they are permitted to send him fifty rubles a month. Food and clothing packages are not accepted in the large city prisons; the smaller provincial jails are not so strict in this respect. Before his transportation to camp, the prisoner's receipt is taken away from him. While he is en route, which may be for a month or two, he is without any money. And he is also without money so long as he remains in a transit camp, like that at Vladivostok, which may be for half a year or more.

When he reaches the labor camp he can report to the camp's economic department the amount of money he left behind in detention prison. Usually it takes more than a year before the rest of his money is transferred from the prison to the camp. In camp too the money is not paid out to him, but a personal account is set up for him. From this account he may draw fifty rubles a month in cash, which he may use as he pleases.

The camp, that is, the NKVD, hires the prisoners out to work in all sorts of state enterprises. In Kolyma, where there is no native population except for the settlements of the primitive Yakuts, the entire economy is based upon prison labor. Prisoners are employed in every sort of work through-out Kolyma. For each convict workman the business pays a fixed sum to the camp. There is a definite quota for the day's work which each prisoner is required to perform.

A prisoner working in the woods must fell, saw, and pile three, four and a half, or six cubic meters of wood, according to the thickness of the forest.

If he works in the gold mines, he must obtain an average of twenty grams (0.7 oz.) of pure gold a day, or deliver enough wheelbarrows of ore from the mine to the refining apparatus to yield twenty grams of pure gold.

A prisoner working as a doctor in the hospital must treat a ward of at least fifty seriously ill patients. Each prisoner who works as a nurse is in charge of a fixed number of patients.

When the prisoner meets his daily quota he receives pay from the camp; the amount differs very much according to the type of work, but may not exceed one hundred and fifty rubles a month.

The highest wages are paid to gold-mine workers. A doctor receives ninety rubles a month. An ordinary nurse gets twenty-four rubles a month, a registered nurse forty-eight. A medical attendant receives fourteen rubles a month, a field worker averages forty to fifty, a woodsman sixty to seventy, a construction worker fifty rubles a month—provided always that the prisoner is able to meet the high labor quota. He must fulfill his quota 100 per cent. If he does 99 per cent of his quota, he is paid nothing. If he exceeds 100 per cent, his wages are increased. There are jobs where you can never earn anything because it is virtually impossible to meet your labor quota. Among such jobs—for women—are pick-and-shovel work, snow-shoveling and haying.

Women in Kolyma work at all heavy jobs under the same conditions as the men, with the exception of the gold mines, where only men are employed.

What can a prisoner in Kolyma buy for his money? If he fulfills or more than fulfills his labor quota, he can use the camp commissary three times a month. In this store he can buy twenty-five ounces of bread three times a month and, if it is available, one and three quarters ounces of tobacco twice a month. In the extremely rare event that he exceeds his quota by 50 per cent, he has the right to buy two pounds and three ounces of bread three times a month and slightly more than an ounce of sugar twice a month, in addition to the usual tobacco ration. He pays the state-fixed price for these articles. If the percentage of his labor quota is 110 per cent, he will, therefore, spend 8.40 rubles for bread and 12 rubles for tobacco. If his percentage is 150, he will spend 12 rubles for bread, 12 rubles for tobacco, and 0.60 rubles for sugar.

Figuring average earnings at fifty rubles, the prisoner is left with from thirty to thirty-five rubles. Anything else he wants he must buy illegally at black-market prices.

The camp supplies every prisoner with about five ounces per month of wretched soap. Female prisoners therefore always spend a part of their money for soap; men never do. This accounts for about ten rubles.

Among the prisoners bread is sold at a price of ten rubles for seven ounces. A matchbox full of tobacco is the same price. There is naturally a great deal of simple barter: seven ounces of bread for a matchbox full of tobacco.

Only smokers are allowed to buy tobacco at the prison commissary. Nonsmokers, even though they have fulfilled their quotas, are not entitled to tobacco. When a shipment of prisoners arrives in camp the economic department immediately records the smokers and nonsmokers. Unsuspecting newcomers state truthfully which they are. At this point the deals begin. There are prisoners working in the economic department also. They make an agreement with a nonsmoker, list him as a smoker and divide the tobacco with him so that they can use the tobacco in trade. Light smokers get out of the habit because the prisoners are without tobacco half the time anyway. They then trade away most of their tobacco, although as a matter of form they will light a cigarette now and then in order not to be denounced as nonsmokers—which they otherwise would be by other envious nonsmokers who surrendered their ration.

In principle prisoners at Camp Elgen were allowed to receive packages from relatives. In practice such packages arrived very seldom, and the same was true of letters. Anyone who received news from home as much as once or twice a year considered himself lucky. Many never succeeded in resuming connections with their families, especially when a father and mother had both been arrested and the children placed in a state children's home.

All letters of the prisoners were subject to censorship. Prisoners were not allowed to write about living, working, or food conditions, nor to say anything about other prisoners. The name of the camp also could not be mentioned. All the mail went via postbox numbers—for example, Magadan, Box

No. 522—although in reality the camp might be four or five hundred miles from the port of Magadan. Half of the letters were not sent off because the camp censors, who were none too good at reading, were too lazy to read through them all. The letters which were sent out had to pass the military censorship of Kolyma, which checked on all letters, even those of free citizens. There, half of the remaining letters disappeared, again because of the personal deficiencies of the censors. Some of those that passed the censors reached their destination, some did not. The Soviet Union is large, and the postal system is incredibly inefficient and careless. (No letters at all could be sent abroad. Nor was there any other way to transmit information abroad, since every letter to a foreign country by a Soviet citizen is subject to special censorship in peacetime as well as in wartime.)

In addition to these human obstacles to correspondence there were the special conditions in Kolyma. Six months of the year there is no shipping, since the Sea of Okhotsk is frozen over; hence there is no communication with the "mainland." When a package for a prisoner finally arrives it has often been on the way for more than a year. Half the contents is missing, as proved by empty or half-empty bags. The package is handed to the prisoner by the chief of regime, an officer of the guard, who first removes forbidden articles such as books, sharp or pointed objects, indelible pencils, eau de cologne (because it is alcoholic), medicines, and so on. If there are cigarettes in the package he will condescend to accept a present of a pack, and it would be wise to press it upon him.

As soon as anyone receives a package the entire camp knows about it, and the recipient is deluged with congratulations—each well-wisher secretly hoping that he will be offered at least a cigarette, if not something to eat. Even when the package is exclusively food, the recipient dolefully remarks that all he got were a few warm things to wear—the object being to discourage his comrades' hopes from the start. They don't believe him, of course; they recognize such remarks as a polite rebuff.

Late at night they hear the crackling of paper from the lucky bird's cot, and the forgotten aroma of sausage is wafted through the barrack. Everyone sniffs, everyone's mouth waters; sighing, the others draw their blankets over their heads.

The prisoners trade not only among themselves, but with the free citizenry also. In Kolyma all goods are rationed because of transportation difficulties; the inhabitants were familiar with ration cards long before the war. Free citizens buy textiles and food at state prices and sell them at black-market prices to the prisoners. Such practices are forbidden, but the prisoner cannot protest, since he is breaking the law in trading with a free citizen. These transactions must be managed behind the backs of the guards; but there are always opportunities for at least a few prisoners, and they then pass on the goods to the less privileged prisoners—adding their own profit to the purchase price, of course.

Camp Rations

It is impossible to live on the camp ration for prisoners, for more than two years, at any rate. By the third year whoever tries it is a physical wreck; by the fourth he has become incapable of work; and by the fifth year he bites the dust, or more often the snow.

Daily Bread Ration for Prisoners in Kolyma

FULFILLMENT OF LABOR QUOTA	WOMEN	MEN
100% or better	21.0 OZS.	28.5–32 OZS.
70% to 99%	17.5 OZS.	25.0 OZS.
50% to 69%	14.0 OZS.	17.5 OZS.
Disciplinary ration	10.5 OZS.	10.5 OZS.

The higher bread ration for men applies to miners. As soon as a male prisoner is sent to lighter work in the woods or on construction, he receives the meager women's ration.

For all prisoners, per day: 3.5 ounces of salted fish; 2.1 ounces of cereals—barley, barley-groats, millet, or oats—0.17 ounce of meal or starch; 0.5 ounce of vegetable oil; 0.34 ounce of sugar; 0.106 ounce of herb tea; 10.5 ounces of cabbage leaves, brined.

Menu for Prisoners

BREAKFAST: Half a herring or 1.75 ounces of salt fish; sweetened tea; one-third of the bread ration.

LUNCH: Cabbage leaf soup, one pint. Groats. One-third of the bread ration.

SUPPER: Cabbage leaf soup, with a few grains of some cereal and boiled-down fishheads floating in it. One-third of the bread ration.

Year in and year out, on weekdays and on holidays, the diet is the same. Its monotony alone, aside from its lack of vitamin C, tends to bring on scurvy. To combat the disease the prisoners are given a dose of "concentrate" in the camp dining rooms. If you don't drink your glass of concentrate, you don't receive a wooden spoon for eating. This concentrate is an extract of pine; it is a beverage bitter as gall, but it has actually proved to be effective against scurvy and is manufactured in the local vitamin factory of Taskan, on the Taskan River, a tributary of the Kolyma.

The lack of vitamin B has resulted in mass cases of pellagra. A prisoner with a serious case of pellagra must give up 1.75 ounces of his bread ration and is given instead a brew made of flour and yeast, which is supposed to restore the missing vitamin B.

In spite of these measures, one of the most frequent diagnoses of the cause of death in prisoners is polyavitaminosis—lack of vitamins. Another frequent cause of death is dystrophia alimentaris, that is, starvation.

In evaluating the prison rations it must be kept in mind that these rations are for people who perform the heaviest kind of physical labor twelve, fourteen, and sixteen hours a day in a country which during the eight months of winter has the lowest temperatures of any inhabited country on the face of the earth.

Bread

Misha was a young man of about twenty. He had kept his courage up through prison, camps, and gold mines. And he had had the devil's own luck; he contracted an inflammation of the lungs which brought him into the hospital. The hospital was the dream of all prisoners. With his strong young organism, he had conquered the disease, while most of his fellows on adjoining cots had escaped to a better hereafter with half a dozen or more years still owing to the state.

In order to make sure God knew whom He was dealing

with when these deserters reached Heaven, a card made of wood was tied to one of their big toes, reading: "Prisoner X, born . . . died . . . diagnosis . . . paragraph . . . term. . . ."

Now, after all the stabbing pain, the agonized coughing and the delirium, Misha could think of only one thing—his limitless hunger.

Everybody in the camp loved him, loved the trace of recent childhood that still lingered in his thin, boyish face, in spite of years of imprisonment. But no one could help him, because all were gnawed by hunger; all could think of only one thing: more bread, a little more bread.

After his recovery he was sent to "light" work—wood chopping. One day he could stand his hunger no longer. None of the guards was in sight. He took a supply of firewood which he had cut secretly, loaded it on his back and tramped off, puffing and sweating, through the deep snow. The settlement of free citizens was several miles away, and he had to hurry in order to get back to his place in the woods in time for the return to camp.

A good-natured housewife paid him for the wood with a warm meal, which he devoured on the spot, and gave him some white bread to take with him on the way. She watched him with a smile as he joyfully stuffed the precious food into the left breast pocket of his wadded jacket and raced off toward the woods.

The brief winter sun was already sinking behind the crimson-stained hills of snow. Tonight he would eat his fill for once. He did not know that he had already been missed. And he was hurrying so that he did not notice the guard ahead of him. When the soldier raised his rifle, Misha failed to see him. And when he heard the hoarse cry, "Halt," he was so startled that he stumbled on a few steps. The soldier fired.

That evening the prisoners, each as weary and hungry as Misha had been, carried the body of their young comrade into camp.

The soldier made his report to the camp commander: shot while trying to escape. The commander nodded. Nothing unusual. After the soldier had closed the door behind him, the commander read the dead boy's name again. He knew few of the prisoners by name; there were far too many of them. But apparently he must suddenly have remembered that bright face of the young boy, so different from the dull gray despairing mass of the prisoners.

In spite of the poor light in the morgue, he saw that the boy had been shot in the chest. From the front, not from behind. Naturally he was not going to make a fuss on account of the death of a contrik. But at least he could transfer the soldier who had done this.

Someone raised the kerosene lamp. He suddenly saw the doughy, bloody mass bulging out of the boy's jacket.

"What is that?" he whispered.

"That is what he died for, Citizen Commander. A piece of bread."

(Told to me by a friend of the boy who worked as a medical attendant in the prison hospital where I was employed in 1945.)

The Day in Elgen

In summer the day in Elgen begins at five o'clock, in winter at five-thirty. An iron rod is beaten several times in succession against a dangling length of iron rail, the kind of rail the carts in the gold mines run on. Presumably these iron rails are delivered along with the barbed wire whenever a camp is established, for there is such a length of rail in every camp in Kolyma, and everywhere it gives out the same wailing, hateful sound that so tears at one's insides that probably no prisoner ever forgets it for the rest of his life.

At the sound the uniformed women guards are at the side of our cots, pulling the blankets away from us. "Come on, come on, get up, faster, faster." It is better to choke back the swear words that are on the tip of your tongue and get into your long, clammy wadded trousers, whose original black is by now brightened with innumerable patches in various colors. Then you rush into the washroom where the battle for the foot-rags is already in full swing and where you can swear as hard as you like. You find that your footgear, which you carefully tied together in the evening, is now scattered into two different corners and is cold and wet.

Then we line up in front of the barrack in rows of five, each of us armed with her drinking cup and ration ticket. When all are together at last and our feet have congealed to their usual low temperature, the guard gives the order to march. She leads us in close formation to the dining room. There some seventy of us line up in front of the counter for our bread. If we were allowed to go individually to the dining room, the line would not be long enough and we might forget for a moment that we were in a regimen camp.

The bread is distributed by a gray-haired old invalid with sharp eyes, a sharp tongue, a thin sharp nose, and thin sharp fingers. In front of her lies a book like the commander of the guard's book, listing the names of all the prisoners by brigades. You give her your name and she begins thumbing through the pages while seventy women wait. She pushes back her glasses, stares at you to make sure you really are the person you claim to be, sets her glasses back on her nose, and hands you the ready-cut seven ounces of bread. It is a middle section, of course; not everybody can have an end of bread. Ends are for her special friends; she cannot befriend everyone. It is impossible to explain to someone who has not been in camp or prison what the end of a loaf of bread means. The end is crisper, it looks more attractive and it seems to be heavier. But more than that, an end mysteriously fills you more than the middle section of the bread, although it too weighs only seven ounces (200 grams). A middle section is a stab-wound to the heart; it is a confirmation from Providence that you are abandoned for good and all. It is the beginning of a day on which everything will surely go wrong. And you almost always get a middle section.

Not only on account of the ends is the distributor of bread one of the most-hated women in camp. She also has the right to allow for three grams of crumbs and moisture for each two hundred grams of bread, so that in reality she need give out only one hundred and ninety-seven grams. What happens to all the crumbs and to the moisture, which is not lost at all, since it is well known that she covers the loaves at night with damp cloths in order to replace whatever moisture may have evaporated? Those extra three grams go into her own stomach, or she makes gifts of bread to her bosom friends. It's easy to see how she has filled out since she has held this post. The worst-hated people in camp are the well-fed.

After the bread is taken care of, the same line forms at the next counter—except that the line has now grown longer by the addition of squads from other barracks. Our breakfast ration ticket is torn off and our drinking cups are filled with a slightly sweetened, faintly tinted, lukewarm liquid, which is supposed to contain the third of an ounce of sugar we are entitled to every day. Then half a herring is slapped down on the counter. Good Lord, are these herrings all head? What has happened to the tail ends? Of course you really know. The cooks have their favorites too, and they can't have everyone for a favorite. The tail end of a herring is almost all edible, except for a tiny portion, while the head amounts to the same in weight, even though so little of it can be eaten. There are quite a few prisoners who save their herring heads, boil them in water and then eat this "soup." It cannot be said that they are any the fatter for it, or any the healthier.

As the regulations require, we eat our breakfast in the cold dining room, crowded together on a bench at a more or less clean wooden table. Then, strengthened by our hearty meal, we rush back to the barrack, finish dressing, perform the sacred duty of putting our cots in order, find some pretext for squabbling with one of our neighbors, and then the clanging rail signals that it is time to leave for work.

Once again we line up in rows of five in front of the barrack, and after a suitable wait the guard leads us to the square in front of the gate. There are six or seven hundred women waiting to go out. Every brigade is guarded by at least two male soldiers. The soldiers are not here yet, so the prisoners wait. As yet only the *naryaditsya*, who is responsible for the distribution of work, is on the spot. She is one of the most influential prisoners in the camp, for she makes up the lists of the various labor brigades, although of course she is subordinate to her free superior, the chief of labor distribution. Unlike her superior, she knows every prisoner in the camp, and a casual remark of hers at the right time very frequently determines where a prisoner will be sent to work. She can make proposals for transfer of workers, and since most free camp administrators are notoriously lazy and careless, these proposals are as a rule adopted without question. This applies also to proposed transfers to other and more remote camps. Naturally the naryaditsya offers her suggestions on the basis of her personal impressions. To make sure that these personal impressions are good, and in the hope of getting or keeping a better job, the prisoners shamelessly shower presents and flattery upon her. This is the more necessary because she usually is called upon to assist in the daily "shakedown" or search of the prisoner's person, and she only pretends to search those prisoners who have kept on her good side.

Shakedowns are an important part of life both in prisons and camps. Female prisoners may be searched only by women. Since there are usually not enough women supervisors in the camps, the camp administration also uses prisoners who are in turn checked upon by soldiers of the guard. There is a shake-down every time the prisoners re-enter the camp, that is, once or twice a day. In addition, at least every two months there is a thorough search of the barrack and of all the prisoners' belongings. This operation is always carried out in the middle of the night and usually lasts several hours. Suddenly the entire barrack will be full of guards who chase the frightened women off the planks and begin rummaging through bundles and mattresses in all corners of the barrack at once, so that the prisoners cannot pass things around to conceal them. Nevertheless, almost all the prisoners own a homemade knife fashioned out of a piece of sharpened iron. At night this is carefully stuck into a crack between the planks. The reason for this is that you can make your bread ration go farther by cutting it into slices than by breaking off pieces.

Shakedowns are particularly rigid before and during the state holidays on May 1 and November 7; apparently the administration then fears some demonstration on the part of the prisoners, although the idea of a demonstration on these or any other days never even enters the prisoners' heads. The two cases of genuine counterrevolutionary demonstrations which took place in two women's camps were carried out, significantly enough, by criminals. They hung up a placard reading, "Long live fascism!" They were shot, and their names and the announcement of the executions were read to us at the evening roll call.

Ordinarily the guards turn up scarcely anything in the course of these searches: writing paper, pencils, cotton bags, homemade sewing needles, contraband food which may have been bought with endless trouble and excitement from the earnings of two or three months, and money in excess of fifty rubles. For there is a regulation that no prisoner may have in his possession more than fifty rubles—even though he may have been paid more than that in wages. What we hated worse than the coarseness of the guards, worse than the confiscation of the little things we needed, worse than the humiliation of the whole procedure, was the fact that we were robbed of our all-too-brief night's sleep. For all through the years in camp we suffered from chronic fatigue.

To get back to our departure for work. Sometimes it was supervised by the camp commander or the chief of labor distribution herself; in this case a few lockup sentences would certainly be handed out for unauthorized talking, smoking, or lateness. Wrapped in warm furs and felt boots, these well-nourished officials performed this burdensome duty a few times every month. They have long since stopped seeing the thin, mournful faces of the wretched creatures who stand huddling in the cold, silent and resigned. They do not know the individual prisoners and do not want to know them. They know only that there are a certain number of prisoners who have to work until they collapse. If they collapse there will be others to replace them, and these others will be equally unknown, except as statistical units. Prisoners who break down go to the hospital. Then it is the medical section's business either to send them back into the gray mass of the camp, once more fit for work, or to write them off in File No. 3 (the death file). The camp commander has not made the camp or the prisoners; the soup was cooked by the NKVD and she only adds the spice.

At last the convict doctor comes out to the square in her white gown. She has rushed out of the infirmary, where at the last minute she excused or did not excuse a sick prisoner from work for a day, and she now has to inform the naryaditsya of her decision. Meanwhile the guards, who are addressed as "Citizen" (the prisoners are not allowed to address a free person as "Comrade"), have come up in their long, warm soldier's cloaks or sheepskins, their bayonets fixed to their rifles. The prisoners wait. They have no furs or felt boots; they have only the patience of despair.

The big wooden gate is thrown open. The soldiers line up on both sides. The naryaditsya with her list and the commander of the guard with his register is also there. The first brigade of field workers is called. They go forward a few steps. Then each member of the brigade, called by name, replies loudly giving her name, and goes out through the gate to the road, where the brigade is again lined up by fives. As they go out the commander of the guard counts the number in the brigade, say forty prisoners. When all forty are outside in eight rows of five, the guards count them once or twice more. Then one of the guards goes back to the commander and signs for the reception of forty prisoners. Then the first field brigade marches off. The other six hundred women wait, poorly clad in summer and winter. The prisoners must perform outside work until the temperature reaches fifty degrees below zero centigrade ($-58°$ F.). According to the official medical reports, most of the cases of frostbite among prisoners do not occur during work, but in waiting to leave and to enter camp. Nevertheless, this same ceremony is adhered to in all the camps. It is part of the "regimen." Usually it takes more than an hour before the camp gate closes behind the last prisoner. Although we have been up since five o'clock, the work day is reckoned as starting at seven o'clock. We work from seven o'clock until twelve; then there is an hour's rest at noon, and we work again from one until eight.

The first brigade of field workers receives the order, "Forward, march," and starts off. Since all the prisoners are frozen from standing still, they try to warm up by marching quickly. But all of them cannot keep up the pace. The average age of the criminals is about thirty, while the average age of the contriki is forty or more. The older women lag behind; the spaces between the rows of five become uneven. But that is not permissible. The guards shout thunderously, "Halt," and again we stand freezing, shifting our weight from one foot to the other. "Don't string out," we are ordered, and again we start on our way. But the younger women are dissatisfied with the slower pace. They begin cursing furiously at the breathless, gasping older women. Talking during the march to work is forbidden. We have scarcely taken twenty paces when we are ordered to halt again. The guards can well wait. They are warmly dressed, and all they have to do is keep us in order. It does not matter at all to them whether they do so standing still or walking, on the road or in the fields, whether there are spectators present or not. Passers-by take no notice of us anyhow. The overwhelming majority of the population of Kolyma are prisoners or former prisoners, and these gray rows of five are as familiar a sight as the hills, the marshes and the snow.

"So you want to chat?" the guard says, grinning at us, who are freezing. Now a number of pithy curses directed at him are heard. That does not trouble him at all. He waits, and so do we. Once a criminal has started cursing, one word is not enough; she spouts a rain of imprecations before she shuts up again. Then we go on once more, until the first rows get too far ahead or the last rows lag two paces behind. A brigade with guards takes some fifty minutes to cover a distance that a person could normally walk in twenty minutes.

When we reach the field we are turned over to the labor brigadier, a free citizen, who assigns each prisoner her work.

In the fields of the Elgen state farm cabbage is the principal crop. In the difficult climate of these regions even the undemanding cabbage requires careful and involved tending. Elgen has greenhouses and hotbeds where the cabbage plants are raised.

The cabbage seed is sowed in the greenhouses. Then each seedling is transplanted to a small pot made of a mixture of peat and cow manure. The pots are placed in the hotbeds where they remain until planting time, usually May 28; by then the plants are four to six inches tall. When being set, the plants are put into the ground inside their fertile pots, the bottoms of which have been chopped off so that the roots can develop more freely. There are frequent night frosts in June, but these rarely harm the young cabbage plants since they have been gradually hardened to the cold. However, hailstones the size of pigeon's eggs often fall in July and damage the crop.

Against the various noxious insects, such as cutworms and

cabbage worms, Paris green, a solution of carbolic acid and soap, and a spray of corrosive sublimate are used. The plants are fertilized with as much cow manure as is available, and with nitrates. The earth around the small plants is loosened and heaped up by hand with a small, sharp hoe. The second and third cultivations are done with a special plow.

The hardest part of the job is watering, which is done by women prisoners who carry watering cans all over the huge fields. The harvesting is done in September, when the land is already covered with snow. The cabbage heads are knocked off their short stems with spades.

In winter the prisoners cut the peat, which is used along with cow manure and horse manure to prepare the soil. They also make the fertile pots and do the sowing, which must not take more than two weeks. Soaked by rain and eaten by mosquitoes, they tend the cabbage; then, with hands and feet numbed by cold, they harvest it. In return they receive the large, bitter dark-green outer leaves, while the plump white heads find their way to the kitchens of the free population.

And in spite of all that they say: "This is *my* field." Or: "See how fine *my* cabbage is."

The guards are interested only in seeing that no one leaves the field, or that no unauthorized person approaches the prisoners. But if the unauthorized person has a little talk with the guard, and if a bottle of highly-prized alcohol changes hands, then the guard fails to notice anything when the unauthorized person picks out a woman for himself and disappears with her for half an hour.

For the rest, our lord and master is the brigadier. The brigadier takes care that the labor force placed at his disposal turns out a definite amount of work, for which he is responsible to the agronomist. The labor force is always reckoned very close, so that in order to meet his quota the brigadier must drive the prisoners to the highest possible productivity. It does not matter whether he is personally kind or brutal. If he himself has a lazy nature, he will always think the prisoners are shirking their work and are far too slow. If they stop once in two or three hours to roll a cigarette, and he happens by just at this time, he will shout that they have done nothing all day but stand around smoking. A decent brigadier will overlook his workers' "pause for a smoke," in which the non-smokers take part, of course; it is still called a pause for a smoke even when, unhappily, nobody has any tobacco—a state of affairs that often lasts for months. When after five or ten minutes such a brigadier "happens" by, everybody knows that it is now time to get back to work.

The fields of Elgen are surrounded by virgin forest, from which they have been wrested by toilsome clearing. The forest was driven back, but the swamps remain, and the drainage ditches in the fields were dug mostly by women. Of all the prisoners' work, ditch-digging is the most dreaded. Even tough, hardened Russian women do not have the strength to dig up nine cubic yards of earth in a day. That is the normal quota for prisoners, and it does not matter whether the prisoner is a man or a woman; prisoners have no sex. But no woman can meet the quota. And so, when the women toss their clanging spades into a heap in the evening, they know they have not earned their seventeen and a half ounces of bread. They walk wearily back to camp with aching backs, lie down on cots whose hardness they no longer feel, and as they fall asleep they think, "I won't get up tomorrow no matter what they do to me. I can't do it. This is the end."

But in the morning when the iron rod clangs against the rail, they start up out of bed and do all the things a prisoner must do, and it is not the end, not yet, not for months and years. It is not so easy to die.

They take the hated spades in their hands and dig and dig. There are two hundred acres of fields at Elgen, and these required many long ditches. One morning the free brigadier came by, looked on for a while, spat and went away. A few hours later he came back to inspect the work, and this time he cursed, loud enough for the guards to hear him. But while he was invoking the devil and the devil's grandmother and sparing neither the Mother of God nor all the ancestors of all prisoners and ditch-digging prisoners in particular, his eyes rested on one small woman who held a spade far too large for her. Tears and beads of sweat mingled on her face and trickled into the ditch, but she did not take the time to wipe them away. The brigadier's eyes were sad as he walked away over the fields.

He was not an NKVD man, nor a member of the guard, and he had no connection with the administration. He was a farmer who had been recruited, tempted by the higher earnings possible in this remote region. He had heard, of course, that Kolyma was penal territory. But after all, Siberia itself is penal territory, and Kazakhstan and Karaganda and the Urals and Arkhangelsk and Murmansk. There are penal territories everywhere in the Soviet Union. In those other areas, however, there is little contact between prisoners and the civil populace. In Kolyma you could not escape the prisoners. He had not known that every free citizen who takes a job in Kolyma, no matter what his trade, must participate in the exploitation of prisoners. He had not realized that the free citizens of Kolyma were there to drive harried, emaciated, dead-tired prisoners to their work.

He earned more money than he could have in his home

village, but it gave him no pleasure. Although he had come solely with the intention of saving, he began senselessly drinking his money away. There was no meaning to thrift, and in Kolyma everyone drank—not only because of the bitter climate. In Russia everyone drinks too much, but in Kolyma all drank without measure. It was as if they had to drown something inside them with huge quantities of liquor. Nobody spoke about it, and everybody drank. And no matter whom they toasted, they never spoke a toast for the NKVD—in spite of the extra rubles they earned here in Kolyma.

When the brigadier came back at night to measure the day's work, the women were all sitting in a circle around a fire. It was too dark for them to dig any more, but until the prescribed number of hours were up the guards were not allowed to take the brigades back to camp.

The brigadier sat down with them. "Tired, girls?" he said. This time he did not curse them because there were no guards near by. He rolled a cigarette, and half a dozen eyes gazed longingly at his tobacco pouch. "Here, have a smoke." Greedily, their hands reached out. A shy voice asked, "Ivan Alexandrovitch, how are our percentages?"

They knew they had not completed their quota. He knew it too. He knew it was impossible for them ever to do it.

Three times a month he had to turn in production figures, on the basis of which the prisoners received their camp bread card. Three times a month he sweated over those figures. He hated the figuring. He was a farmer, and so he knew what work was. These women had worked, and therefore they deserved their bread. His figures were always a triumph of the imagination—and they added up to a hundred per cent for all the women.

He growled something inarticulate and disappeared into

the darkness, for the guards were coming to line the women up by fives for the march back to camp. But the very sound of his voice reassured them. He would not leave them in the lurch this time either, for he was a good brigadier and a good man. Kolyma had not yet wholly killed his compassion.

For unending months the women wore themselves out digging ditches. Then one day a steam shovel was brought in which dug in a few weeks more than the women had been able to do in a year.

The twentieth century is the century of technology as well as of bloodshed. When will technology reach Kolyma and relieve the women prisoners who draw heavily laden sleds with the traces across their own chests, as once the Volga boatmen drew the barges; who fell trees in the forest and carry them out on their own shoulders, no matter how many times their knees give way under the weight? How many snow-shovelers must go blind every year because there are no snow-glasses?

A Day Off

During the summer there were no free days for prisoners in Kolyma. But in the winter months, from November until April, the prisoners were entitled to three rest-days a month. However, part of these days off were killed by the camp administration, which sent the prisoners out for several hours to do maintenance work and cleaning in the camp, to shovel snow or saw wood or wash floors.

At one time I was in a small camp called Volchok, on the edge of the forest, about two and a half miles from the main Elgen camp. Here we lived without guards. We were enjoying one of our rare days off, and were lying on our cots, tired and hungry as ever.

One of the girls, a young thief, had brought in two

drunken truck drivers. Since she could handle only one of them at a time, the other looked around. And suddenly he came stumbling straight toward me. "Little countess," he hiccupped, "I want you."

My face was gray from the smoke of the eternal kerosene lamp; my jacket was covered with so many multicolored patches that it was impossible to tell what its original color had been; my hands were cracked and calloused from the work and the cold. I turned my head away to escape the reek of alcohol and moved as close as possible to my bedmate. She put her arm protectingly about me, but that did not stop him from molesting me. Then several women fell upon him and with a few vigorous Russian curses shoved him out of the barrack door.

A few minutes later he was back at my cot again.

"Little countess," he said, "tell me what you want. I'll bring you anything, anything you wish."

Like most truck drivers he had been, and presumably still was, a bandit; with the help of a few of his fellows he could no doubt get at any of the stores of clothing and food.

"I don't need anything," I answered.

"You don't need anything?" He stared in amazement at the starved figure of the countess before him.

"You don't want to tell me, *Grafinushka.*

"Yes, I'll tell you," I sighed. "But you can't get me the thing I want."

"Yes I can, yes I can," he said eagerly, moving dangerously close again. "Just tell me. I'll get you anything."

Speaking very slowly I said, "The only thing I want is—a bunch of grapes. Fresh grapes. . . ."

For a moment he stood numbed with astonishment.

"Grapes," he mumbled thickly. "Grapes? Has anyone ever heard the like? What a countess!"

Shaking his head, he reeled out into the deep snow.

Incentives

If a prisoner does not meet his labor quota 100 per cent, he cannot keep body and soul together very long. Therefore it is to his own interest to use every ounce of his available strength to earn his daily twenty-one (for women) or twenty-eight and a half (for men) ounces of bread.

The managers of Dalstroi, the trust in charge of exploiting Kolyma, are interested in fulfilling the plan by more than 100 per cent. In the first place, they will thereby serve the state; in the second place, they earn decorations; and in the third place, the state then showers the top rulers of Kolyma with annual bonuses amounting to fifty and a hundred thousand rubles apiece. Moreover, they like the sound of the title "hero of labor," although their labor consists solely in dreaming up newer methods for extorting a little more work from the prisoners.

They count first of all upon the prisoners' hunger. A prisoner who does 110 per cent or better of his quota is allowed to buy at the camp commissary three times a month.

Every summer, when the gold season fever grips Kolyma, meetings are held after work and the prisoners are informed that the administration is considering rewarding all prisoners with good work records by allowing them to become colonists. For example, if a prisoner still has three years to serve, he can become a colonist for six years instead. The hours and places of work of colonists scarcely differed from those of the prisoners, but they earned more and lived outside the camp. Otherwise they were strictly supervised by the

NKVD and could be locked up in camp again at any time. Such a type of colonization actually existed during the early years of construction in Kolyma, but in 1937 all the colonists were sent back into the camps. Since then the word colonization has been used only as bait; it is brought out of moth balls every summer in order to spur new and credulous prisoners to greater efforts. The older prisoners merely listen to the promises of colonization with a contemptuous smile, knowing that nothing more will be said or heard about it after the gold season is over.

There was another bait called "early release." Of the more than one hundred thousand prisoners, two hundred were picked out and released shortly before their term was up. The list of the names of these people, who were called two-hundred percenters (*dvukhsotniki*) were posted in the dining rooms of all the camps, so that the rest would learn from the example of these superproducers. On closer examination you discovered to your surprise that a prisoner who had worked as a chambermaid for some NKVD chief was listed as a two-hundred percenter in woodcutting, for which meritorious accomplishment she was being released before completion of her sentence. Most of these people were criminals who had distinguished themselves in the service of the camp authorities by special cruelty toward their fellow prisoners, and who were falsely listed as miners; or else they were brigadiers who had made a name for themselves by denunciations and ruthless driving of their workers.

Such lists produced few results.

The prisoners were all weary and needed rest. And so, in March and April, before the beginning of the gold season, the OP was set up. This is the Russian abbreviation for health center. A select group of prisoners was put into the best barrack in the camp for two or three weeks. They were freed from work, except for a few hours of snow-shoveling or sawing wood. They received two portions of *kasha* (groats) a day instead of one, and an additional seven ounces of bread.

The group selected for OP was determined by the doctor and the commandant together, but the latter had the decisive word in each case. The doctor chose the feeblest and most run-down prisoners, while the camp commandant preferred to reward the prisoner brigadiers and the workers with the highest labor percentages—in other words, the healthiest and strongest prisoners. What was the use of feeding up the moribund, who in any case wouldn't be able to work much longer? And so, for the sake of appearances, a few of the more wretched prisoners were sent into OP, while the main body consisted of the healthy oxen who would now be given an opportunity to gather strength before they started their difficult job—of spurring on their comrades in misery.

Another candy-coated pill was the camp's "cultural education section," for which the Russian abbreviation was KWTshe. It met in a special barrack called the "clubroom." Prisoners, headed by a free citizen, made up the group. Its main function was to spur the prisoners on to greater efforts. Political clarification came first. While it was almost impossible before the war for prisoners to obtain a newspaper, during the war we were kept informed on troop movements almost as regularly as free citizens. Although we were condemned as counterrevolutionaries, spies, and traitors, all of us strongly desired to see Hitler defeated. In spite of all we had gone through, prisoners scarcely differed from free citizens in this respect. And the prisoners were equally ready to do their share and give their last strength to help defeat Hitler. Therefore the culture section organized labor competitions—the counterpart of the "socialist competitions" among the free citizens. The members of every single labor brigade had to volunteer in writing to exceed the virtually impossible labor quotas. These solemn promises were given at a public meeting. Who would refuse to do his bit? Obviously, only people who did not want Hitler beaten, who were bent on displaying their counterrevolutionary attitude even in camp. Such people might as well bury all their hopes of liberation. For counterrevolutionaries, even though they were already prisoners, were frequently tried anew for alleged counterrevolutionary utterances or actions, so that after they completed their first term of five years they would be sentenced to five or ten years more. An army of prisoner stool pigeons was employed by the NKVD to watch the prisoners.

The results of the labor competitions were posted on large bulletin boards in the camp yard. Twice a year the inmates were assembled in the clubroom at the end of the workday and the administration publicly thanked the brigadiers and brigades with the highest labor percentages. These commendations were entered in each fortunate prisoner's file—the *lichnoye dyelo*. This solemn ceremony generally concluded with a "concert" by prisoner talent. Usually it was terrible.

For a high average production, a special pass was given out. The good workers—*otlichniki*—who possessed this pass could lose it again for any infraction of the rules which resulted in a lockup sentence. The pass entitled them to buy tobacco at times when there was not enough to go round, and bearers of the pass were given preferential treatment at the annual renewal of equipment.

Signing up for the war loans was handled in a fashion similar to the labor competitions. First there was an appeal to the prisoners' patriotism. Then it was pointed out that only incorrigible counterrevolutionaries would fail to make their contributions. But of course subscription was voluntary.

Then a prisoner from the economic department came to the barrack with a list. The list contained the name of each prisoner and, in a column next to it, the amount of money she had in her personal account. Subscriptions had to be twenty-five rubles or more. The commander or the administrative chief leaned idly and apparently indifferently against a pillar while the voluntary subscriptions were taken down. At last it seemed finished.

The commander peered over his shoulder at the bookkeeper. A few stubborn women had crawled into their cots and were pretending to be asleep. Loudly the commander called out the names of the nonsubscribers. Guilty and frightened, they pushed past him to the table where the bookkeeper sat with her list. "Only if you want to, of course; it's all voluntary," the commander said with a cold, cruel glint in his eyes.

Tobacco is also used as an incentive to make prisoners work. The prisoners are almost all mad for tobacco. Theoretically every smoker who delivers 110 per cent of his quota can buy three and a half ounces of tobacco a month. But in practice ample quantities of tobacco are available only in the gold-mine camps. Tobacco is weighed out to the gold miners directly at their places of work. And during the hundred days of the gold season the slogan for the prisoners is: "One gram of gold equals one gram of tobacco."

The Storytellers

In the large main camps there are a few books available to the prisoners. But very few prisoners make use of these books. They are too tired and it is too dark in the barracks for them to want to read late at night. Moreover, some of the prisoners from villages, and the great majority of the criminals, cannot read at all. And so the storyteller is an important personage. The storyteller is the only person in camp who is loved and respected by all prisoners equally, no matter whether they are contriki or criminals. For every prisoner wants to forget reality, and the storyteller gives him forgetfulness. When the storyteller speaks, the barrack no longer seems so dark and cold; the loneliness of the forest is no longer so hostile and oppressive; the hard, tough osier rods bend into basketry more easily. The cursing and the animosities die down for a time, and the longing for bread or a little tobacco lets up. It is altogether remarkable that these prisoners, who endure all the suffering that men can think of to impose upon other men, who have before them years of daily torment—that these prisoners can still weep over the fictional tragedy of a fictional love.

The best storyteller I met in all my years in camp was Maria Nikolayevna M, a Moscow schoolteacher who in prerevolutionary times had belonged to a small revolutionary splinter group. After the civil war was over this group was quickly absorbed by the Communist Party. But in 1937, when the hunt for enemies of the people was on and all old sins were recalled, she was sentenced to ten years imprisonment. She spent part of the time in a *polit-izolator,* and then was sent to camp in Kolyma.

She was so emaciated that it was hard to see how she could drag about the weight of her clumsy clothing, let alone her own body. But in that pathetic body and inside that little head with its close-cropped dark hair there dwelt a warm, unconquerable human soul. The atmosphere of the camp, with its merciless law of hunger, cruelty and self-preservation, was something she simply refused to recognize. She lived, worked, and talked as she had been accustomed to do for almost fifty years of life in the free world. When she worked in the fields, she devoted herself to the task with the precision of a scientist in his laboratory. "Maria Nikolayevna, this is no flower garden," her partners at work would groan when she lovingly patted and firmed the earth around each cabbage seedling. "If you do it that way we'll never make our percentages."

"Percentages, percentages?" Maria Nikolayevna would murmur testily. "What is all this about percentages? If a job is to be done it ought to be done right. Percentages!" The result was that she usually worked alone, for the others fled from her in order to have a decent amount of work to show at the end of the day. She, who was more diligent than any of the others and who always did the best and most thorough work, always had the lowest percentages. For labor quotas in the Soviet Union, for free people as well as for prisoners, are based upon quantity rather than quality.

The injustices that are an inherent part of camp life were so intolerable to her that for the hundredth time she would speak up for the victims of injustice, even though for the hundredth time her protest would be futile. Her free superiors found her protests a nuisance, and the prisoners felt no gratitude toward her for these efforts. Generally she was regarded with indulgent contempt—until she began to tell stories.

The best time with her was in winter when we were weaving wicker baskets. Then nobody ventured to speak sarcastically to her, although she would carefully examine each rod to see whether it was quite right. The brigadier himself obviously hung around the workshop because he too wanted to listen to her. For words came to Maria Nikolayevna as though the story she was telling lay printed on the work-bench before her. She had an innate gift for storytelling, and a marvelous memory besides. Once she recited the whole of Pushkin's *Eugene Onegin* without omitting a line; and her recitation conjured up the sophisticated dandy of the early nineteenth century so that we saw him before us, standing right by the kerosene drum that served us for a stove, sur-rounded by half-finished baskets. I doubt that any people anywhere ever drank in the music of Pushkin's verses as greedily, as thirstily as these unsightly figures whose gray faces were smudged by the eternally sooty kerosene lamp.

I shall never forget the day I spent with Maria Nikolayevna in the snow-covered woods, where we were gathering the frozen willow rods. It was light work, and dreadful work. There is plenty of willow in Kolyma, but only a few of the branches are suitable for basketry. And so we would go slowly from tree to tree and bush to bush, looking for the usable rods, until we had ten bundles apiece, each bundle a generous armful. Light work—so light that it was impossible to warm up. Walking slowly through the woods and plucking twigs with the temperature forty degrees below zero—with such work the blood froze in your veins, your numbed hands refused to bend, and the frost cut like knives into your ill-protected feet.

Both of us had selected the same area, and while we looked for switches a few yards apart we exchanged a word now and then. The frosty air carried everything we said a great distance through the frozen forest. But the more the cold bit into my body, the more taciturn I became, until at last I fell silent. Nothing in the world continued to interest me except the thought of a fire, and there was no use lighting one be-cause we had to be continually moving around.

Sometimes I desperately jumped up and down in the snow, or ran a ways into the woods where Maria would not hear me crying like an infant from the pain of the cold. But these outbursts lasted only a few minutes, for the quota, the sacred quota, had to be met; by the time darkness fell I must have ten bundles finished.

Once or twice, when I came near Maria, she took my arm and danced wildly around in the snow with me until we were gasping for breath and shouting with laughter that could scarcely be distinguished from sobbing. But at least that warmed us for a few minutes.

Once more we searched for switches, and then I heard her say, "Do you know Turgynyev's prose poem, 'How beautiful, how fresh were the roses'?" I said I did not. From what source she drew the strength, the warmth to recite, I cannot say. But I know I forgot everything and did not even notice when the snow slid down off a twig and trickled down the back of my neck; for suddenly the snow was filled with the fragrance of roses and Turgynyev's words drew a magic circle around us which none of the world's misery could breach.

When she had finished reciting, I went up to her and embraced her. As long as we could keep alive an awareness of beauty, as long as such feelings could flower at forty degrees below zero, there was nothing that could break us. And so I embraced her, although such demonstrations were rare indeed among prisoners. I shall never forget those roses of Turgynyev amid the ice of Kolyma.

A Petition

It was the time of the morning departure from the camp to the gold mines. Several thousand men stood in rows of five and waited. The camp commander with his various assistants stood watching to see that every man who could stand on his feet was sent on his way through the gate.

Someone moved away from the gray army and went up to the commander.

"Citizen Commander, may I have permission to give you a petition?"

The commander nodded.

A skeletal hand, all splits and cuts, took a sheet of paper out of a ragged jacket whose filthy wadding was working through in a hundred torn places. He placed the paper in the commander's fur glove. Apathetic, hopeless, hungry eyes, sunk deep in their sockets, watched the commander's expression as he read.

The commander skimmed through the petition and instantly roared to the commander of the guard: "Here, ten days in the lockup without work for this fellow."

Ten days in the lockup—that meant ten days at ten and a half ounces of bread and a bowl of soup, ten days in an unheated dark cell on bare boards, without a blanket, while the autumn blizzards drove snow through the wooden walls. Ten days of fighting the cold, of fingers and toes aching until they became numbed, until turning over and tramping up and down no longer helped, and the exhausted, cowering heap of rags in the corner shivered only now and then in the cold.

But no trace of disappointment gleamed in the apathetic eyes which now turned from the commander's red, angry face to the face of the guard. Those eyes had hoped for nothing— and were no longer capable of fear.

A superfluous kick sent the prisoner reeling through the low door into the darkness of the cell. It did not even occur to him to dodge the soldier's boot.

Five days later he was called out to the camp commander.

Stumbling on his frozen feet, dizzy with hunger, he stood at the desk of the man who was lord and master over three thousand prisoners.

"Now tell me, you son of a whore, what do you mean by writing such a petition? You want me to transfer you to the status of a horse! What do you mean by that, you so-and-so and so-and-so?"

The creature that had once been a man answered:

"It's very simple to explain, Citizen Commander. If I were a horse, I would have at least one day off in every ten. Now I have no days off.

"If I were a horse I could rest now and then while at work. As a prisoner I cannot.

"If I were a horse, I would be assigned to work equal to my strength. As a prisoner I am always hungry, and when I do not meet my labor quota I get less bread, so that I do still less work, and in the end I get so little bread that I can hardly stand on my feet.

"A horse has his stable and his blanket—I haven't had a new jacket for two years because my percentages are too low.

"A horse doesn't have to work more than fourteen hours a day. But I am kept in the mines fourteen and sixteen hours, especially when I haven't met my quota.

"If drivers beat a horse too hard, or drive him too much, they are punished. For a horse is precious in Kolyma. But who punishes the guards and brigadiers who beat and kick me because I've become too weak to do my work well?

"What is a prisoner in Kolyma? Nothing. But a horse—a horse is something!

"So you can see for yourself, Citizen Commander, how much better off I would be if I were a horse."

"Back to the lockup! Take him away! To the lockup!"

The Life of Slaves

For a moment the prisoner's eyes rested longingly on the hot, crackling stove. Then, with bowed head, he stumbled in front of the guard through the snow and back to his icy cell.

The commander sat alone at his desk. Involuntarily, he read again: "I request transfer to the status of a horse." And underneath his answer: "Ten days in the lockup. By order of the commander."

Thoughtfully he toyed with the red pencil. And suddenly he wrote in large letters across the petition:

"Economic Department. Issue to prisoner: One wadded jacket (new). Ration Category I (highest) for one month. October 5, 1944. By order of the commander."

And since prisoners work in the economic department, this story became well known. It was told to me by the book-keeper of the camp—Camp Burkhala in the northern mining district of Kolyma—whom I tended when he was confined to the prisoners' hospital.

9. Sickness, Self-Mutilation, Suicide

Camp Medical Organization

DURING OUR FIRST FEW DAYS in our first labor camp at Magadan, the group of new arrivals with whom I had come were assigned to digging and cleaning up in the camp yard. It was early June, but the wadded jackets that made us look like shapeless bundles were very welcome. As soon as we dug up a few shovelfuls of earth, we struck ice. I felt a thrill of awe. There is a difference between reading about permafrost in geography books and standing upon soil that thaws only to a depth of ten inches or so even in midsummer. The perpetual frost has been forced down a little deeper only where the soil of Kolyma has been worked by tractor-drawn plows.

In the meantime our documents had been checked over and all the women who had had any medical training, whether as nurses or medical students, were assembled in a square in front of the city hospital. At that time the city hospital was still located near the women's camp. Since then it has been moved to a building—a really imposing one by Kolyma standards—at the other end of the city, near the port. There, perched on a hill, it looks down upon the bay and its encircling hills.

We were the first contriki, aside from doctors, who were being admitted to medical work—as older inmates told us with envious amazement. It was not that the regimen had been relaxed in any way. But the lack of medical personnel in the face of the constant influx of prisoners was so pronounced that there was nothing else to do. At this time, however, we were employed to tend only prisoners, not free citizens.

Every camp has its infirmary and its small hospital of several beds Distant spur camps are visited once or twice a month by a medical assistant who bandages wounds, distributes pills, and excuses sick prisoners from work if they are running a fever. Severe cases he has transferred to the hospital in the main camp.

In the infirmary and hospital a prisoner doctor usually does all in his power to give the sick the care they need. It is not his fault that the most essential medicines are not available, nor is it his fault that the rations for the sick are wholly inadequate.

Especially severe, infectious, or chronic cases are transferred to the large prisoners' hospitals. The largest of these is the Central Hospital of the USVITL. Until 1942 it was located in Magadan; then the hospital building was used to house troops and the hospital itself moved out to the twenty-third kilometer from Magadan, where it occupied a large group of buildings with over eight hundred beds. In 1946 it was moved closer to the gold-mining region on the left bank of the Kolyma River, where a large bridge on the road to the northwest crosses the river. This time barracks which had been used by troops during the war were converted into a hospital.

The hospital now has about a thousand beds. It is divided into all the special departments of any great hospital, and there are prisoner specialists to staff those departments. A number of doctors have since been released from imprisonment and continue to work there as department heads.

The working heads of the departments are prisoners, who are generally subordinate to a free department chief. Medical attendants, nurses, and orderlies are prisoners.

This hospital is generally well provided with all types of medicaments and pharmaceuticals. Modern methods such as X-ray treatment and pneumothorax are also used. But all these measures are of no use because the principal evil cannot be remedied—the chronic undernourishment of the patients. The cooking in the hospital is more careful, and somewhat more nourishing foods, such as cornmeal, rice, bilberries and even small quantities of canned meat, find their way into the menu, but the portions are as tiny as those in camp. There are always shortages resulting from theft by the prisoner personnel, who are supposed to get only the ordinary camp fare, but who appropriate some of the patients' rations.

At the time I was there, the prisoners' hospital in Magadan was Section Ten of the city hospital. It took up several barracks which were surrounded by barbed wire and were complete with watch towers and a commander of the guard. The whole was called San-Okp and was under the supervision of the chief doctor of the city hospital whom I have already mentioned, Fomenko. This tall, soft, fat man with his egg-shaped head, fleshy nose, and big hands looked more like a butcher than a surgeon. He was among the few Soviet citizens who wore a hat; when he examined a prisoner he kept it on his head. He also seemed to think it too much effort to take his stethoscope out of his pocket in behalf of a sick prisoner. Instead he put his huge, fleshy ear to the patient's back, which was covered with a towel for the purpose. This procedure did not increase the accuracy of his diagnoses.

It was through my work in the prisoners' hospitals that I learned a great deal not only about the various women's camps and their inmates, but also about the male prisoners in all the camps of Kolyma, Indigirka, and Chokotsk. I was able to piece together some picture of the fate of thousands of prisoners. In addition, communication by the grapevine has reached a high development throughout the Soviet Union, particularly among prisoners. This is a consequence of the dictatorship's policy of keeping secret things which in other countries are published in the newspapers. Simply because they are wrapped in secrecy, no matter whether they are important or unimportant, such affairs arouse interest and speculation among the people. It is the nature of secrets to be found out and passed on in whispers, under oath of silence.

It is inevitable that a nurse in the prisoners' hospital, who closes the eyes of hundreds of prisoners and delivers to the office a monthly statistical report on her ward, will get a very good idea of the mortality rate among the prisoners. It is inevitable that she will draw conclusions on conditions of camp life, work, and food from the wretched appearance and physical state of lice-ridden prisoners. It is inevitable that she will learn about the beatings of prisoners when she bandages their flayed backs.

Subjects spoken of reluctantly are confided to a nurse by men on the point of death. Even the most innocent nurse would begin to wonder why during 1939 and 1940 the hospitals swarmed with patients who had been sentenced in 1937 and 1938, while after 1941 it was rare for a prisoner sentenced during those years to show up in the hospitals. It was certainly not because all of them had suddenly stopped getting sick, but because they had meanwhile died in the gold mines.

Not only patients told their story and the stories of their comrades. In the course of my work I also associated with free doctors, medical inspectors, and chiefs of the public health organization. While I was wearing my white gown they forgot that I was a prisoner. With cynical frankness they spoke of incidents and conditions in the various camps under their jurisdiction. To emphasize how hard they themselves worked in their own zones they tossed off shocking figures on the wretched conditions in other zones.

When a doctor complained about the sanitary conditions in his camp, the chief of the public health administration would put him in his place. "Your camp? Why, it's a paradise compared to the others. You ought to see the camp where they bathe once every six months and the prisoners wear their loused-up jackets over their bare bodies. Were you ever at the Fifty-sixth Kilometer? [At the fifty-sixth kilometer west of Magadan there was a men's disciplinary camp where a great epidemic of spotted typhus broke out in 1940.] That's where you would see lice, my friend. . . ."

Before even a single prisoner from our corrective labor camps was admitted to the camps of the katorga convicts, we learned about the mass deaths in those camps through the reports of the chief of the public health organization, for our hospital was under him. This same chief ordered the pharmacist of our hospital to prepare anti-itch materials by the pound, for all the katorga convicts were afflicted with scabies as well as dysentery.

In addition, secret reports and statistics were given to prisoner stenographers to copy or tabulate, because the free citizens are incredibly lazy and have grown accustomed to putting off as many of their duties as possible upon prisoners.

That summer day we started work in the prisoners' hospital of Magadan. The sickly old head nurse who had commandeered me for her ward had spoken of a women's ward, but I saw no sign of women. It was just a trick on her part, the head nurse said, smiling as she handed me the white gown and a square of muslin for a cap—in the Soviet Union there are no starched caps for nurses. Any nurse who was willing to work in a women's ward would do a good job in a men's ward, she said. Later on I had to admit that she was right. When dealing with prisoners, it was more pleasant to nurse the men patients than the sick women. But at the time I didn't like the idea and I felt apprehensive as I walked into the ward behind the head nurse.

Not much could be seen of most of the prisoners. It is a habit typical of prisoners to crawl out of sight under the blanket whenever they have the opportunity. They keep even their heads covered, not only for warmth, but in order to see and hear nothing of their surroundings, which they fear and which they want to have no part of for as long as possible. This attitude is particularly characteristic of patients suffering from avitaminosis.

But the first patient on the left, a swollen colossus whose gaunt head, sunken, yellowish face and blue lips made a remarkable contrast with his dropsical limbs, examined me suspiciously with dark, slanting Tartar eyes.

On the average there were fifty patients in a hospital barrack. This was the internal medicine section. It was headed by a free woman doctor (at that time Dr. Passelkova), who was assisted by a male doctor, a prisoner. Every section had two prisoner nurses who were alternately on duty twenty-four hours at a time. Of the twenty-four "free" hours, part was lost in roll calls, the ritual of marching out to work, waiting for guards, and standing in line for food. The nurses were supervised by a free head nurse who was also in charge of the prisoner orderlies. There were usually four orderlies to a section, two for the day and two for the night shift.

In the beginning it was extremely difficult to get used to a twenty-four hour stretch of duty. At night the doctor and a guard made the rounds through all the wards at different times. If a nurse was found asleep, a report was made to the chief doctor next day, and the guilty nurse lost her hospital job. I worked for two years without a single day free; substitute nurses were later introduced, but at that time there were none. Although you get accustomed to the routine to some extent, the body goes on suffering from these unnatural hours. In spite of habit, you crave sleep every night, not every other day.

The mortality in our ward amounted to ten or fifteen deaths a month out of fifty beds, a figure that I found fairly consistent in other hospitals where I later worked. In the surgical wards it was somewhat higher, in the women's wards considerably lower. But only about half of the prisoner deaths occur in the large hospitals; the other half of the deaths take place in the camps, the camp hospitals, and the invalid camps. The latter have particularly high mortality rates. Incurable chronic cases are transferred to these invalid camps, where they lie on planks, three decks one above the other, and where every morning several corpses are taken out of the barracks. For a long time there was such an invalid camp at the twenty-third kilometer north of Magadan; later it was moved to the seventy-second kilometer northwest of Magadan.

Every time a new shipload of prisoners arrived at Magadan, we received the first batch of patients direct from the port, the second batch from the quarantine camp to which all male prisoners were taken and where a medical commission examined them before they were shipped on to the various gold-mine camps.

This medical commission, which was similar to the one that examined newcomers to the women's camps, spent exactly long enough on the examination of each prisoner to apply the stethoscope to the region of the heart and to the right and left lungs. Then the prisoner was classified into one of several labor categories:

1. Heavy physical labor (TFT).
2. Medium physical labor (SFT).
3. Light physical labor (LFT).

In practice the camp commanders rarely adhered to these categories, for one reason because they had no light work to assign. There were two additional categories to which prisoners were assigned upon release from the hospital:

4. Working invalid.
5. Nonworking invalid.

The working invalids were better off, since they were frequently used for clerical or other such work inside the camp.

New hospital patients were first taken to the bath where they were washed and had all their hair shaved off. The doctor on duty was in charge of assigning the patients to the proper ward. He would deliver the certificate of admission to the nurse of the ward in question, and this nurse then had to fetch the prisoner from the bath.

During the first month of my work in the hospital I went to the anteroom of the bath one day. The bath attendants—all criminals—were lounging around as usual. I asked for my patient. "He's in the bath, nurse," they told me cheerfully.

I went into the dim room and saw a man, stark naked, sitting on the bench along the wall. Angrily I turned to the two attendants who had followed me in and said, "Why haven't you at least put a shirt on him?"

Their answer was a broad grin. Then I saw that the man on the bench was dead. He had died before his bath, and the attendants had placed him there on the bench for my benefit. They laughed for days at the success of their joke.

We gradually lost the sense of shock and reverence for death which people normally feel. Either you couldn't stand it or you became hardened. Many prisoners who had eagerly sought work as medical attendants soon gave it up because they could not stand it. The superstitious peasant girls, especially, could not bring themselves to carry the dead into the morgue at night.

The Patients

Most of the patients from the ships were carried in suffering from bloody dysentery (hemocolitis), from which they seldom recovered. They lay side by side and watched one after another of their comrades giving up the fight. They looked straight into my eyes and said, "I'm next, nurse." There was no use lying to them; they knew their fate as well as I did. And when I came in with the apparatus which was used at the last hour to inject quarts of physiological saline solution under their skins, they whispered, "So it's time now." Many of them fought desperately against these saline injections because they had seen their fellows die shortly after them.

In spite of the wretchedness of prisoner existence, almost all of them clung to life. Only among criminals whose condition was hopeless did I observe unusual strength of character. When they realized that nothing could help them, they did everything they could to bring on death more swiftly.

One day Petya, the pickpocket, who was the best attendant I ever worked with, was sitting beside a dying fellow criminal. For days the man had refused all medicines and injections because he knew they would only postpone but not prevent his death. Now he asked for the "bottle." Petya wanted to help him with it, for he had long been too weak to move at all. But he signed to Petya that he wanted to hold the heavy glass urinal alone. With a smile of forbearance Petya humored him, but he prepared to catch the vessel which he was sure would drop from the patient's feeble hand.

With a last surge of strength the bony fingers gripped the vessel, and before Petya could stop the man he swung the "bottle" with all his might against his own forehead. He lost consciousness at once, and half an hour later he was dead, as he had wished to be.

Most criminals, for whom brawls and stabbings are a part of daily life, are remarkably squeamish about injections. If a big, brawny tough turns white and almost faints when a tiny sample of his blood is taken for analysis, it is a fair guess that he has been convicted of several murders. None of them can stand the sight of his own blood.

Treatment of these criminals is complicated by the fact that they are all weakened by excessive use of alcohol and every other imaginable intoxicant. For anesthesia they require far more than the usual quantity of ether. Ordinarily they are very meek while in the hospital, but when they are feverish they curse in the lewdest possible way and work themselves into such fit of rage that they have to be tied to their beds.

One night a pneumonia patient suddenly sprang out of bed, ran to the window and smashed the pane with his fist. I grasped him by the sleeve, but he shook me off like a flea and jumped through the window and out into the snow. His only injuries were a few minor cuts, but his action would have cost me my job if all the patients, who were awakened by the shattering of the window pane, had not testified that I really tried to stop the man.

The prisoners most susceptible to disease were those from Central Asia—from Uzbekistan, Turkmenia, Tadzhikistan, and Khirgiz—and the Caucasians, Georgians, Armenians, Chechens. . . . Brought from the subtropical climate of their homelands to the coldest regions in the world, they died like flies. All their vital forces were numbed as soon as they went out into the terrible cold. They did not try to defend themselves. They let themselves be driven out to the gold mines. There they simply did not move. They stood motionless, their arms crossed, their bowed heads hunched between their shoulders, waiting for the end. They made no response at all to orders and curses. Blows were useless—it was as hopeless as asking tin soldiers to bestir themselves.

The decent guards, who realized that these people could not be made to work because in this cold they simply stopped functioning, used their rifle butts to drive the prisoners around and around in a circle, not out of cruelty, but out of pity, because they simply could not look on while the men stood numbed until they fell over like so many dolls. "Another frozen to death," the prisoners would note. "Thermoshock," the doctor would record.

When one of them entered the hospital, it was certain that he would leave it feet first. While their Russian comrades fought for life to the last breath, they waited submissively for death. This fatalism, this utter capitulation to the thought of death, made saving them impossible, although Russians with similar cases would overcome the disease. While the Russian patients swallowed their pills with a childlike faith in their curative powers, the Central Asians took the medicine with skeptical indifference, convinced that it would not help at all.

Their traditions forbade them to undress in the presence of a woman, even a nurse. It was a battle every time to give them an injection or an enema. On the other hand, while we had to insist on the Russian patients' washing, these Asiatics were extremely careful about personal cleanliness to the last minute of their lives.

Many died of tuberculosis, many of intestinal diseases, many of pellagra. But the real sickness was the cold, the sunlessness, and the actual imprisonment. These people, many of whom had been nomads, could not endure confinement.

Of the many hundreds of patients whom I tended in the hospitals of Kolyma, I particularly remember one of my first patients. His name was Radin. He said little about himself and his past, but other patients told me in a respectful whisper: "Radin is a brigadier general; he was commander of all the Caucasian troops. An old Bolshevik, one of the most famous commissars of the Civil War. . . ."

Now he lay in bed, his face gray and sunken, with the broken nose he had received from his interrogators in Lifortovo, the Moscow military prison. Sometimes, in the course of conversation, the dark eyes under the steel-gray brows would flash for a moment, betraying the powerful personality that this wreck of humanity must once have possessed. When I asked his age he said he was sixty, and gave me a searching look. I did not think to question his statement. Later I found out that he was only forty-six; he kept his real age secret because he was ashamed of how much older he actually looked as a result of prison and the interrogations.

Fifteen years of camp lay before him. But in the sixth year of his imprisonment a miracle happened. War with Germany had started. In 1942 a telegram arrived ordering him to be sent back to Moscow on the first plane. (There is a regular air route between Magadan and Khabarovsk.) In the hour of extreme peril, when the Germans were at the gates of Moscow, poor Radin and his military experience were remembered.

They took him out of a snow-shoveling job at some camp. His once tall figure was stooped; he had become a toothless, ragged, filthy vagabond. And there was no longer any light at all in his eyes. Once more he was taken to the prisoners' hospital so that he could be patched up somewhat—he had a terrible case of scurvy. A mild, indifferent smile from toothless jaws was his response when he was told that Moscow apparently intended to rehabilitate him. Rank, decorations, honors —these things could no longer tempt a man whom hunger and cold had reduced utterly. In fact, he seemed to fear such distinctions. For this man was already beyond worldly things. He no longer wanted to have anything to do with people; the one thing he cared for at all was rest, peace. And so he refused to leave his cot in the hospital. One plane after the other departed without him, and whenever he was asked whether he felt strong enough for the trip, he gave a miserable shake of his head.

At last one day, with an absent, unhappy expression, he put on the new uniform which had been given him to replace his rags. Then Radin flew to Moscow—no longer the commissar of the Civil War, no longer commander of the Caucasian troops, but Radin the convict from Kolyma.

A new patient. Accompanied by the orderly he staggered into the barrack, crawled onto his cot and lay on his face, groaning. His temperature read 103.7.

Since I had to take down the data on his case, I asked him to turn over. He groaned in protest. I looked at his certificate from the camp infirmary: pleuritis exudativa. You don't generally lie on your face with pleurisy. Perhaps the high fever had clouded his mind. I tried carefully to move him to a different position, but he howled in pain. Perhaps some incompetent medical attendant—there were many such at the camp infirmaries—had given him an injection which had become infected.

I removed the clothes from his back. What I saw was a suppurating, brownish-red wound, surrounded by proud flesh, and a series of welts and bloody bruises radiating out over his whole back.

"How did you get this wound?"

"A carbuncle," he replied.

"What happened to it?"

"I broke it open," he whispered into his straw pillow, his eyes shut.

"How so?"

He was about to answer. Then he suddenly opened his feverish eyes, saw the attendant behind me and the strangers on adjoining cots, and he hesitated. Finally, in a changed voice, like someone reciting a lesson, he said:

"I broke it open myself. With my sack. We walked here. The sack rubbing against my back opened it."

I looked at his certificate again. The camp he came from was twenty-five miles from the hospital. Walking that distance with a case of pleurisy, a fever of 104, and in a blizzard, was quite a feat.

"Who was with you?"

"The guard."

A pause. I looked questioningly at him. He said nothing. I looked pleadingly, insistently. Still he said nothing.

"Rest now," I said, carefully covering his flayed back. As I bent over him, he forced his dulled eyes open and murmured, "He kept saying I was walking too slow. . . ."

I asked no more questions.

When the ward doctor came back to the tiny ward office after examining this patient, he gave vent to his feelings in some violent words. Then he noticed my presence and apologized. He sat down at his desk and again began cursing. He apologized a second time. Then, twirling the ends of his mustache between his fingers, he swore again.

"There's no need to apologize," I said. "That is all that can be said about that carbuncle."

At night, when everyone was sleeping and I sat at the sleepless man's cot, his fear left him and he talked. I suppose also that he felt that he was not long for this world, so that there was little he need fear. And so, in painful gasps, he told me that the guard had wanted to get the uncomfortable march over with as soon as possible, and so he had driven the sick, feverish prisoner on for hours with blows of a club. At the end of the march he had threatened to break every bone in the prisoner's body if the man reported at the hospital that the guard had beaten him.

The club therapy might well have been fatal anyway for a case of pleurisy. But in this case every blow had fallen upon the suppurating carbuncle, and the outcome was blood-poisoning.

Our outraged ward doctor, himself a prisoner, made a report to the free head doctor. "What good are our hospitals and a medical staff and expensive American medicines when any guard can beat a prisoner?" he asked at the conclusion of his report.

The head physician at that time was Doctor Ruban, a humane person who at once declared his readiness to do something about the affair if the patient would make a statement. But the patient refused to repeat what he had told me. The moment he saw a free citizen before him, all the fright of the defenseless prisoner surged back into his mind. He answered all questions with the monotone phrase: "I did it myself, with my sack; I did it myself, myself."

So we let him die in peace, and the guard went on beating prisoners undisturbed, for the testimony of a prisoner doctor would not be sufficient for bringing charges against a free citizen.

The Search for Forgetfulness

During the war there were two things always available to the free populace: lipstick and liquor. Russian women like to wear heavy make-up, which sits strangely on them because they have so few decent clothes to go with it.

A quart of alcohol, the equivalent of two quarts of vodka, cost five hundred rubles at a time when the state bread price was about two rubles a pound. Few prisoners or released prisoners had that much money. But they craved drink. They grasped at every opportunity to forget reality even for an hour.

Every now and then eau de cologne was available in the rations of the free citizens. It was never used as a cosmetic, but as a drink.

During the war an antifreeze was imported from America for use in the motors of tractors and automobiles. It was plainly marked "Poison," and the drivers were warned against it. Nevertheless, dozens of them died from it because they could not resist the temptation to get drunk on this antifreeze. The stuff brought about a complete breakdown of the kidneys and death within twenty-four hours.

Another favorite intoxicant was chloral hydrate, which was constantly being stolen from the pharmacies and was called by the prisoners "dry spirits." Prisoners who took overdoses of it suffered paralytic symptoms which often lasted for six months and more.

In their desperate search for oblivion prisoners often stole varnish, which was also fatal. I recall a big tall man who was brought into our ward unconscious after he had plied himself with varnish. We went on pumping out his stomach until his last gasp; then I shut his eyes and spread the blanket over the dead body. "Released before his term was up," a patient on an adjoining cot remarked.

The entire ward had of course been watching the process with excitement. Silently they looked on as I packed up the tube and the glass filter and went back to the office. I had reached the door when I remembered that I had forgotten a bottle of spirits of ammonia on the table near the dead man; I had been using it for cleansing his stomach. In Russian this unpalatable liquid is called *nashatyrny spirt;* the word sounds like spirits. As I went back and picked up the bottle, a general disappointed sigh passed through the room: "Oooh."

Utterly amazed, I turned to face the patients. They had just seen a man dying in torment because of his craving for intoxicants. The stinging odor of the murderous varnish still filled the air, and the corpse was not yet cold, and in spite of that they begged me: "Come on, nurse, leave the bottle here. Oh, we were so sure you'd forgotten it. Just one drink, nurse, don't be so stingy."

Without a word I pointed to the dead man. They waved their hands contemptuously. "We can only die once. If we must die, let it be with music. We'll end up in the *sopki* anyway." (*Sopki* was the name of the hill at the foot of which the prisoners were buried.)

With saddened eyes they watched me until I left the ward.

The pharmaceutical cupboard of the ward could not be left unlocked for a moment, for both the orderlies and the patients were always on the alert for the chance to make away with anything that even resembled alcohol. Every tincture prepared with an alcohol base, from peppermint to belladonna, would vanish at once, and undiluted, down their thirsty throats. In the hospital laboratory specimens of kidneys, hearts, livers, and so on, were preserved in alcohol. Once, when the laboratory assistant, a man of almost sixty, came down with a spell of melancholia, he drank up the preserving fluid, and the specimens were left dry.

Codein tablets were hoarded by the patients so that they could get a jag with a large dose.

If you did not watch carefully, a bribed male nurse would dip absorbent cotton into the ether bottle and slip it to some critically ill patient, who would then hide blissfully under the covers to give himself an ether drunk.

The only prisoner doctor not here for counterrevolutionary activity was a drug addict who had misappropriated morphine and been sent up on the simple charge of "theft." His sentence was ten years, and all his petitions for revision of his case or for pardon were without effect.

Camp is not exactly the place to be cured of drug addiction, and since as a "criminal" this man had good connections and greater mobility than other prisoners, he managed to keep himself supplied with morphine. But medicines were very scarce and the stock of morphine in particular was subject to strict control. He had to go to more and more desperate lengths to obtain his drug. Finally the privilege of working as a doctor in the camp was taken away from him, and the genial, highly cultivated man went into a rapid decline. In the end he became a human wreck and was sent off to the invalid camp of Mariinsk.

An Orderly

The orderlies were always selected from among the ward convalescents, with criminals preferred. But I remember an old Ukrainian peasant who was serving ten years as a counter-revolutionary and who was an orderly in our ward for a while after recovering from a severe illness.

He was a prudent fellow who had once owned his own farm. Now he was always glum; since he had worked in the gold mines, nothing could shake his quiet despondency. Just once I saw this old man beside himself with excitement.

Between the hospital barracks, tiny fields of oats were planted. They did not ripen, but the fresh greenness of the young oats enlivened the dreary hospital yard. A small plow was obtained to turn the soil; it was a wretched, ancient piece of iron, but a plow nevertheless. One day several of the hospital workers were outside, standing helplessly around the small Yakut pony which they had hitched to the plow.

Suddenly the old orderly came running out in his white gown. He pushed the baffled workers aside, clucked encouragingly to the pony and took hold of the plow. How he clutched it! His hands gripped the iron handles with voluptuous pleasure. His stooped, forlorn body was transformed. Erect, with head raised, he walked behind the plow with long, sure strides, his eyes filled with such joy that it was transmitted to everyone who saw him; they stopped and looked in silence at this convict peasant who was absolutely drunk with the happiness of holding a plow in his hands after so many years of deprivation.

When he had to give it up at last, he returned to the barrack, once more a lifeless, silent man—a peasant forever torn from his beloved, the earth.

The Free Doctors

There was wide variance in the attitudes of the different free doctors. Most of them did everything in their power to alleviate the lot of the prisoners, for in the main they were imbued with the true spirit of the medical man. Their object was to save human lives, no matter whether they were treating a free man or a prisoner.

In general the male doctors took their duties much more seriously than the women. Curiously enough, the women doctors became calloused much more quickly than the men to all the human tragedies they daily witnessed. In their relationship to their patients they were much more subject to whims, chance impressions, sympathies, and antipathies than the male doctors, and they were far more susceptible to the toadying and hyprocisy of patients who by such means tried to win their favor.

Almost all the free doctors, both male and female, came to Kolyma fresh from their state examinations. The Soviet medical student who finishes his studies cannot enter a post of his own choice in any one of the state hospitals or clinics. (Private practice is theoretically possible, but it is taxed so highly that it is impossible for a doctor to live by it.) The new doctors are sent by the state to places where there is a shortage of medical men—that is, to remote regions.

And so they come to Kolyma quite inexperienced, and are at once given responsible posts as department heads in the prisoners' hospitals. The best of them take advantage of their collaboration with convict doctors, who are usually men with many years of practice behind them, to learn from the older men. Of this type, were my first department head, Pesselnikova, as well as Yekaterina Ruban, a gynecologist, and her husband who was a surgeon and for a time head physician of the hospital. All these doctors learned a great deal at their work and had a dedicated attitude toward medicine.

On the other hand there were some who shifted the whole burden of medical work to the convict underling and busied themselves solely with administrative affairs. As a result, they remained as inexperienced as they had been upon their arrival, while they exploited the accomplishments of the convict doctors to make careers for themselves. Worst of all, they would sometimes make use of their authority as "freemen" to interfere with the convict doctors' methods of treatment—frequently with disastrous results for the patients.

Yekaterina Vassilyevna Klimenko came to Magaden fresh from medical school and swiftly advanced to become department head of three hospital barracks with one hundred and fifty beds. She owed this post not to her own medical skill, but to the fact that she had married an influential member of the NKVD. After her marriage prisoners as well as free citizens were terrified of her, and her slightest whim became law in the hospital. Sometimes this position of power worked to the advantage of her patients, for her department was served first when there were shortages of medicines, linens, or fuel. And her section was naturally the first to be reconstructed so that the patients, instead of lying in one large room, had three wards separated by thin board partitions. The small office where she spent her six-hour working day was painted with oil paint, a rare and highly desirable article in Kolyma.

At nine o'clock in the morning she arrived at her office. She was a buxom, pink-complexioned blonde with pale-blue, slightly squinting eyes. She was always enveloped in a cloud of perfume, and wore an elegant fur coat which she exchanged for the spotless white gown that hung ready for her.

After signing the prescription book and the case histories of patients who were being discharged, she went into the ward, where she directed her attention less to the patients than to the floor. Upon the cleanliness of that floor depended the weal or woe of both the orderly and the nurse on duty. She left examination of the patients to her convict colleague, who also informed her about interesting cases.

If a dying patient was being given a last injection of camphor, she hastened back to her office—this being a sight she preferred to avoid. If she were told beforehand that such a patient would probably not last another half hour, she kept out of the ward altogether.

After going through the same exhausting routine in the other two barracks, she returned to her office. From then on she kept watching the clock—alternating between the cuckoo clock on the wall and her own gold wrist watch. In the intervals she opened her charming, pouting lips and yawned widely, vaguely covering her mouth with a small white hand marked by tiny dimples. She had the manner of a lazy, well-fed cat. She never raised her somewhat nasal, eternally bored voice, not even when she sent an orderly to the gold mines for some minor offense.

She came fully awake only when she talked about needlework, which she had her nurses make for her in large quantities. Patterns, yarn, color-combinations were the things that passionately interested her. Nurses who did not know embroidery, no matter how conscientious they were about attending their patients, were treated by her with contemptuous tolerance; those who could do needlework could neglect their patients as much as they wished and still be sure of the favor and protection of this so-called doctor.

In the women's ward there were always a few patients who looked and were remarkably healthy. These were kept busy embroidering tablecloths and tapestry hangings—in the style of our grandmothers.

All the ladies of Magadan society were wild about this hobby and competed with one another—to the great joy of those prisoners who could do such work, for they could thereby earn additional food. It was amusing to see the wives of NKVD officers outbid one another in sending secret presents to the "counterrevolutionaries"; officially such gifts were strictly forbidden, of course. But the ladies were so excited at the chance to enrich themselves cheaply—for in their eyes this superfluous and generally tasteless needlework represented wealth—that they forgot their ostentatious hatred and contempt for the contriki.

When the hands of watch and clock finally approached the longed-for hour, Yekaterina Vassilyevna lifted her dignified bulk out of the chair, had the nurse remove her gown and help her into her fur coat, and without acknowledgment tripped off on her pretty little feet—Russian women often have remarkably small feet.

Certainly the most singular phenomenon among all the free doctors with whom I worked was the chief woman physician of the prisoners' hospital for the northern gold-mining region. Nina Vladimirovna was a Caucasian woman from Ossetia. The savagery of her native Caucasian mountain village repeatedly broke through the thin veneer of higher education that she had acquired in Moscow.

This younger generation of Soviet physicians learn their profession the way a trade is learned. They do not attend the university, where they would have an opportunity to broaden their general culture; they go to a medical institute where they are taught nothing but professional subjects.

At twenty-eight Nina Vladimirovna was the head of a hospital for five hundred patients, which she always spoke of as "my" hospital. She behaved like a *pomeshchitsa,* a great lady and landowner of Tsarist times, and considered the entire staff of the hospital her personal serfs. With her fleshy hand, covered with black down, she once took hold of a neglectful orderly and pulled his hair until he screamed. At another time the statistician, a prisoner who had held that office for many years, aroused her displeasure. She threw the telephone at his head. When a doctor dared to contradict her, she threw ink eradicator into his face. She bawled out the doctors and nurses in the presence of the patients—using expressions that would have done credit to an old sailor. "Idiot" and "ass" were, with her, practically endearments.

Since the dozen-odd barracks of this hospital were located in total isolation in the midst of the forest, there were neither guards nor a camp administration. She united in her own stout person the threefold power of head doctor, camp commandant, and commander of the guard.

She lived in a frame cottage consisting of three rooms and a kitchenette that was attached to the hospital barrack. An elderly male prisoner kept house for her. This man, although he received a full measure of slaps and scolding, was her spy in the hospital and her confidant concerning all her private affairs. His position with her was unassailable, all the more since he had a considerable talent for business speculations, which he carried out partly for her benefit, partly for his own, using articles which generally turned out to be hospital property.

If you wanted to keep your post in this hospital, you not only had to put up with Nina's whims and explosions, but you also had to curry favor with the woman. You were never safe from her day or night; she would appear suddenly in your ward at the most unlikely hours, and not the slightest fault escaped her fiery black eyes. Ignoring the sleeping patients, she would work herself up into a fit of rage, to which the sleepy nurse, orderly, or alarmed doctor would listen in tremulous silence. She was likely to switch off her fury with equal suddenness if someone came along whom she liked— but one couldn't be sure how long her friendliness would last.

If you came into her office with prescription books or other documents that required her signature, you never knew how the interview would turn out. It was best to find out what her highness's mood was beforehand. If someone had put her into a bad humor she might suddenly stamp her feet, clench her fists, and chase everyone out of the room—except the temporary object of her good will, to whom she would shout an imperious, "Stay!" Then that person would have to sit by, an embarrassed witness, until her furious curses gradually dissolved into hysterical sobbing and she would cry out with tear-stained face that all were conspiring against her, and plotting her ruin.

At the same time she was an excellent administrator; during the period of her "reign" the hospital was in exemplary condition. Her energy and tenacity were inexhaustible. Once she set her mind on something, as, for example, building a greenhouse to raise tomatoes, she would if necessary obtain the glass from Magadan more than three hundred miles away. Naturally, a good part of the tomatoes were eaten by herself and her superiors in the camp and public health administrations of the gold-mining region, and very few of the tomatoes reached the patients. But had it not been for her, no patients at all would have received so much as half a tomato. During the summer months she had a prisoner apply himself exclusively to fishing. She also benefited from this, but it was owing to her initiative that the diet of at least the weakest prisoner-patients received the valuable addition of fresh fish.

She felt neither hatred nor contempt for the prisoners, no more than a landowner of earlier times would have hated his serfs. She looked upon them as tools supplied by nature to increase her wealth, as the prerequisites for her position of power. But she was able to pity them, and in spite of her tyrannical ways she felt a great deal of affection for prisoners who had worked with her for some time.

Every spring at the beginning of the gold season there came a day when the hospital was surrounded by guards, under the personal charge of Captain Selesnyov, the administrative chief of the northern gold-mine area. All the prisoners who could stand on their feet were rounded up, loaded into trucks and sent off to the mines.

Nina would battle heroically for the workers whom she would normally swear at. This one, she would say, looked strong but was inwardly rotten with disease; some other men were far too old for the mines; still others had to stay because the hospital simply could not get along without them. All her pleas, explanations and demands bounced off the broad back and the gilt epaulets of Selesnyov, the man with the immobile face whom no one ever saw smiling.

And when at last the trucks with "her" prisoners rolled away, Nina would stand looking after them, her eyes filled with tears.

The health inspector for Elgen was a gray-haired old man whose fate had somehow taken him to Kolyma. He did not fit in with the administrative set-up at all, for he was a thoughtful, kindly person.

At that time I was working in a forest camp where, in addition to wood chopping, I had to care for the sick. I complained to him that there were a great many sick prisoners in camp, very few of whom were ever excused from a day's labor. He nodded understandingly and said, "The camp exists to turn the screws on the prisoners tighter and tighter, and we medical men exist to patiently loosen them again just a little bit. We are not permitted to do more."

Self-Mutilation

> *Work is a matter of honor, the heroism*
> *and the glory of every Soviet citizen.*
> STALIN

Even in camp we were never spared the banners, slogans, mottos, and quotations from Stalin which are the universal madness of the Soviet Union.

Above the entrance to the dining room were the words: "He who does not work shall not eat."

There was no doubt that you went hungry in camp if you did not work. Unfortunately those who worked also went hungry.

On all the walls were signs: "Place yourself in the ranks of the best workers." The best workers were those who were still fresh, whose energies had not yet been sapped. There was no advice on how a prisoner who had undergone many years of near-starvation was to get up the strength to be a "best worker."

"Two-hundred percenters, teach the others to imitate you!"

The recipe: do as little as possible and bribe the brigadier with money or alcohol, preferably both, so that he will credit others' labor to you, thus making you a two-hundred percenter. Women could repay such a service on the part of the brigadier without money or alcohol.

"Honest work is the way to early release!"

In some countries there are dog races in which the dogs pursue mechanical rabbits running on a track. The moment the first dog reaches the goal, the current is turned off and the rabbit disappears before the eyes of the bewildered racer. It it as easy for a Soviet prisoner who works honestly to win an early release as it is for the dog to catch the rabbit.

"Cleanliness makes for health."

Unfortunately, cleanliness alone won't do it.

Only the doctor can release a prisoner from work. Refusal to work is punished by a sentence in the lockup. A notation of the case is made and signed by the camp commander, the commander of the guard, and the doctor. From three to five such notations are sufficient to bring a work-shirker to trial. In peacetime he was given additional sentences of from five to ten years on the basis of Paragraph 58, Article 14: counter-revolutionary sabotage. During wartime counterrevolutionaries who refused to work were shot; criminals usually got off with an additional sentence of ten years.

In general, cases of refusal to work among the so-called counterrevolutionaries are comparatively rare. It is the criminals who try to evade all kinds of work. They have usually turned to crime because of their dislike for work, and regular work is agony for them. For a few weeks at a time they will pitch in and break all records at work—and then they are through with it. They loaf around devising plans for getting into the hospital. Some of them drink salted water. They swell up and are excused from work. Some may steal a syringe from the infirmary and inject kerosene under their skin. This results in bloody boils which keep them in the hospital for weeks.

Or in the morning, before departing for work, others may wrap a wet foot-rag around one of their feet. In the evening they come back with third-degree frostbite in their toes. The same trick can be used on the fingers.

There is another method that many criminals have recourse to. They lay their left hand on a block of wood and with an axe cut off their three middle fingers, leaving the little finger and the thumb. With two fingers they cannot hold a wheelbarrow in the gold mines, but when they are ultimately released they can still do other kinds of work with a crippled hand.

Acid and crayon are rubbed into the eyelids, producing a syndrome similar to that of trachoma. The criminals also have a recipe, which they keep strictly secret, for producing symptoms typical of syphilis.

Out of the stems and roots of *makhorka*, a kind of ersatz tobacco, they make an infusion which produces heart murmurs and fever. They also rub their armpits with onions or garlic before their temperature is taken. This produces a higher reading, but onions are worth fifty rubles apiece in Kolyma and are very rare. Another method to raise the temperature is to rub the mercury end of the thermometer when they are unobserved. The friction heats the bulb and makes the reading higher.

Sciatica is one of the favorite camp sicknesses, but a good many prisoners have to limp dejectedly off to work because they tried to make too much of a good thing and pretended to have sciatica on both sides—which is impossible.

A great many prisoners simulate insanity, some for years. There are special insane asylums for prisoners. But even genuine and proved mental disease is no grounds for the release of a prisoner in the Soviet Union.

Prisoners are never informed beforehand when they are being transferred from one camp to another. When the trucks are ready and waiting, the prisoners destined for shipment are bruskly ordered out of the barrack with their bundles and loaded like so much baggage. If a criminal has an idea that the new camp will be worse for him than his present one, he will at the last moment cut open the surface of his abdomen. Criminals are so skillful at this that they never injure their internal organs. In fact, such cases are so frequent that the prisoner is not even sent to the hospital. The gaping wound is sewed up in the camp infirmary, and if the criminal has bad luck he will at most gain half an hour by his self-mutilation. Then he will be tossed into the truck.

Female criminals trying to escape transportation will strip off all their clothes and crawl naked up to the top of the board platforms. Crouching there they will respond to all orders to go to the truck with a torrent of curses. Finally two guards will come, tie the screaming and kicking woman's hands and feet and throw her into the truck. Usually some sympathetic person will toss her clothes in after her, so that she can dress during the ride.

Every prisoner welcomes a broken arm or leg—and the bones of sufferers from scurvy break easily. Here, too, the prisoners will assist chance if they have the opportunity. For example, they will hold their leg between moving hand-trucks in the mines.

Especially envied are the prisoners with large trophic boils, which also are common to scorbutics. However, such boils have to be extraordinarily large to win a prisoner release from work. The smaller scorbutic sores, which may persist for years, do not count.

Deafness, dumbness, and paralysis are sometimes simulated for years, since many of the camps are without qualified doctors. In the hospitals false paralysis is uncovered in the following fashion. The malingerer is placed on the operating table and given a slight anesthesia. The moment he wakes up, when he is not yet fully conscious, he is placed on his feet and his name is called. Automatically he will take a few steps. As soon as he becomes fully conscious he will let himself collapse to the floor—but by then it is too late; the doctors have already had convincing proof that his legs are quite capable of supporting him.

Proved cases of malingering and self-mutilation are punishable, and if there is a medical report on the case, the prisoner will have at least two years added to his sentence. But doctors rarely make such a report if there is any way to avoid it. And the regulation that self-mutilators are allowed no more than thirteen days in the hospital is generally evaded.

Suicide

The last way out is suicide. This is a way never chosen by the criminals, though it is occasionally taken by male counterrevolutionaries and less frequently by female counterrevolutionaries. The chief reason for the relatively low rate of suicides is the fact that prisoners are never alone. In the barracks and at work they are constantly surrounded by other prisoners or by guards. The very fact that thousands of others are enduring the same fate tends to suppress the thought of suicide.

There is an incessant flow of rumors to the effect that revision of cases, amnesty, relaxation of the rules, or improvement in the rations are "on the way." No one believes these rumors; they are laughed at, but they nevertheless leave a lingering spark of hope.

Women are far more enduring than men. A man can reach a point of exhaustion where he no longer recognizes anything but food and sleep. A woman will still try to preserve a remnant of her humanity. And women are also more adaptable to unaccustomed physical labor. Strictly speaking, wood chopping is lighter than the work in the gold mines, from which women are exempt. But the transition from working as a stenographer, housewife, or teacher to wood chopping is no easier than the transformation of an intellectual into a gold miner. In almost every case it was the intellectual who chose voluntary death by freezing, hanging, or plunging from the tower of the refinery into the depths of the mine, rather than endure the slow, deadly torture of the camp.

Members of the family are not informed, no matter whether death is "natural" or violent. The fact is entered into the statistics, and the prisoners' documents are transferred to another file which bears the identifying mark: "File Number 3."

The Morgue

"Petya," the nurse called, laying the used syringe into the sterilizer to be boiled. Petya, the orderly, a pickpocket who was serving his fifth camp sentence, although he was just twenty-five years old, stuck his shorn head with its prominent ears in at the door of the office.

"Petya, Volkov asked me to wish you a long life."

Petya was not particularly shocked at thus learning that Volkov had died. Since he had been working in this ward of the prisoners' hospital, he had seen so many die that death no longer made any impression upon him.

"Shall we take him out tonight, nurse?"

The nurse looked at the clock with its iron weights shaped like pine cones. How had such clocks got to Kolyma, she wondered? It was shortly after midnight.

"Yes, in two hours you can take him to the morgue. Why leave him lying with the patients all night? Where is Nyura?"

"Washing the floor."

"She'll just about finish by then. Bring me a board for Volkov."

While she wrote the dead man's name and dates on the

little board, Petya busied himself with the body. The shirt and underwear had to be removed, for they were hospital property—prisoners were buried naked. Then he drew the blanket over the sunken, yellowish face with its closed eyes.

"A good nurse," Petya murmured to himself. "She even closed his eyes. The others don't trouble about it."

Respectfully, he watched her writing the last words on the board. Petya could not write. Then, with a piece of bandage, he tied the slat to the body's big toe. After that he looked around for Nyura.

Nyura was fifteen years older than Petya, but he loved her dearly. She was contrik, not a criminal. All her life she had worked hard. Her youth had been spent in a small village. Later, in the turmoil of revolution and civil war, she came to the city and worked in a factory. By the time of her arrest she was the mother of four children and lived in a small worker's flat in a town in Byelorussia. But her mother was Polish, and in 1938 in the Soviet Union that was as dangerous as having a Jewish mother in Hitler Germany. Convicted of counterrevolutionary activity and sentenced to ten years in camp, she was transported more than eight thousand miles to Kolyma to pay for a nonexistent crime.

Nyura worked on the assumption that all men were good who did not emphatically prove that they were not. And even when they did, she was still in doubt, still wondered whether she might not have been mistaken. A friendly manner was as much part of her as her pink skin, the wrinkles at the corners of her gray eyes, and the clean shawl which she wore tied with neat severity around her straight blonde hair.

She worked as an orderly in the hospital, but no one ever dreamed of addressing her with the customary, *"Sanitarka."* Everyone called her Nyanya, the name Russian children give their "nannies"—and to her, all—doctors, patients, and Petya the pickpocket—were her children. Her voice was not especially tender or pleasant, nor were her hands; but it had a kindly sound, as her hands had a kindly touch. Other mothers who had been parted from their children became in their sorrow harsh and embittered. But Nyura, who had wept over her children continually during the first months of her imprisonment, could not lock up her maternal feelings within herself.

Petya was as devoted as a dog to her. Most of the women he had known were prostitutes and thieves. Kicked about from early childhood, without a home or parents, he had spent his boyhood riding the "rods" of railroad cars. He never cared where the trains were going, as long as it was somewhere in the south; he could spend the winter in a warm climate, begging for his food, and if the going got tough he could steal what he needed.

Sometimes he would band together with one or two other boys, until they got separated somewhere in the vast expanses of the country. Once he was caught and taken to a children's colony. But for him the steppes were home, the starry sky a roof; he had spent his days dozing on cliffs above the Black Sea, and the rattling of railroad-car wheels was music to him. He could not endure the monotonous work and discipline of the educational colony, and on the first warm day he ran away.

Next time he was sent to prison for theft, and from prison to a penal colony. Branded as a criminal, he became a criminal. From then on he worked together with members of the "profession." Adult criminals taught him the tricks of the trade. Camp was his school, bandits were his teachers. In

1938 he was sent to Kolyma as a recidivist, a criminal with several convictions.

After recovering from an illness he stayed in the prisoners' hospital as an orderly. He was a dour-looking fellow with dark, sullen eyes and a harsh twist to his mouth. He spoke as little as possible—until Nyura came.

Nyura was like a little stove, and like a freezing animal he crept close to her to receive her warmth. Silently he crouched near her, incapable of saying what he felt for her, for this was the first time any human being had been simply good to him. Gradually words came to him, words he had not known were in him; gradually he learned how to smile as he had never smiled before. Petya, who always had shirked work, would run headlong out into a blizzard, eagerly swinging the hated water pail, because Nyura needed water and Nyura must not carry anything if he could do it for her.

Now she was moving along the floor with her scrub cloth, reaching under the cots that stood side by side. The patients were all asleep except for a dropsical cardiac patient who was in a half-sitting position—a block of wood had been placed under the straw mattress to prop up his back—and who sat brooding, his inflamed eyes open, his breathing rapid and painful.

Opposite him stood the cot with the dead man. Above the table in the center of the barrack hung the burning electric bulb, shielded for the night with a scrap of blue muslin. Now and then the cardiac patient looked at the cot where Volkov lay beneath his blanket. Volkov was so emaciated that only his head made any hump under the blanket. Not that he felt particularly sorry for Volkov; the man had been an unpleasant, quarrelsome patient. But to die like this, in this barrack, all alone, without a single familiar face, a single

263

hand to cling to when the end came—the cardiac patient groaned softly to himself.

Nyura was finished with her work. Petya went out behind the barrack and dumped the dirty water. This was forbidden, but it was snowing anyhow and the spot was almost instantly covered by fresh snowflakes.

Then they placed the dead man on a stretcher, spread the blanket over the stiff, naked body, and carried him out. Only the left foot with the board attached to the big toe showed out of the blanket—but the Kolyma winter could no longer harm Volkov's feet.

They put on their wadded jackets and tramped out into the snow. The commander of the guard glanced quickly at the stretcher and let them pass. The morgue was outside the hospital zone. They walked down the deserted road, past the laboratory and a two-story dwelling house, until they came to the small, isolated frame building.

Outside, a figure was leaning against the doorjamb. Petya started in fright: the figure was a corpse. He overcame his fear and knocked. It took some time before Kolya, the convict guardian of the dead, opened the door.

"What kind of helper have you got there?" Petya asked.

Kolya grinned. "That's the best way to keep the guards away. Never fails. Not one of them comes by when I have a cadaver standing out there. They used to come sniffing around here now and then. Now I can have a glass in peace whenever I want, and when Katya is on the night shift and drops by we aren't disturbed when we . . ." Leaving the sentence unfinished, he ran his tongue over his full lips and glanced at Nyura out of the corners of his eyes to see whether she might be interested in having a little love among the dead.

But Nyura's eyes looked past him at the corpses which lay

piled up along the walls all around the dissection table. Now Volkov lay there too as though he had never breathed or spoken. His arm dangled down and his head hung over the legs of the corpse beneath him.

"They'll be up for autopsy tomorrow," Kolya said, prodding the pile of frozen corpses with his toe. "I'll have to warm the place up so that they'll be thawed out in time." He busied himself about the small iron stove. "If you want to have a smoke, Petya, you two can stay here a while."

He opened a door which led to a small partitioned-off room behind the dissection room. There was a cot in it. On shelves around the walls stood glass vessels containing hearts, kidneys, and stomachs in alcohol. Kolya closed the door behind them and went back to his corpses.

They were alone. But Petya did not roll a cigarette. He looked at Nyura, then at the closed door and the cot. On the window sill a kerosene lamp was smoking. He blew it out and took hold of the woman. At first Nyura resisted; then she yielded.

When Kolya let them out, Petya mumbled casually, "The lamp went out, Kolya. I guess it's out of kerosene."

"That's all right," Kolya growled understandingly, and he closed the door behind them.

This time, as they passed the corpse leaning against the doorjamb, Petya threw it a look of gratitude.

10. The Tradition
of the Potemkin Villages

Wallace in Magadan

NONE OF THE numerous high commissions ever aroused so much excitement as Wallace's visit to Kolyma during the war. Some time before the visit took place, a persistent rumor warmed the souls of the freezing prisoners; in return for help in the war the Soviet Union was going to cede Kolyma to the United States. Even the soberest and most reasonable of the prisoners conceded the possibility, and long discussions were held as to whether in that case the prisoners would also be turned over to America. It was a typical prisoners' fairy tale, as absurd as it was tenacious. And it received a tremendous stimulus when news came of the impending visit of the American Vice-President.

Wallace traveled through the Asiatic portions of the Soviet Union in order to observe the capacity of Soviet industry. I do not know what he saw in the rest of Soviet Asia, but in Kolyma the NKVD carried off its job with flying colors. Wallace saw nothing at all of this frozen hell with its hundreds of thousands of the damned.

The access roads to Magadan were lined with wooden watch towers. In honor of Wallace these towers were razed in a single night.

At the edge of the city there were several prison camps, among them the large women's camp with its several thousand inmates. These prisoners worked in various places throughout the city. Every prisoner who was there at the time owes Mr. Wallace a debt of gratitude. For it was owing to his visit that for the first and last time the prisoners had three successive holidays. On the day of his arrival, the day of his visit and the day of his departure, not a single prisoner was allowed to leave the camp.

This was not enough. Although the route for Mr. Wallace and his suite was carefully prepared in advance, there was still the possibility that by mischance the visitor would catch sight of the prisoners in the camp yard—which would not have been an edifying spectacle. Therefore, on orders from above, movies were shown to the prisoners from morning till night for three days. No prisoners went walking in the yard.

To some extent the prisoners of Magadan did repay him, but probably Mr. Wallace did not know it. How could it occur to him that the actors whose performance he enjoyed one evening in the Gorky Theater of Magadan were mostly prisoners? He never met any of these actors, because immediately after the curtain fell they were loaded aboard a truck and returned to the camp. After all, it would have been embarrassing if one of the actors had happened to know English and had mentioned to Mr. Wallace that he was one of hundreds of thousands of innocent prisoners serving a ten-year sentence in Kolyma.

And how could Mr. Wallace know that the city of Magadan, which had risen so swiftly out of the wilderness, had been built exclusively by prison labor; that women prisoners had carried the beams and bricks to the building sites?

He probably did not realize that he had sowed confusion among the prettily dressed swineherd girls at the model farm on the twenty-third kilometer from Magadan by asking them a harmless question about the pigs. For these girls were not swineherds at all; they were a group of good-looking office girls who had been ordered to play a part especially for Mr. Wallace's visit. They took the place of prisoners who actually did take care of the swine. However, the interpreter saved the situation and the visit went off smoothly.

Mr. Wallace was also gratified to note the rich assortment of Russian merchandise in the show windows of Magadan. He made a point of going into a store to examine the Russian products and to buy some trivial item. The citizenry of Magadan were even more amazed than Mr. Wallace at the Russian goods that appeared overnight in the shop windows, because for the past two years all the—strictly rationed—goods which could be bought had been of American origin. But the NKVD had gone to the trouble of digging stuff up from the remotest stores and precious private hoards in order to impress Mr. Wallace. A citizen of Magadan with presence of mind slipped into the store at the same time as the important visitor and bought a food delicacy that had long since vanished from the channels of trade. Another wanted to follow his example, but by that time Mr. Wallace had left, and this citizen was laconically informed that the articles were "not for sale."

Then Mr. Wallace went home and published his enthusiastic report on Soviet Asia. The watch towers were put up again, the prisoners sent out to work again, and in the empty shop windows were to be seen nothing but a few dusty and mournful boxes of matches.

Devyatka

Devyat means "nine" in Russian. A certain store in Magadan is popularly called *devyatka,* that is, the "store for the nine." Only nine families carry the special pass which entitles them to make purchases in this store.

Who are the privileged persons in the "land of the workers and peasants" who have access to the treasures of this luxury store, where even during the war everything was available, from oranges, chocolate, and foreign preserves to the most select textiles, fine shoes, and American cigarettes—all things that the ordinary Soviet citizen has not even dreamed of having for thirty years? Who are the "heroes of labor" who, with their families, are entitled to special rewards? They are:

1. The chief of the Dalstroi Trust, the supreme head of Kolyma, Indigirka and Chukotsk—Lieutenant General Nikishov.
2. His deputy, Colonel Gakayev.
3. The chief of the political administration.
4. The chief of procurement.
5. The chief of the NKVD troops in Kolyma.
6. The chief of the guard troops in Kolyma.
7. The chief of the regular troops in Kolyma.
8. The chief of the economic department.
9. The chief of the health department of all the camps of Kolyma, Indigirka, and Chukostk.

Not another soul can enter this store, no matter how honestly he may have earned his money. This accords beautifully with the basic principle of full-fledged socialism, which according to Stalin has already been attained: "From each according to his abilities; to each according to his needs."

Article 119 of the Constitution of the USSR:
The citizens of the USSR have the right to recreation

Colonel Gakayev, who has been promoted to the post of Nikishov's deputy, was formerly administrative chief for the northern gold-mining district of Kolyma (SGPU). The administrative seat is Yagodnoye, a fair-sized settlement with pretty frame houses at the foot of the mountains.

Gakayev, a Caucasian by birth, was as feared as any Asiatic despot. With an unscrupulousness and brutality which has scarcely been equaled even by the other slave drivers who rule in this area, he fulfilled and overfulfilled the plan for the extraction of gold. This won him a nice bonus of fifty thousand rubles in a single year.

Not only the prisoners were exposed to his fits of Caucasian savagery; the free populace of his realm had constantly to expect some new chicanery, for he never tired of inventing some way to cheat them. The greater part of this population, of course, consisted of former prisoners who were employed partly in the gold mines, partly as white-collar workers and laborers of all sorts in Yagodnoye itself. Gakayev not only organized their working hours, but their leisure hours as well.

Every Sunday a dozen trucks stood ready to take these workers to the gold mines where they refined gold all day long as "voluntary shock-troop workers."

270

The Tradition of the Potemkin Villages

The streets of Yagodnoye were utterly deserted on Sundays. No one dared to go out. Even people who had medical certificates stating that they were not to be employed in such "voluntary" work, and even those who were indispensable in the city, such as doctors, were afraid to venture out on the streets. If anyone encountered Gakayev on a Sunday he was out of luck. Gakayev would put up with no discussions; he would requisition the nearest car, order his victim into it, and half throw him in if he did not move fast enough. All the while he would rain juicy curses upon the man and threaten to bring him to trial as a saboteur.

In Yagodnoye there was a volleyball court—volleyball being a favorite sport in the Soviet Union. It was seldom used, for the summer in Kolyma is all too brief, but now and then a few young men would get together there for a game. After all, they had to do something else besides work, play cards, and drink. So they thought, at any rate, and after spending a Sunday at the gold mines they relaxed by playing ball in the milky light of the bright summer nights, when there is neither twilight nor darkness.

Gakayev did not think they ought to relax. He came by one evening, saw the young men at their game, and was so furious that for a moment the usual curses froze on his lips. The next moment he made up for this omission by roaring with redoubled volume; his bull neck swelled and flushed red with rage. So that was the way they had worked at the gold mine—so hard that they had energy to squander on volleyball!

Next day, on orders from Colonel Gakayev, the volleyball court at Yagodnoye was blown up.

11. After the War

The "Overtimers"

Prisoners the world over count the years, months and weeks, and finally the days, to their liberation. I had taken a matchbox and put in one match for every month of my term. Five years are sixty months—sixty matches. Every month I would take out another match. One day in the summer of 1942 I threw away the last match.

And then nothing happened.

As ever, the rail screeched for us to march out in the morning; as ever, the guards cursed; as ever, the overseers bawled in a hundred different inflections: "Davai, davai! Bystrey, bystrey!" (Get going, get going! Faster, faster!) As ever we sweated under the burden of logs and sacks and bricks, disputed for the butt of a cigarette that had already been smoked by four others, froze wretchedly in front of the camp gates until we were at last allowed to pass through, were counted and counted and counted, stared into the scraped soup-bowl to see whether by some miracle it would fill up again, until a punch in the ribs from someone impatiently

272

waiting to eat would knock us off the bench and we would crawl back to the planks and the bedbugs—as ever.

A year and a half after I had discarded the sixtieth match the commander of the guard handed me a slip of paper at evening roll call and asked for my signature. It read:

"The prisoner, Elinor Lipper, sentenced to five years in corrective labor camp, has completed her term of punishment. However, she is to be retained in camp until the end of the war. She has been informed of this decision."

And days, weeks, months, years passed, hope passed, life passed. Faster, faster. Get going, get going. Weariness, hunger, cold. To lie for once in a clean bed, to be alone for a day, to live for a single day without hearing the clang of the rail. . . . What does an apple smell like? Do railroads still run somewhere in the world? In this wilderness there was not even a sparrow. But there was a sky, with a roaring, glistening triangle in it. Three planes, the center one laden with gold, escorts to either side. Gold for America. . . .

Years passed. May 1945 came—the day of victory, with meetings and speeches. Prisoners embraced one another, their eyes filled with tears of happiness, of hope.

And nothing happened.

Days and weeks and months and years passed. The year of victory, 1945, passed. The year 1946 passed. That was the tenth year of my imprisonment. Old prisoners died, old prisoners were released, and again and again the ships spewed forth from their holds new prisoners. One woman prisoner more or less—who cared?

To all my letters, petitions, inquiries: "When will you release me?" I received the stereotype reply: "We are waiting for an order from Moscow."

Slave and starve, slave and freeze, work faster, faster, get going, get going!

"Hello there, Elinor, I have a book that would interest you."

"Interest me? The devil with your book. I want freedom."

"Elinor, there's a movie at the club tonight."

"The devil with your movie. I want freedom."

"Elinor, they say the overtimers are going to be released soon."

"The devil with your fairy stories. I don't believe anything they say any more."

A prisoner who has served his sentence is not released automatically. The camp sends a conduct report to the proper authorities and must receive a confirmation of release. During the war the *bytoviki* were released. These were persons who had violated the law in some manner, but who were not convicted either as counterrevolutionaries or as ordinary criminals. They formed a very small percentage of the camp population. Criminals were also released, with the exception of those convicted of banditry. Of those convicted as counterrevolutionaries, only those charged with being members of the family of convicts, with being SOE's (socially dangerous elements) and with having failed to make a denunciation, were released during the war.

All other persons convicted on some counterrevolutionary charge or sentenced by the OSO (the invisible panel of judges) were not released at the termination of their sentence so long as the war lasted. They were all informed that they were being held in camp until the end of the war. These people were called *peresidzhiki,* "overtimers." However, they were not released immediately after the end of the war

274

either; their releases began to come through by list in the spring of 1946, and went alphabetically, so that persons whose names began with A or B were at liberty by May, while those at the end of the alphabet were kept in camp until late fall. But even then some individuals who had been convicted as Trotskyists were still detained. When I left Kolyma at the end of 1946, they were still waiting for a decision, although many had already served ten years instead of their original sentences of five years.

After Release

Every prisoner who is being released receives a paper known as Form Number 25. It is valid only at the place of issue and does not permit the recipient to travel to other places. Only after some time has passed does the former prisoner receive his internal passport. (No Soviet citizen receives an external passport except those few whom the government is sending abroad.) This internal passport is marked with a rubber stamp which is called the "minus 135." This means that the bearer may not settle in any of the 135 largest cities of the Soviet Union, or within sixty miles of them, nor in any border areas or administrative centers. He is also forbidden to return to his former residence. When this document is made out, the former prisoner must indicate where he wants to settle; if the place is approved, it is written down in his passport.

The state pays a released prisoner's traveling expenses from the camp to his place of settlement. Wherever he goes, he is at once branded as a former convict. These regulations apply to the entire Soviet Union.

The prisoner who is released in Kolyma is subject to additional restrictions. If he is under fifty and not officially declared an invalid by the medical labor commission, he may not leave Kolyma. Persons over fifty will not be allowed to leave if their skills happen to be urgently needed in Kolyma, that is, if they are doctors, geologists, engineers, chemists, bookkeepers, cooks, tailors. . . .

There is a special category for released prisoners of German origin who before their arrest possessed Soviet citizenship. Among these are Volga Germans, Siberian Germans, German exiles and immigrants, and German Jews. All of them are forced to sign a statement to the effect that they will be settled as colonists in Kolyma, usually for a period of six years, sometimes for an unlimited time.

Except for the women and a few others, they are settled in Tyenki, a remote area (of Kolyma!), where they must live in community barracks. Almost all the work is heavy physical labor. They do not have the right to leave their assigned place of work, and they are closely supervised by the NKVD.

Released foreigners who never possessed Soviet citizenship are deported to their native lands. This is what happened to me.*

Since the number of free citizens has gradually swelled with the release of prisoners, there are now gold mines where

* This law is observed in the case of the nationals of a few countries only—France, Holland, Switzerland, e.g., whose governments must still be reckoned with by the USSR. As indicated above, thousands of German nationals who fled to Russia after 1933 were imprisoned, and the survivors, when released, had to stay in the USSR. This applies also to many Spanish "Loyalists," and to thousands from the countries of eastern Europe now behind the Iron Curtain. All these comprise the overwhelming majority of foreign radicals trapped in the USSR. This explains why so few books like this have been written—so few have returned to tell. The author's release was due to the active intervention of the Swiss authorities, because she had become a Swiss national by marriage in 1935.

only free workers are employed. Among these are the Verkhny At-uryakh mine in the northern mining district; the near-by Nizhny At-uryakh mine, also called the Maxim Gorky mine, is worked by prisoners.

There is a tendency to employ only free citizens in the entire northern mining district, while in recent years prisoners have been sent out to still more remote mines—along the course of the Indigirka, where there are also large gold mines and prison camps, and to the Chukotskiy Peninsula on the Arctic Circle, an independent administrative district (Chukstroi) which is to be removed from the supervision of the Dalstroi Trust.

The Mill Grinds

Aside from criminals, peasants formed the main body of so-called counterrevolutionary prisoners during the thirties. After the assassination of Kirov in 1934, large contingents of workers and intellectuals were sent to the camps. At the end of 1936 and in 1937 and 1938 there began an endless stream of counterrevolutionaries from all classes of the population and from all the towns and villages of the Union republics. In 1939 and 1940 came the Poles who were arrested in large numbers after the partition of their country. In 1941 they enjoyed an amnesty, since they were to be formed into a Polish army of liberation to fight Hitler.

People from the Balkan countries, many of them Jews, who had fled before Hitler's armies, were arrested immediately after they crossed the borders of the Soviet Union and were sentenced to either three years as border violators or to eight years as suspected spies. Both groups had to do time for eight years, since the border violators were not released during the war. In 1940 a ship arrived in Kolyma with six hun-

dred such refugees. At the end of the war sixty returned to
their native lands; in the gold mines of Kolyma the others
had given up the lives they had hoped to save by fleeing to
the Soviet Union.

In 1941 a new category of prisoners came in, the *ukazniki*.
A ukase was issued which provided that any worker who left
his job in a war plant, no matter for what reasons, was subject to from six to eight years of imprisonment. Hundreds of
young girls between the ages of eighteen and twenty were
sent to Kolyma for running away to their villages because
they could no longer endure the starvation in the cities where
they had been forced to work. Some had only gone back home
for a few days to visit a sick mother, but the factory manager
would not give them any days off and when they returned
they were arrested. They came as adolescents and were instantly transformed by Kolyma into full-fledged prostitutes.
Thousands of workers were sent into the Kolyma camps as
ukazniki, for some petty misdemeanor. These prisoners
were given amnesties when the war ended in 1945, but those
who had not been physically wrecked were morally shattered.

In 1944 and 1945, when the Soviet armies were advancing
westward, prisoners came from the liberated areas. Thousands
of young Latvians and Lithuanians were first kept prisoner
in Kolyma and then forced to become colonists under the
name of "special contingents."

Thousands of people who had unwillingly endured the
German occupation were convicted of treason and sent to
Kolyma on ten-year sentences solely for this reason, or because they were victims of the flourishing practice of denunciation.

At this time other hundreds of young girls between the
ages of seventeen and twenty-two were sent to Kolyma on

charges of treason. These were western Ukrainians—after the war Poland ceded western Ukraine to the Soviet Union—who had belonged to the *bandyerovtsi* organization. Polish partisans later told me that this organization had committed the most frightful and inhuman crimes against both Polish and Soviet citizens, and that it had carried out many pogroms, urged on by the Germans, the Ukrainian nationalists, the priests, and the members' own savagery. They had been arrested and were being punished. But why had Soviet officers, interrogating seventeen-year-old girls, broken the girls' collarbones and kicked in their ribs with heavy military boots, so that they lay spitting blood in the prison hospitals of Kolyma? Certainly such treatment had not convinced any of them that what they had done was evil. They died with tin medallions of the Virgin on their shattered chests, and with hatred in their eyes.

And then, in 1946, the homecomers came to Kolyma. These were women and girls whom the Germans had carried off from the Ukraine to Germany, where they had been put to work in Nazi munitions plants. The war had ended and the slave laborers, homesick and eager, at last boarded the trains for the Soviet Union. The same fate was reserved for them as for the unfortunates who had been taken prisoner by the Germans—for a soldier of the Soviet Army was not supposed to have been taken prisoner; he should have fought to the death.

There were no prisoner-of-war camps for Germans in Kolyma, but there were such camps for Japanese prisoners. Their camps were isolated from the Russian penal camps. The inmates worked only eight hours a day, and their own former officers, who did not have to do any physical work, functioned as brigadiers. Usually they were employed in road building. They received a fixed rice ration which was independent of the amount of work they did. Later, however, they shifted to bread—apparently bread was more satisfying under the climatic conditions, which the Japanese found very hard to adjust to.

Before the war, during the war, and after the war, continuous new hordes of prisoners were ground to dust. The snows of Kolyma covered the graves; the gold mines along the Indigirka swallowed more and more prisoners; the vast Arctic peninsula of Chukotsk, rich in coal, uranium, and other metals, demanded more and more laborers.

No one knows their names. No one can count the dead.

But the Soviet Union is rich and mighty, and the Soviet people stand united behind their Leader. So it is said, so written. United? Who then are these twelve million prisoners —a figure the NKVD officials repeatedly confirm—who are constantly filling the prisons and camps of the Soviet Union? If they are really opponents of the regime, then the government can rule only by suppressing with brute force twelve millions of the people in whose name it rules. On the other hand, if they are innocent victims, as in fact they are, who can assert that this regime and its leaders are what they say they are, the liberators of the people?

Last Encounters with Kolyma Prisoners

In the X-ray room of the Central Hospital of the USVITL on the twenty-third kilometer the patients from various wards wait in the dark anteroom. Only when the barrack door is opened to admit a new patient does light fall for a moment upon the waiting group. All the women are wearing hospital clothing, men's undershirts and long underwear, tied with ribbons at their ankles; over this costume they have draped a sheet or blanket.

Beside me a young woman is coughing, the barking, hoarse, tormented cough of the tubercular. Several criminals are exchanging the pithy curses which are used by these people in place of the normal greetings. From her subdued sighs I gather that the young woman is not yet used to such expressions, which means that she cannot have been in Kolyma very long. We strike up a conversation.

She arrived with the last shipment and was sent directly from the port to the hospital. Sentenced to ten years imprisonment, she still does not know what camp means. Probably she will never find out. Since she is obviously tubercular, she will be sent from hospital to hospital, from invalid camp to invalid camp, and will go on coughing and spitting blood until the end. Usually death is quickly merciful to such patients, for the Yakut climate and the Soviet starvation rations speed them on their way.

She contracted tuberculosis, not in Soviet prisons, but among the Nazis. She was seventeen years old when the Germans carried her off from her native Ukraine to the Ruhr, where she was forced to work in the Krupp munitions factories. It was there that the fever and coughing began; she was hospitalized and spent months in bed. After a while she was sent back to the factory, and worked until the war ended.

Because she coughed she was unable to join in the group singing with the other Russians returning home from Germany in flower-bedecked trains. But she dreamt of her home village in the Ukraine, which she would be seeing again within a few days; of the fragrant bread that is baked there; and of cream and ham and fragrant red cabbage soup, soup with plenty of meat in it. Perhaps there were scarcities now because of the war, but people would certainly go to a little trouble about a girl whom the Nazis had made sick.

People went to a little trouble. Everything was well organized. At the border they were transferred to another train, because the gauge of Russian railroads is wider than the European. This train was not decorated with flowers. Instead the windows were barred and the doors locked from outside.

The songs died on the lips of the dismayed homecomers. Henceforth they were treated as convicts, although they knew nothing of any charges against them and had never seen a judge. Not until they reached Magadan were they informed that they had each been sentenced to ten years in camp as traitors.

That was the Soviet Union in 1946.

The Story of a Lithuanian Jewish Woman

When the Germans occupied the capital of Lithuania in 1941 they drove all the Jews into the ghetto. Among these Jews was a kindergarten teacher and her two small children. Her husband was taken away and shot during the first days of the occupation. She existed for a while on what scraps of food were available, and then one night she and her children, with all the other inhabitants of the ghetto, were driven out to a huge pit on the outskirts of the city. There mothers, children, and old men were lined up on the edge of the pit. She stood clasping her five-year-old daughter, who clung to her neck with both arms, and holding her sobbing eight-year-old boy tight against her.

"Mama," he screamed when the shots rang out. "Ma——" Then he fell silent abruptly and the mother heard his small body fall with a thud upon the other bodies in the pit. At the same moment the clasp of the little hands around her neck loosened, and she herself plunged into the pit on top of the bodies of her children.

At night she awoke among the dead. She had not been hit; before a bullet reached her, the death of her children had blanked out her consciousness. Half suffocated, she struggled up through the bodies to the air, to life. There were no Germans in the vicinity; they had moved on, to other murders. She escaped unobserved into the woods. Kind people took her in and kept her hidden throughout the war.

And then one day in 1944 the Red Army came and liberated the country. She was able to leave her hiding place and go back to work in the Soviet Republic of Lithuania. But everything here reminded her of what had happened, of her dead husband, of the pit, of the last cries of her murdered children. None of her friends or relatives was still alive. She alone had been rejected by the mass grave. She could no longer endure it; she could not stay here.

One day she learned that a brother she had long thought dead had survived the years of horror and was living in Rumania. She applied for a passport to Rumania. But passports for foreign travel are not issued to Soviet citizens.

By chance she heard that a number of other Jews in a predicament similar to hers were planning to leave the country secretly by plane. She decided to go with them.

The authorities allowed the plane to start; then it was immediately forced to land again. The NKVD had of course found out through informers about the daring plan, but they wanted the fact of an actual flight for their trial. All the inmates of the plane were arrested and sent to prison. After a few hearings the NKVD obtained a confession from the Jewish kindergarten teacher of her criminal intention to emigrate to Rumania. She was sentenced to ten years in camp as a traitor. It was 1946 when this verdict and sentence were passed.

The night before I was to be shipped out of Kolyma, I said good-by to her in the barrack of Magadan women's camp. She sat on her cot swaying back and forth as though she were rocking a child in her arms, and murmuring, "Why didn't I remain in the grave, why didn't I die right off along with my children, why . . . ?"

In describing my experiences in Kolyma I have had to forsake chronological order to give a picture of the total scene. I am now going to summarize my terms in Kolyma camps in their proper order.

I spent the first two years in Kolyma in Magadan women's camp (Shen-Olp) and worked in the prisoners' hospital, which was near the camp, but in town.

After the outbreak of the war I was shipped on a tugboat to Balagannoye, and from there by truck through the forest to Camp Talon, which is on the Tauy River, twenty-three miles from Balagannoye. There I worked as a snow-shoveler, wood chopper, porter, fieldworker and finally as a nurse in the infirmary. After about a year I was sent back, this time in a rattling hay wagon drawn by a Yakut pony whose facial expression remarkably resembled that of us prisoners. The little beast looked weary, cross, hungry and not eager to work. For hours we shook and swayed through the forest, and once we even had the opportunity to pluck a few handfuls of berries along the roadside. The forest floor is covered with berries in this region—bilberries, two different sorts of blueberries (*golubika* and *zhimolost*), a tasty yellowish-red berry, aromatic as a pineapple, which is called in Russian *morozhka,* and finally hawthorn hips, which taste very good after they have been nipped by frost. In Balagannoye we were again placed aboard a tugboat, of which I have the most unpleasant memories. It was raining, the boat rocked madly, and I was never so seasick in my life. Just as I had reached the point where I thought I was going to throw up my very stomach, we docked in Magadan.

Then my health broke down and I entered the Central Prisoners' Hospital, which was now situated on the twenty-third kilometer out of Magadan. When I was on my feet again, I went back to the women's camp at Magadan. For two months I worked in the icy vegetable storehouse (for the free population), sorting potatoes. More than half of them had been allowed to rot or freeze, but there were no potatoes for prisoners; the authorities preferred to let them spoil. For months I went out with my brigade every day at dawn, marching through the sleeping city of Magadan to the stinking potato storehouse. But soon I was to remember that interlude with longing, for I was shipped to Elgen.

Everything I had hitherto experienced paled before the horrors of Elgen, where I spent two years, living in each of the three spur camps as well as in the main camp. At first I was in the foreigners' camp, five miles from Elgen. I worked there in the woods, and at a primitive workbench where I made wooden shingles, what were called Finnish roofing shingles. After work I walked back and forth the five miles to Elgen hospital to fetch the most necessary medicines for the sick prisoners in my camp, who were in my charge. Then I was in swift succession shifted to the main Elgen camp, where I worked at ditch-digging, then to the agricultural base, the branch camp of Volchok, two miles from Elgen. Here I worked in the fields from sowing to harvest time, and also gathered willow branches in the woods around

Elgen. Often we had to march six miles in our shapeless footgear before we reached our place of work. The following winter I escaped wood chopping and became a basket weaver. In the spring I was in another spur camp, Polevoi Stan, three miles from Elgen in the opposite direction. There I worked at sowing. And so it went, back and forth between main camp and spur camps, from one job to the next, and to this day I cannot say what was the worst: the incessant hunger, the unbelievable cold of winter, or the clouds of mosquitoes in summer.

By an extraordinary piece of good luck I fell ill and was sent to the Central Prisoners' Hospital of the northern mining district (112 miles from Elgen and three miles from Yagodnoye). After my recovery I worked there as a nurse for a year and a half. Naturally I was in constant contact with sick prisoners from the gold mines. But my work as a nurse, which I loved, was constantly interrupted by a stubborn fever and attacks of weakness. Finally, after a two-day journey in an open truck, I landed again in the hospital on the twenty-third kilometer. The eighth autumn of my stay in Kolyma I was again in Magadan women's camp, this time employed as a cleaning woman.

And then the thing happened which I had no longer dared to believe possible: I was placed aboard a ship, and after an odyssey of another nine months I was returned to freedom, to my home. Home!

12. The Road Back

Aboard Ship

A SHIP LAY in the port. Along the side of the ship tiny dark creatures crawled upward. But they were not actually crawling up the side; it only looked that way from a distance. In reality people were climbing the almost vertical rungs of the iron gangplank.

My sack with my few indispensable belongings on my back, I nervously, hesitantly placed one foot after another upon the narrow rungs. Higher and higher. Once I looked down at the narrow strip of water between pier and ship, and I felt dizzy. I was no longer in condition for mountain climbing. Mountain climbing? When had I ever done that? When I was in Switzerland?

Keep in mind that you are traveling on orders from Moscow! Where to? No information given. What for? No information given. Was I on the road to freedom? But the guards did not for a moment leave our small group of prisoners. We were finally stowed away in a hold of the ship.

Here was a hell where people fought with one another for a drink of water. I looked around at the gray-faced male

287

prisoners in our locked storeroom, seasick, vomiting from the planks on the floor, or doubled over the battered pail where they must also relieve themselves before the eyes of the two women who were locked up with them. I looked at them lying above and on top of one another. Their hands had stubs where fingers had been frozen off; their legs were covered with sores. There was one young boy with the nose of a skeleton in a living face; the nose had been frozen off. They stared lustfully at the women; for seven years they had not seen a woman. At night they took turns mounting one of the women, shamelessly, barely covered by a ragged blanket, while the rest looked on greedily. I was the other woman; I cowered in my little space, unable to sleep for fear, fending off the hungry beasts with my feet, my elbows, my repugnance of them.

Voyage to freedom? We arrived only at Bukhta Nakhodka, where a place on the floor awaited us in the overcrowded barrack for prisoners in transit.

Bukhta Nakhodka

During the war Vladivostok was declared to be exclusively a war port. The transit camp was therefore liquidated and shifted a day's journey farther north to the port of Bukhta Nakhodka, also on the Pacific Ocean. Conditions there did not depart from the tradition of Vladivostok. The barracks were bug-ridden and overcrowded, the food repulsive, the water in terribly short supply.

Just once the frightful conditions in that camp led to a senseless, in fact, insane act of terrorism, which of course went unreported in the Soviet press. In 1945, after the liberation of Latvia and Lithuania and the incorporation of those countries into the Soviet Union, thousands of young Latvians were arrested on charges of collaboration with the Germans, or of having served in the German Army. The charge was undoubtedly true of a large number of them; many of them had their blood group tattooed on their arms, which proved that they had been members of the SS. But many of them also were young boys who had been snatched from their schoolrooms and forced to serve in the army, mainly in the German antiaircraft artillery.

Without distinction, all were shipped to Bukhta Nakhodka, and from there to Kolyma. They were not to be tried until they reached their destinations.

First they were placed in the Russian labor camps. As foreigners they lived in separate barracks, but were driven to work in the gold mines with the other prisoners. Gradually they were transferred in small groups to prison for a brief pretrial examination, and all were systematically convicted of violations of Paragraph 58, Article 1—treason—and sentenced to ten years.

Suddenly, in the first half of 1946, this process was stopped. No one knew the reasons, of course, but some pressure from abroad was assumed. In any case, no further verdicts were handed down, and those who were not yet sentenced were released. However, they were not given complete equality with the free population; they were called "special contingents" (abbreviated SK), lived in community barracks and were settled at certain places which they were not allowed to leave. Even though they were now free, they worked mostly in the gold mines, but their hours of labor and their earnings were on a par with those of other free citizens.

Those of the special contingents who had not yet been transferred to Kolyma were released in Bukhta Nakhodka and employed at work in the port.

In the spring of 1946 the highest authorities in Bukhta Nakhodka were alleged to have received an anonymous letter demanding that no more prisoners be sent to Kolyma and that Bukhta Nakhodka be cleared of all prisoners.

Whatever the case, at this time the ocean freighter *Dalstroi* was in port temporarily, on her way to Magadan. Her cargo as usual was to consist partly of prisoners and partly of explosives, large quantities of which were used in the gold mines.

Several tons of the explosive, ammonal, were already in the hold, but no prisoners had yet boarded the ship. It was about midnight, and just the captain and a few sailors were on board. Suddenly the ship exploded. The unknown person who set off the explosion was undoubtedly blown to bits. The blast whirled the captain high into the air and tore him to ribbons; a part of his body was identified on a hill five miles from the scene. The helmsman, who had just left the ship, saw the pillar of flame shoot into the air and instantly cut the rope that held the ship to the pier. As a result, it was driven somewhat offshore; otherwise the destruction would have been even more frightful than it was. This same helmsman raced to the nearest prison camp, pulled open the gates, and screamed: "Save yourselves if you can." The prisoners fled wildly through the gates; the camp guards shot down the helmsman.

Everything was destroyed for a radius of three miles. Countless victims were buried under collapsing houses. All the children in the state kindergarten were killed. How many lives were lost as a result of this act of terrorism cannot be estimated, for no figures were ever published.

Most of the prisoners' barracks were at some distance from the port and few prisoners were hurt. Those who had run away assembled outside the danger zone and were brought back to camp afterward. In the women's camp zone all windows were blown in and many women were thrown to the ground, but none were killed. But the knowledge that they were penned in caused frightful panic among the prisoners.

It was taken for granted that the act had been done by a Latvian or Lithuanian of the special contingents who were employed at the port. The subsequent arrests in the summer of 1946 were in accordance with this guess.

The port was repaired, and thousands of prisoners continued to be shipped out to Kolyma through the transit camp of Bukhta Nakhodka.

The women prisoners in the transit camp with whom I shared the filthy barrack floor—the planks were overcrowded—were still overwrought from the horror of the explosion. During the two days I spent there, they talked of little else and never tired of telling new details.

I ate a farewell soup of rotten potatoes which smelled of sewage. Then a short march and we stood—at the railroad station! There was a locomotive, a genuine locomotive. The first one I had seen for eight years. I wished I could pat it. But my feelings of tenderness vanished when I entered the prison car.

The Prison Car

It had been an ordinary passenger car originally. They are called *stolyupinskye* in Russia and were invented in Tsarist times. The outside windows were barred, a close meshwork of iron rods. Guards paced up and down the corridor. The compartments were windowless except for a tiny eight-inch square, barred. The compartments were entered by a barred iron door which was kept locked throughout the journey.

There were iron bars instead of glass panes in the windows to either side of this door. Should it be necessary, that is if a lockup sentence has been imposed upon the "travelers," a second solid iron door can be rolled across these bars and the door itself, so that the prisoners sit in darkness.

The lowest berth in the compartment consists of two wooden benches. Above are two more wooden benches, connected by a sheet of iron. Above these again are a third tier of two more benches. Thus the compartment is divided into three layers. There is a kind of manhole at the door through which the second and third tiers are reached.

Into such a compartment as many as twenty-five people were crammed. And the journeys lasted four, five, and six days in succession, from one prison to another. Food during the journey consisted of seventeen and a half ounces of bread, a small piece of salted fish, and now and then a teaspoonful of sugar. Usually the sugar was confiscated in whatever transit prison we happened to be staying.

An officer from the Bukhta Nakhodka transit camp threw us a last look as we sat there like animals in a cage. Something in his look encouraged us.

"Where are we going, Citizen Officer?"

"To Kazakhstan," he replied in a low voice.

"How long will we be traveling?"

He hesitated for a moment. "About twelve days," he said, and looked away.

How could a man have such honest eyes and lie so? We suffered the torments of prison cars and transit prisons for more than two months before we reached Kazakhstan. It was not the congestion in the compartments or the hunger that bothered us most, it was thirst. We screamed ourselves hoarse for a drop of cold water, while the food and the steaming tea kettle for the guards were carried along the corridor past us. There was water at every station, but not for us.

"You dogs, you give us salt fish and nothing to drink," a voice screeched.

The guard in the corridor came threateningly to the barred door. "What did you say, you slut?"

"Nothing. I want a drink."

"You'll have to wait."

At last they came. Two guards with a single pail of water. A slot in the barred door was opened. They counted the number of inmates in the compartment. Then one of the guards dipped a tin cup into the pail and handed it through the opening while the other counted the cups. A single cup was used to serve a hundred convicts in succession.

As in ordinary railroad cars, there was a toilet at either end of the car. In the corridor stood the guards, yawning with boredom. It was only a few steps from the door to the toilet. The prisoners pleaded, begged, shouted, screamed:

"Let us out, let us out."

Many were sick, many suffering from diarrhea from their diet of black bread, salt fish, and unboiled water. But the prisoners were allowed out to the toilet only twice every twenty-four hours, although it was only a few steps and the guards stood idly in the corridor all day long. Those were the regulations. It was rare for the sergeants in charge of the shipment of prisoners to relent and allow the prisoners out a third time. And so the prisoners whimpered and whined, howled and cursed, as they were transported like wild beasts from one prison cell to the next. And when they could no longer endure it and were forced to relieve themselves in the compartment, they were kicked and beaten with rifle butts.

Vladivostok

After a day's journey the gates of Vladivostok Prison closed behind us. Into the barred room where we were waiting to be searched came a buxom young peasant girl who hitched her skirt up high, revealing a pair of plump thighs, and began washing the floor. Now and then she peered up curiously from under her mop of blonde hair at our group of newcomers.

"Dochka (little daughter), how old are you?"

"Sixteen," she answered amiably as she wrung out her scrub cloth.

"How do you happen to be in prison?"

"I've got to do six months' time," she answered indifferently, wiping away the perspiration from her forehead with a damp, red hand.

"What did you do? I suppose you snitched something?"

"Nothing of the kind." She was indignant at the imputation of stealing. "I skipped out of the trade school." We looked puzzled. "You see, we weren't asked whether we wanted to go to the school. It was opened after the war. Somebody drew up a list and then we were sent there from our village school. But I didn't like it a bit in trade school, and the food in the city was bad, so one day I made up my mind to go back to our village. I planned it with two other girls. They were only fifteen and they only got five months because they said I put them up to it. And I got six months as the leader. We never even reached home; they caught us before we got there."

"How do you like it here in prison, Dochka?"

"Oh," she said, "it's not so bad. I work cleaning up. I only have to stay in the cell at night. And then there's Mitya, the cook's helper. . . ." She reddened and giggled in mild embarrassment. "He's always getting me something extra to eat."

As though to corroborate this, the door opened, and after making sure that there was no guard around, Mitya came in with a bunch of carrots which he cautiously removed from under his shirt and handed to the girl.

He was at least twice her age, an unprepossessing fellow with pussy pimples on his neck, a low brow, cunning eyes, and a gap in his mouth where two front teeth were missing. With the cynical grin of the professional criminal he took hold of her, reached down for her breasts and patted her buttocks. Nonchalantly, she let him. She did not look up at the repulsive fellow, but kept her eyes fixed on the juicy carrots he had brought her. Eagerly she sank her healthy white teeth into a carrot.

Sixteen years old—and already she understood that to be fed sufficiently in prison you had to put up with all sorts of things. And what could be more troublesome to a growing girl than hunger? She had also learned that she would not have to work so hard if she let an overseer fondle her now and then. And so, a few months later, she would return to life in firm possession of a new wisdom—that a woman need neither go hungry nor work as long as there were men ready to pay for a little so-called love.

We spent ten days in prison in Vladivostok, during which we sat four to a cell six and a half feet wide and nine feet long, without exercise and without light. Then we were loaded into the prison car again.

Khabarovsk

A colorful band of prisoners rode with us to the transit prison of Khabarovsk. Some of them were Japanese in fantastic high fur caps and long, fur-trimmed coats; the rest were juvenile delinquents between the ages of twelve and sixteen. They were pallid, thin, stunted children. Almost all of them were to serve three-year sentences for theft.

We had already eaten up the bread which was supposed to last us for three days. If it was almost impossible for us adults to husband our rations, how could these starving children possibly do it? Moreover, they would steal each other's bread, so that each knew his bread was safest in his stomach.

Twice a day, like all the rest, they were let out in pairs to go to the toilet. On the way there the tormented little fellows ran as fast as they could. They tried to prolong the short walk back through the corridor, especially when they passed the women's cages, for they hoped to be given a scrap of bread or a little tobacco. Fifty pairs of youthful eyes looked in on us with curiosity and expectancy, some impudent, some pleading, all hungry. Long, tattered trousers hung down over their torn shoes; their little gray hands were invisible inside the sleeves of men's jackets that reached down below their knees. Their bloodless lips poured forth a stream of obscene remarks, emphasized by gestures and filthy curses such as even grown-up criminals seldom used in the presence of women. Then they disappeared behind their own barred door, where they fought for places and where now and then a small boy who could not defend himself bawled loudly.

The train stopped at the railroad station in Khabarovsk. The guards of the transit prison took charge of us. One door after the other was opened and individuals called out by name. One after the other the boys jumped down from the high step to the snow-covered platform. They were not burdened by a bundle, for they had no possessions at all. Their hands buried in their long sleeves as in a muff, they crouched in the snow side by side, with bowed heads, as they had been ordered to do. Those whose ears were not covered with a rag turned blue with cold.

Then we all ran on the double to the van, the "Black Raven" which was to take us to the transit prison.

Of all the ten Soviet prisons I was in, Khabarovsk was by far the cleanest, except for the bedbugs which are everywhere. Our meals, though inadequate as usual, were at least not prepared from spoiled food, and the sugar which was withheld by most transit prisons was promptly distributed every day. It was even possible to get to see the doctor the first day, so that the little Tartar girl who had had scabies since we left Bukhta Nakhodka was able to obtain salve to rub on her hands, which had raw, suppurating sores from scratching, and on the rest of her itching body.

Irkutsk

After another few days we went aboard the prison car once more, this time for a five-day journey to Irkutsk. Several young prostitutes from our cage, heavy-breasted women with plump calves and picturesquely tattooed arms, who wore their bright shawls askew over one ear, put themselves at the disposal of the guards; supposedly they went into the guards' compartment to wash the floor. They returned with an ample supply of tobacco which they gave away freely to us and to the noisy boys in the adjoining cage, for prostitutes are the most generous of all prisoners. One night the transport commander, a glassy-eyed, drunken sergeant, came reeling into our cage, pushed all the women off the bench except for a seventeen-year-old girl, and lay down with her in a tender embrace. We utilized the occasion to beg permission to go out to the toilet once more, and did so—accompanied by envious glances from the men's cages.

The transit prison of Irkutsk, notorious since the days of the Tsar, has lost nothing of its dreadful reputation among prisoners. The jammed cells were swarming with bedbugs and lice, and the door is opened only once a day to remove the bucket, a frightfully stinking bucket that must take care of the needs of eighty prisoners for twenty-four hours. There is no place to wash and the prisoners are not allowed to go out for a walk.

One of the women had given her wet felt boots to a prisoner who worked in the kitchen so that she could dry them and bring them back to the cell in the evening, when her work was over. Meanwhile the inmates of our cell were transferred to another building which lay across several snow-covered yards. The barefoot woman asked the guard for permission to fetch her boots first. The soldier would not hear of it. She crawled up on the planks. He pulled her down by force, thrust her through the door and dragged her across the stone floor of the dark corridor. Then, with blows and curses, he drove her across the snow.

"They shout about the fascists—but this is what they do themselves!" the woman sobbed as he gave her a last push that sent her flying into the cell.

Novosibirsk

Our next stop after several days of traveling was a cell in the transit prison of Novosibirsk. On the two tiers of planks the women prisoners lie jammed together. This is a perfectly ordinary Soviet prison cell: dark, with a small barred window high up in the wall, so covered by its wooden shutter that only a tiny patch of sky can be seen, but nothing of the cells opposite or of the prison yard. In one corner is the bucket, and in all corners are rats who jump squeaking over the faces of the sleepers. Yet they are less disturbing than the bedbugs which are there in armies, and which can neither be driven away nor caught.

Something squeaks on the top tier. Those are not rats; they are the ten-day-old twins who are being shipped with their mother from one camp to another and must wait in between in the cell of the transit prison. For although women prisoners are forbidden all relations with the opposite sex, the slogan of the criminals remains: "They have robbed us of our freedom, but not our nature." And during the long years of camp life many children are born, in spite of the close guard —and frequently with the co-operation of the guards, who are highly susceptible to the charms of convict prostitutes.

I lay sleepless on the boards. Suddenly I felt a peculiar warmth on my left side. I had just been baptized by an eight-month-old boy who had first seen the "light" of the world in a prison. His mother had been pregnant at the time of her arrest. Where was she to get diapers for him? The boy had rolled off the rags she had placed under his thin legs—in the transit prison there are only the rough planks, no straw sacks and no blankets. In his sleep he had snuggled with his swollen, rachitic little stomach against me. Now he began to cry. I awakened his emaciated mother, who with a sigh thrust her empty breast into the hungry little mouth.

On my right lay a Ukrainian peasant woman, her arm around her five-year-old girl, who lay beside her eight-year-old sister. Beside them the sixteen-year-old daughter moaned in her sleep.

During the war this woman had lived in a region that was occupied by the Germans. This made her suspect, like thousands of others who had survived the German occupation. Perhaps she had sold milk or eggs to the Germans. When Soviet troops liberated the area, she was ordered to move to Siberia.

She packed her slender possessions and, with her three children, set off for Siberia. This is called "free" exile. For a few years she managed to eke out a miserable living. Then she felt such homesickness for the rich and fruitful soil of the Ukraine that one day she again packed her bundle, took her three children by the hand and returned to her native village. But she was not long to enjoy the bliss of working in the fields of home. She was arrested, charged with "escape from exile," and convicted. Her sentence: "Five years of administrative exile to Siberia."

This time she was not allowed to travel to Siberia as a free citizeness. She and her children were transported in the prison car from one transit prison to the next, and her ultimate destination was a far more inhospitable region than the one she had fled from.

Such traveling by stages takes many months; for weeks and weeks the prisoners sit in the transit prisons waiting for the next transport. And so the children lived in the cell, stared at the tiny patch of sky, pulled each other's louse-ridden hair until adult prisoners broke up the quarrel, and lifted each other on the stinking bucket. While the five-year-old stood by hungrily, the eight-year-old stretched on tiptoe to look out of the peephole and see whether the prison soup was coming. And when the two smallest children in their ravenous hunger would fall upon the soup and snatch an extra cabbage leaf, the sixteen-year-old girl would rap them on the forehead with her wooden spoon, for she and her mother were just as hungry as the little ones.

Once a day there was a fifteen-minute walk in the prison yard. Then, blinking in the unaccustomed daylight, the children would tramp with the other prisoners through the snow, their freezing hands hidden in the overlong sleeves of their ragged jackets, around and around, around and around . . . until the guard drove them all back into the close confinement of the cell and closed the iron-plated cell door, while the youngest child still looked back longingly.

And in the town, only a few houses away from the prison, there hung a touching placard, a placard that is encountered again and again in all the cities and villages of the Soviet Union. It shows Stalin with a little girl in his arms, and below there is the inscription: "Thank you, Comrade Stalin, for a happy childhood."

Chelyabinsk

We arrived in Chelyabinsk on a holiday, Constitution Day. With bloodhounds at our heels, driven on by surly guards, we tramped for miles through the flag-draped streets of the town. Some of the prisoners were handcuffed to one another in pairs. In the first rows marched a group of juvenile thieves. Adult passers-by glanced quickly at us and hurried by. Prisoners are too common a sight in Siberia to attract attention. And it would be dangerous to show sympathy for them.

A little girl of about three pointed a finger at us and asked in a loud, high, surprised voice, "Mama, what are they?" "Oh, they're from the prison," the mother answered indifferently, drawing the child back into the vestibule of her home.

But a group of boys accompanied us at some distance, across the street from us. Shouting and howling, they glided their sleds over the firm ice of the pavement. And they repeatedly waved and shouted to the boys their age who marched in our ranks. "Come over here. Come and play with us." But the boys in our ranks only looked longingly at them, although they were itching to hold a sled in their hands, to take a run and then slide, slide, gloriously down the smooth, long street. They knew what those other boys did not understand—that if they so much as stepped out of line, it would be considered an attempt to escape, and the guards might shoot without warning. Gradually the town boys dropped behind, and we continued on along the deserted streets on the outskirts of town to the transit prison, five miles from the railroad station.

After we had been registered, the men and women were separated. We were taken out to a courtyard, in the middle of which was a circle about thirty feet in diameter, enclosed in a double barbed-wire fence. At the entrance stood a guard in a long, stiff fur coat which reached down to his ankles. He also wore a fur cap pulled low down over his ears.

Perspiring from our long march, we threw our sacks down in the snow and sat on them. But after ten minutes we were so thoroughly frozen that we got up in spite of our fatigue and began trotting up and down between the round walls of barbed wire. It was the usual story: first the men were sent to the bath and then the women. The bath was small; it could hold only fifteen people at a time—and hundreds of prisoners were waiting. However, it was one of Chelyabinsk's specialties to make prisoners wait out in the snow in December. And so we trotted up and down. Darkness fell and we were still trotting. A floodlight illuminated our frozen faces,

faces that in spite of their numbness reflected our helpless fury. For three hours we waited in the snow.

In the chilly bathing room with its ice-cold stone floor we poured two basins of lukewarm water over our bodies and then stood naked for about half an hour, waiting for our clothes, which were meanwhile being deloused in the disinfection room. If only we were in our cell and able to rest. We had long since forgotten that we had eaten nothing all day long.

Once in the cell we had difficulty finding a place to sit on the floor. So the first night passed, and then four more days and nights. And then again we tramped the five miles back to the railroad station and the prison car. For an entire day we stood on a siding in Orenburg. The train to which our car was to be attached had left without us.

Sol-Ilyetsk

Fifty miles from Orenburg we were unloaded again. After being marched to the prison we were given baths—in the usual fashion. Then we were distributed among various cells. I had just stretched out on the planks when the door was opened and the guard ordered the inmates of the cell to get ready for bathing. I informed her that I had just come from the baths. "This is bath day for the cell. Regulations. Get ready." And so I bathed a second time—in the usual satisfactory fashion.

Most of the inmates of this cell were contriki. Some of them came from regions which had been occupied by the Germans; members of the families of some of them had not returned to the Soviet Union after the war ended. The woman beside me, who had originally been sentenced to five years, had just received an additional two years for bartering a blanket that belonged to the camp.

All asked anxiously whether they were being sent to Kolyma. I consoled them with the Kolyma formula which customarily drives newcomers to despair: The first five years are the hardest; then you get used to it.

I had had ten years! They looked at me with the same reverent expressions with which I, too, many, many years ago, had looked at the first prisoners who told me of their long years of imprisonment. And when they asked me how these years could possibly pass, I answered with a verse from a song that all prisoners in all camps and prisons hum when they lie on the planks and stare up at the ceiling:

> *Wherever you look*
> *The world is dead*
> *And slowly, so slowly*
> *The day passes by.* . . .

Our sacks on our smarting shoulders, we ran down an ice-covered slope toward the railroad station. Those in front slipped and fell. Those behind piled on top of them. In a moment there was an inextricable knot of shouting, raging prisoners, cursing guards, and dogs mad with excitement.

Finally we reached a small square, from which a wooden stairway led up to the tracks. This was the railroad station. At a stand several fat peasant wives, completely swathed in bulky clothes, were offering some kind of food for sale. Yet, again and again free citizens would come up to us, imagining that we wanted to sell the bread we had been given for the journey, which we all held tightly clasped under our arms. They did not realize their error until one of the guards shouted, "Beat it, citizen." Then they would turn hastily and regretfully away.

We had been marched to the station almost an hour before the train pulled in. A biting wind from the Ural Mountains swept over the unsheltered square. A tiny Kalmuk boy who was on his way to the prison in Tashkent stood with hunched shoulders, motionless in the cutting frost. His dark, slanting eyes over the prominent cheekbones, the flat-cheeked, yellow-skinned face and the broad nose, were drawn and squinting with pain of the cold. The wind tugged at his ragged trousers, revealing the bare flesh of his legs, and penetrated through the holes in his shoes. We shook him, swung him back and forth, pushed him forward the few steps we were allowed to move and yet preserve a fitting distance between ourselves and the free citizens. He resisted and looked at us silently, pleadingly. He did not understand Russian, and every step he took on his freezing feet cut like knives. But if he did not move, his feet would be done for. Again and again we pulled him up when he tried to crouch down in the snow, surrendering to the cold. At last the train came; at last his name was called. As he clambered up into the car with numbed, awkward feet, his bare legs were again visible, exposed to the cold.

Aktyubinsk

This was our last ride in the prison car. One hundred and sixty-five miles southeast of Orenburg we were unloaded. With some difficulties, for waiting at the station were only the militia with a group of prisoners from the local militia prison. The militia were not the proper authorities to take charge of us. But the commander of the prison car refused to accept the militia's prisoners unless the militia received us in exchange. Finally they struck the bargain.

The locomotive whistle had already blown for the second time when, with a sigh of relief, we jumped down on the platform. We had missed by a hair riding on another five days to Tashkent and waiting there in the prison to be shipped back. That had happened to another group of our prisoners from Kolyma who had been separated from us in one of the transit prisons and whom we met up with again a month later. Such extra journeys were no rarity. On the way we had met many prisoners who were not fetched by the appropriate prison official and who consequently were taken on to the next transit prison, one that was often many days away. Aside from the additional torment of a new prison and a longer trip in the prison car, such a prisoner travels without bread, since these additional journeys are not reckoned on in determining his rations. How many thousands of useless miles have been traveled in this way! Who cares? Who pays for it? The Soviet economy.

We spent the night in the militia prison, which was pleasantly situated at the back of a small garden with snow-covered trees. The officer who received us remarked to the guard: "It doesn't matter what cell you put them in. They're going to the German camp tomorrow."

For simplicity's sake, the men were thrust into the lockup, an icy cell with bare walls and a bare stone floor, where they spent the entire night jumping up and down in order not to freeze to death. We stretched out on the floor of a women's cell. But I could not sleep. "German camp, German camp." The words kept going around in my head. Was that to be the end of my journey to freedom?

The Nazi Camp

Camp for Civilian Internees Number 222. Its inmates were Nazis from East Prussia and Upper Silesia who had been arrested and brought here immediately after the Soviet troops marched into those areas. There were about a thousand men and a hundred women in the camp. Like the Kazakhs, the native population outside the camp, they lived in earthen huts, underground barracks of which only the narrow windows and the round, mud-covered roof protruded above the ground. By Soviet standards these earthen barracks were very roomy. Every internee had his straw sack and blankets, and in winter each received a sheepskin and felt boots—articles no Russian prisoner would dream of possessing.

The official hours of labor were eight for healthy inmates and only six for the weak and the old—many of the internees were over fifty. Those who were not employed inside the camp at tailoring, shoe-repairing, or basket weaving; in the laundry, the baths, the kitchen, or at clerical tasks, worked building houses for the city of Aktyubinsk, and in the fields in the surrounding countryside. At a spur camp named Kossukhai about twenty-five miles away the men worked in a coal mine.

The minimum ration was seventeen and a half ounces of bread, and all inmates received this irrespective of their production. In addition there were bread bonuses for good work. The remainder of the food consisted of soup three times a day, grits twice a day, and once a day either a meat sauce made of salted meat of dubious quality, or a bit of fish. In addition the internees received ten and a half ounces of sugar a month, and five ounces of tobacco.

In spite of the shorter hours of work and the better food compared with the Russian penal camps, the great majority of the inmates were in wretched health, and hundreds of patients were constantly in the sick barrack suffering from dystrophia alimentaris—undernourishment. Another scourge was malaria, from which 90 per cent of the inmates suffered. The Germans simply could not adjust to the food or to the climatic conditions—extreme heat in summer and icy blizzards in winter. Their morale was abysmally low.

We had been brought to this camp in order to be repatriated, although we learned this only unofficially. My comrades from Kolyma, whose long road of suffering was at last to end here, were mostly people who had fled from the advancing Nazis. Many of them were Jews who were now locked up in camp with these same Nazis and, to the great satisfaction of the Nazis, subject to the same regimen. In the barracks where they were at first living together there were incessant brawls. The Kolyma prisoners, made savage by years of imprisonment, applied against the Nazis the methods they had acquired from their contact with Russian criminals. At last the camp administration was forced to place them in a separate barrack of their own. They also refused to work along with the Nazis, or to work under a German brigadier, and they won out on this demand as well.

Three months later they were taken to Odessa and from there repatriated via Focsani. By the spring of 1947 they were back home.

Brest-Litovsk

As for me, I stayed in the camp until fall, and spent three weeks being shipped in a cattle car. But my dreams of early freedom ended in a repatriation camp in Brest-Litovsk where I spent another half year while my papers were once more being checked over. It was a mixed camp, with Polish and

German war prisoners and internees who were being subjected to a final check-up before being sent home. Discipline in the camp was loose, for this was not a labor camp. The population was constantly changing, and this circumstance was used by the Germans working in the kitchen to put across all sorts of manipulations with the food, which was incredibly bad.

The attitude of the Poles was essentially different from that of the Germans. They were more dignified, but also adjusted better to conditions; it was easier for them because their language was so close to the Russian. Their hatred of the Germans flared up at the slightest provocation; toward the Russians they exhibited a proud contempt.

There was a group of five hundred Polish officers who had lived in the woods for years, resisting the Germans. When the Red Army entered Poland, they greeted their liberators and placed themselves and their troops, together with the German prisoners of war they had captured, at the disposal of the Red Army. But they insisted on continuing to fight as a unit. The Russians wanted to incorporate them into the Polish legion and would not comply with their desires. The Polish officers suspected trouble. A good many of them could have fled, but they did not want to abandon their men, for whom they felt responsible.

Under the pretext that the Poles needed retraining in a Russian military school, the Russians transported them to Russia, put them into prison and then transferred them to a prisoner-of-war camp.

The End

At last came the day when I rolled across the Russo-Polish frontier in a cattle car. Five days later we were unloaded in

Frankfurt on the Oder. I passed through the gates of three different repatriation camps in the Russian zone of Germany. And then, one brilliant June day in 1948, a flight in an American plane finally ended my eleven years of confinement in Soviet prisons and camps.

List of My Prisons and Camps

Moscow and Transit

First hours: Lubyanka Prison, Moscow.

One year and three months: Butyrka Prison, Moscow.

One month and five days: Transportation in a cattle car from Moscow to Vladivostok.

Six and one half months: Transit camp of Vladivostok.

One week: Transportation aboard the freighter *Dalstroi* from Vladivostok to Magadan.

Kolyma

Two years and three months: Women's camp at Magadan (Zhen-Olp).

One month: Women's camp at Balagannoye.

Four days: Prison at Balagannoye.

Eleven months: Talon women's camp.

Two months. Prisoners' hospital at the twenty-third kilometer.

Two months: Magadan women's camp.

Two years: Women's regimen camp at Elgen, and three of its spur camps.

One and a half years: Prisoners' hospital in the northern gold-mining district.